Ernest Edward Wild

The Common Form Draftsman

A handbook of Queen's Bench forms: being a collection of forms ordinarily in use in proceedings in the Queen's Bench Division of the High Court of Justice: with notes, table of stamps, and index

Ernest Edward Wild

The Common Form Draftsman

A handbook of Queen's Bench forms: being a collection of forms ordinarily in use in proceedings in the Queen's Bench Division of the High Court of Justice: with notes, table of stamps, and index

ISBN/EAN: 9783337324018

Printed in Europe, USA, Canada, Australia, Japan

Cover: Foto ©ninafisch / pixelio.de

More available books at **www.hansebooks.com**

THE COMMON FORM DRAFTSMAN;

A

Handbook of Queen's Bench Forms,

BEING

A COLLECTION OF FORMS ORDINARILY IN USE IN PROCEEDINGS IN THE QUEEN'S BENCH DIVISION OF THE HIGH COURT OF JUSTICE.

WITH

Notes, Table of Stamps, and Index.

BY

ERNEST EDWARD WILD, B.A., LL.M.,
Of the Middle Temple, Esq.,

AND

FRANK SHEWELL COOPER, M.A.,
Of the Inner Temple, Esq. ; Barristers-at-Law.

LONDON:
BUTTERWORTH & CO., 7, FLEET STREET, E.C.
Law Publishers.

1899.

PREFACE.

THIS little book, as it is, perhaps, unnecessary to point out, is not intended to compete with *Chitty's Forms* or any similarly exhaustive work. It merely aims at furnishing in a compendious form a collection of the precedents most frequently required in a solicitor's office in proceedings in the Queen's Bench Division.

It is a common complaint that the forms printed in the Appendices to the *Yearly Supreme Court Practice* * and the *Annual Practice*, useful though they are, fail to meet the requirements of the practitioner in several obvious respects, and it is hoped that this work will supply some of the more marked deficiencies in the sets of forms there prescribed.

The book has been prepared on the assumption that the *Yearly Supreme Court Practice*, or the *Annual Practice*, is in the hands of every solicitor, and consequently it does not pretend to be a practice book. The notes have been reduced to a minimum, and deal almost entirely with the framing of the forms. However, at the head of each form references have, where practicable, been given to the Rules of the Supreme Court bearing on the

---

* The *Yearly Supreme Court Practice*, by Muir Mackenzie, Lushington, and Fox. Price 20s. net. Issued annually. Butterworth & Co.

form in question, so that the practice may be readily ascertained. References have also been given to the forms in the Appendices to the *Yearly Supreme Court Practice* and the *Annual Practice*.

In the great majority of instances the forms have been filled up to suit imaginary cases, a plan which it is hoped will render the collection more useful to the inexperienced draftsman.

In view of the alteration in the practice at Queen's Bench Chambers, consequent upon the introduction of the compulsory summons for directions under Order XXX., special attention has been paid to this branch of the subject, and an endeavour has been made to embody the changes involved,—a task not free from difficulty, seeing that the practice is still in some respects in a somewhat nebulous state.

Great care has been taken to render the index as complete as possible.

Thanks are due to Mr. H. F. TRAILL and Mr. G. L. BORRADAILE, Solicitors, who have kindly read the manuscript of the work, and made several valuable suggestions.

Since the shortcomings of a collection of this nature must necessarily be numerous, any suggestions or corrections, with a view to rendering it more useful and complete, will be gladly received.

1, GARDEN COURT,
  TEMPLE, E.C.
    April, 1899.

TABLE OF CONTENTS.

CHAPTER I.
Writs of Summons.

NO.		PAGE
I.—Writ of Summons, General Form	... ...	1
II.—Ditto ditto Specially Indorsed	... ...	3
III.—Ditto ditto General Form, District Registry		3
IV.—Ditto ditto Specially Indorsed ditto	...	4
V.—Description of Parties		5
VI.—Indorsement of Representative Capacity of Parties ...		6
VII.—General Indorsements. Money Claims where no Special Indorsement		7
VIII.—General Indorsements. Damages and other Claims		8

CHAPTER II.
Special Indorsements.

IX.—Money Due on an Account Stated	14
X.—Work Done under a Building Contract	14
XI.—Carriage of Goods by Railway	15
XII.—Commission on Sale of Houses	15
XIII.—Allotment Money and Calls upon Shares in Company	15
XIV.—Carriage of Goods by Sea	16
XV.—Goods Sold and Delivered and Account Stated ...	17
XVI.—Guarantee for the Price of Goods Sold	18
XVII.—Hire of Furniture	18
XVIII.—Foreign Judgment	19

NO.		PAGE
XIX.—Money Lent and Interest		20
XX.—Return of Deposit		20
XXI.—Money Received by Agent for Sale of Goods		21
XXII.—Inland Bill of Exchange. Indorsee against Acceptor		21
XXIII.—Inland Bill of Exchange. Indorsee against Acceptor		22
XXIV.—Inland Bill of Exchange Indorsee against Acceptor, Drawer and Two Holders		22
XXV.—Inland Bill of Exchange. Drawer against Acceptor		23
XXVI.—Inland Bill of Exchange. Payee against Acceptor		24
XXVII.—Inland Bill of Exchange. Indorsee against Drawer in Default of Acceptance		24
XXVIII.—Foreign Bill of Exchange. Drawer against Acceptor		25
XXIX.—Foreign Bill of Exchange. Indorsee against Drawer and Acceptor		26
XXX.—Cheque. Payee against Drawer		26
XXXI.—Ditto. Indorsee against Drawer and Indorser, with Waiver of Notice of Dishonour by Drawer		27
XXXII.—Promissory Note. Payee against Maker		28
XXXIII.— Ditto. Indorsee against Indorser		28
XXXIV.—Recovery of Land		29
XXXV.— Ditto. Assignee of Reversion against Assignee of Term who has Paid Rent		29
XXXVI.—Rent under a Yearly Tenancy		30
XXXVII.— Ditto Covenant in a Lease		31
XXXVIII.—Rent of Furnished Apartments		31
XXXIX.—Salary and Commission of Traveller		32
XL.—Board, Lodging and Tuition		33
XLI.—Solicitors' Bill of Costs		33
XLII.—Charges for Warehousing Furniture		34

TABLE OF CONTENTS. vii

CHAPTER III.

SERVICE OUT OF THE JURISDICTION, SUBSTITUTED SERVICE
AND RENEWAL OF WRIT.

NO.   PAGE
XLIII.—Writ for Service out of the Jurisdiction, or where
Notice in Lieu of Service is to be Given out of
the Jurisdiction 35
XLIV.—Affidavit in Support of Application for Leave to
Issue Writ (or Notice) for Service out of the
Jurisdiction 36
XLV.—Order Giving Leave to Issue and Serve out of the
Jurisdiction 38
XLVI.—Notice of Writ in Lieu of Service to be Given out
of the Jurisdiction 39
XLVII.—Affidavit in Support of Application for Order for
Substituted Service... 40
XLVIII.—Order for Substituted Service 42
XLIX.—Affidavit on Application for Renewal of Writ ... 42
L.—Memorandum or Præcipe for Renewed Writ ... 44

CHAPTER IV.

APPEARANCE AND PROCEEDINGS IN DEFAULT THEREOF.

LI.—Entry of Appearance, General Form 45
LII.—Notice of Appearance 46
LIII.—Entry of Appearance by Defendant Incompletely
                  Described in Writ ... 46
LIV.—Ditto   ditto   by Partners Sued in Firm
                  Name 47
LV.—Ditto   ditto   under Protest by Person
                  Served as a Partner ... 47
LVI.—Ditto   ditto   by Third Party 47
LVII.—Ditto   ditto   by Third Person to Counter-
                  claim 48

NO.		PAGE
LVIII.—Entry of Appearance by Landlord Named in the Writ		49
LIX.—Ditto ditto Limiting Defence		49
LX.—Notice Limiting Defence		50
LXI.—Affidavit in Support of Application to Appear by Party not Named as Defendant		50
LXII.—Order Giving Party not Named as Defendant Leave to Appear		51
LXIII.—Entry of Appearance by Leave by Party not Named as Defendant		51
LXIV.—Notice of Appearance by Party not Named as Defendant		52
LXV.—Entry of Appearance by Party Served with Order to Continue Action		52
LXVI.—Affidavit of Personal Service of Writ		53
LXVII.— Ditto Substituted ditto		54
LXVIII.— Ditto Service of Writ on Company		54
LXIX.—Affidavit of Service of Writ on a Partner on behalf of the Firm		55
LXX.—Ditto ditto ditto upon Person in Control of Partnership Business		56
LXXI.—Notice of Service upon Person in Control of Partnership Business		57
LXXII.—Ditto ditto on Partnership where Capacity of Party Served is Uncertain		57
LXXIII.—Affidavit of Service of Notice of Writ		58
LXXIV.—Judgment in Default of Appearance. Liquidated Demand		58
LXXV.—Judgment in Default of Appearance. Liquidated Demand. Several Defendants		59
LXXVI.—Interlocutory Judgment in Default of Appearance. Unliquidated Demand		59
LXXVII.—Præcipe of Inquiry		60
LXXVIII.—Writ of Inquiry for Assessment of Damages		60
LXXIX.—Final Judgment in Default of Appearance after Assessment of Damages		61
LXXX.—Judgment in Default of Appearance. Recovery of land		62

TABLE OF CONTENTS.   ix

NO.		PAGE
LXXXI.—Judgment in Default of Appearance. Recovery of Land, Rent, and Damages		62
LXXXII.—Judgment in Default of Appearance against Married Woman		63

CHAPTER V.

PROCEEDINGS UNDER ORDER XIV.

LXXXIII.—Summons for Leave to Enter Final Judgment under Order XIV.		64
LXXXIV.—Affidavit of Plaintiff on Summons under Order XIV.		65
LXXXV.— Ditto Defendant on Summons under Order XIV.		66
LXXXVI.— Ditto Service of Summons and Affidavit under Order XIV.		66
LXXXVII.—Order Empowering Plaintiff to Sign Final Judgment (No. 1.)		67
LXXXVIII.—Ditto Giving Defendant Unconditional Leave to Defend (No. 2.)		67
LXXXIX.—Ditto Giving Defendant Conditional Leave to Defend (No. 3.)		68
XC.—Ditto Giving Defendant Conditional Leave to Defend as to Part of Claim (No. 4)		68
XCI.—Ditto Giving Defendant Unconditional Leave to Defend as to Part of Claim (No. 5)		69
XCII.—Ditto against a Married Woman and Others (No. 6)		69
XCIII.—Ditto in Action on Bill of Costs (No. 7)		70
XCIV.—Ditto Permitting One or More of Several Defendants to Defend		70
XCV.—Ditto under Order XIV. with Directions		71
XCVI.—Ditto for Entry of Action in the Short Cause List		71
XCVII.—Ditto Remitting Action to the County Court		71
XCVIII.—Ditto Dismissing Application		72
XCIX.—Notice of Appeal to Judge from Order of Master		72

CHAPTER VI.

Alteration or Addition of Parties.

NO.		PAGE
C.—Summons to Add a Defendant	... ...	74
CI.—Order Adding Defendant ...	... ...	75
CII.—Summons to Strike Out a Party	... ...	76
CIII.—Order Striking Out a Party ...	... ...	76
CIV.—Consent of Added Plaintiff or Next Friend of Plaintiff	... ...	77
CV.—Authority to Solicitor to Use Name of Next Friend	... ...	77
CVI.—Notice of Application for Appointment of Guardian for Defendant Infant or Person of Unsound Mind...	... ...	77
CVII.—Affidavit on Application for Appointment of Guardian	... ...	78
CVIII.—Ditto for Entry of Appearance as Guardian of Infant	... ...	79
CIX.—Consent of Guardian ...	... ...	80
CX.—Affidavit on Application for Leave to Sue *in Formâ Pauperis*	...	80
CXI.—Ditto ditto ditto to Issue Third Party Notice		81
CXII.—Third Party Notice ...	... ...	82
CXIII.—Order Giving Leave to Issue Third Party Notice...		83
CXIV.—Summons by Third Party to Discharge Order	...	84
CXV.—Judgment by Default against Third Party	...	84
CXVI.—Ditto against Third Party after Trial...	...	84
CXVII.—Summons for Judgment against Third Party after Decision without Trial...	... ...	85
CXVIII.—Ditto for Directions as to Third Party	...	85
CXIX.—Order Ditto ditto	...	86
CXX.—Affidavit on Application for Order to Carry on Proceedings...	... ...	86
CXXI.—Order to Carry on Proceedings	... ...	87
CXXII.—Summons to Discharge Order to Carry on Proceedings	... ...	87

TABLE OF CONTENTS. xi

| NO. | PAGE |

CXXIII.—Summons to Compel Representative of Deceased Party to Proceed... 88
CXXIV.—Certificate of Abatement... 88
CXXV.—Ditto   of Change of Interest 89

CHAPTER VII.

JOINDER OF CAUSES OF ACTION, TRANSFERS AND CONSOLIDATION.

CXXVI.—Summons to Disunite or Exclude Causes of Action 90
CXXVII.— Ditto to Transfer Action 91
CXXVIII.—Order Transferring Action 91
CXXIX.—Summons to Consolidate 91
CXXX.— Ditto   ditto   Another Form ... 92
CXXXI.—Order to Consolidate 92
CXXXII.—Ditto Refusing to Consolidate 93
CXXXIII.—Heading when Actions are Consolidated ... 93
CXXXIV.—Order Staying Proceedings Pending Trial of Test Action 94

CHAPTER VIII.

TRIAL WITHOUT PLEADINGS.

CXXXV.—Indorsement for Trial Without Pleadings— Contract 95
CXXXVI.—Ditto   ditto   ditto   —Tort 96
CXXXVII.—Notice of Trial Without Pleadings 96
CXXXVIII.—Summons for Statement of Claim 97
CXXXIX.—Order on Summons for Statement of Claim (No. 1) 97
CXL.—Ditto   ditto   ditto   (No. 2) 97
CXLI.—Notice of Special Defence... 97

CHAPTER IX.

The Summons for Directions.

NO.		PAGE
CXLII.—Summons for Directions	... ...	99
CXLIII.—Order ditto	... ...	100
CXLIV.—Summons ditto —Commercial List	...	101
CXLV.—Order ditto ditto	...	102
CXLVI.—Notice of Application for Further Directions	...	103
CXLVII.—Order for Further Directions	... ...	104

CHAPTER X.

Pleadings and Proceedings in Connexion Therewith.

CXLVIII.—Summons for Time...	106
CXLIX.—Particulars Exceeding Three Folios	106
CL.—Summons for Particulars	108
CLI.—Order for ditto	108
CLII.— Ditto ditto of Counterclaim	109
CLIII.—Particulars Delivered Pursuant to Order	109
CLIV.—Summons for Leave to Amend Pleading... ...	110
CLV.—Order Giving ditto ditto	110
CLVI.—Summons to Disallow Amendment	111
CLVII.—Ditto ditto Counterclaim	111
CLVIII.—Summons to Strike out Pleading...	112
CLIX.—Ditto ditto where no Reasonable Cause of Action ...	112
CLX.—Notice of Motion to Strike out or Dismiss ...	113
CLXI.—Judgment Pursuant to Order Dismissing Action	114
CLXII.—Notice of Counterclaim to Person not a Party ...	114
CLXIII.—Summons for Leave to Plead after Reply ...	115
CLXIV.—Ditto ditto Deliver Further Defence	115
CLXV.—Confession of Defence	116
CLXVI.—Judgment for Costs after Confession of Defence	116

CHAPTER XI.

Proceedings in Default of Pleading.

NO.   PAGE

CLXVII.—Summons to Dismiss Action for Want of Prosecution   117
CLXVIII.—Order Dismissing   ditto   ditto   ...   117
CLXIX.—Judgment on Dismissal of Action for Want of Prosecution 118
CLXX.—Ditto   in Default of Defence. Liquidated Demand   118
CLXXI.—Ditto   ditto   ditto.   Unliquidated Demand   119
CLXXII.—Ditto   ditto   ditto. Recovery of Land   119
CLXXIII.—Ditto   for Part of Claim Unanswered by Defence 120
CLXXIV.—Notice of Motion for Judgment in Default of Defence 120
CLXXV.—Affidavit of Service of Notice of Motion   ... 121
CLXXVI.—Affidavit of Default of Defence 121
CLXXVII.—Judgment on Motion   122
CLXXVIII.—Summons to Set Aside Judgment by Default... 122

CHAPTER XII.

Discovery and Inspection.

CLXXIX.—Application for Leave to Deliver Interrogatories 123
CLXXX.—Interrogatories   123
CLXXXI.—Ditto   where More than One Plaintiff or Defendant   124
CLXXXII.—Application for Leave to Deliver Interrogatories to a Corporation 124
CLXXXIII.—Affidavit in Answer to Interrogatories, with Objections 125
CLXXXIV.—Application for Further Answer to Interrogatories 126
CLXXXV.—   Ditto   Discovery of Documents   ...   126

xiv   TABLE OF CONTENTS.

NO.	PAGE
CLXXXVI.—Affidavit as to Documents	126
CLXXXVII.—Notice to Produce Documents for Inspection	128
CLXXXVIII.—Ditto Inspect Documents	129
CLXXXIX.—Application to Inspect Documents not Mentioned in the Pleadings, etc....	130
CXC.—Affidavit in Support of Application to Inspect Documents	130
CXCI.—Affidavit of Verification of Copies of Business Books	131

CHAPTER XIII.

Payment into Court.

CXCII.—Application for Leave to Pay into Court after Defence Delivered	132
CXCIII.—Notice of Payment into Court	132
CXCIV.—Authority of Plaintiff for Money to be Paid out of Court	133
CXCV.—Notice of Acceptance of Money Paid into Court	133
CXCVI.—Judgment for Costs after Acceptance of Money Paid into Court	134

CHAPTER XIV.

Admissions.

CXCVII.—Voluntary Notice of Admission of Facts ...	135
CXCVIII.—Notice to Admit Documents	136
CXCIX.—Ditto ditto Facts	137
CC.—Admission of Facts Pursuant to Notice ...	138
CCI.—Affidavit of Signature of Admissions	139
CCII.—Notice to Produce Documents	139
CCIII.—Affidavit of Service of Notice to Produce ...	140

CHAPTER XV.
SPECIAL FORMS OF TRIAL.

NO.		PAGE
CCIV.—Application to Set Down Points of Law	... ...	141
CCV.—Special Case by Consent	...	142
CCVI.—Application for Special Case	...	143
CCVII.—Application for Leave to Set Down Special Case where Person under Disability a Party	...	143
CCVIII.—Memorandum of Entry of Special Case ...	...	144
CCIX.—Agreement as to Result of Special Case ...	...	144
CCX.—Judgment on Special Case	...	145
CCXI.—Issue of Fact...	...	145
CCXII.—Application for Trial of Issue of Fact	...	146

CHAPTER XVI.
DISCONTINUANCE AND WITHDRAWAL.

CCXIII.—Notice of Discontinuance	147
CCXIV.—Application by Plaintiff for Leave to Discontinue	148
CCXV.—Order Giving Plaintiff Leave to Discontinue ...	148
CCXVI.—Application by Defendant for Leave to Withdraw Defence	149
CCXVII.—Judgment for Defendant's Costs on Discontinuance after Notice	149
CCXVIII.—Judgment for Defendant's Costs on Discontinuance by Order	150
CCXIX.—Consent for Withdrawal of Action after Entry for Trial	150

CHAPTER XVII.
NOTICE OF AND ENTRY FOR TRIAL AND PROCEEDINGS IN CONNEXION THEREWITH.

CCXX.—Notice of Place of Trial	151
CCXXI.—Application for Change of Venue	152
CCXXII.—Notice of Trial	152

xvi   TABLE OF CONTENTS.

NO.   PAGE
CCXXIII.—Notice of Trial with Jury by Defendant   ...   153
CCXXIV.—Ditto   Special Jury   153
CCXXV.—Application by Defendant to Dismiss in Default
           of Notice of Trial   154
CCXXVI.—Consent to Countermand Notice of Trial   ...   154
CCXXVII.—Application for Leave to Countermand Notice
           of Trial   155
CCXXVIII.—Notice Countermanding Notice of Trial   ...   155
CCXXIX.—Entry of Action for Trial   155
CCXXX.—Application for Postponement of Trial   ...   156

CHAPTER XVIII.

EVIDENCE.

CCXXXI.—Agreement to take Evidence by Affidavit   ...   157
CCXXXII.—Application for Leave to Prove Particular Facts
           by Affidavit   157
CCXXXIII.—Notice of Intention to Read Evidence-Taken in
           Another Cause   158
CCXXXIV.—Application for Examination of Witness before
           Examiner   158
CCXXXV.—Order for Examination of Witness before Trial   159
CCXXXVI.—Application for Commission   159
CCXXXVII.—Short Order for Commission   160
CCXXXVIII.—Long Order for Commission   161
CCXXXIX.—Writ of Commission   164
CCXL.—Order for Letter of Request for Commission...   166
CCXLI.—Request for Commission   167
CCXLII.—Undertaking by Solicitors as to Costs of Request for Commission   168
CCXLIII.—Order for Appointment of Special Examiners
           to take Evidence Abroad   169
CCXLIV.—Application for Inspection of Bankers' Books   170
CCXLV.—Præcipe of Subpœna   170
CCXLVI.—Subpœna ad Testificandum. General Form...   171
CCXLVII.—Ditto   Ditto   High Court   ...   171

TABLE OF CONTENTS. xvii

NO.		PAGE
CCXLVIII.—Subpœna ad Testificandum. Assizes		172
CCXLIX.—Ditto Duces Tecum		172
CCL.—Writ of Habeas Corpus ad Testificandum		173
CCLI.—Affidavit of Service of Subpœna		174
CCLII.—Notice of Evidence in Mitigation of Damages		175
CCLIII.—Affidavit by One Deponent		176
CCLIV.—Ditto Two or More Deponents		177

CHAPTER XIX.

MOTION FOR JUDGMENT.

CCLV.—Notice of Motion for Judgment		179
CCLVI.— Ditto to Set Aside Judgment Directed (No. 1)		179
CCLVII.— Ditto Ditto (No. 2)		180
CCLVIII.— Ditto for Judgment after Trial of Issue		181
CCLIX.—Application for Leave to Set Down Motion for Judgment		181

CHAPTER XX.

JUDGMENTS.

CCLX.—Final Judgment under Order XIV.		182
CCLXI.—Ditto Ditto against Married Woman		183
CCLXII.—Ditto Ditto on Conditional Order		184
CCLXIII.—Judgment after Trial with Jury		184
CCLXIV.—Ditto Ditto without Jury		185
CCLXV.—Ditto in Court for Amount to be Ascertained		186
CCLXVI.—Ditto after Trial before Referee		186

C.F. b

NO.		PAGE
CCLXVII.—Judgment after Trial of Questions of Account by Referee		187
CCLXVIII.—Ditto of Dismissal on Non-appearance of Plaintiff		187
CCLXIX.—Ditto on Motion after Trial of Issue		188
CCLXX.—Ditto on Warrant of Attorney		189
CCLXXI.—Memorandum to be Indorsed on Judgment or Order where Act ordered to be done		189
CCLXXII.—Order by Consent for Judgment		189
CCLXXIII.—Consent of Defendant to Order		190
CCLXXIV.—Judgment by Consent		190

CHAPTER XXI.

EXECUTION.

CCLXXV.—Summons for Leave to Issue Execution	191
CCLXXVI.—Præcipe for Writ of *Fieri Facias*	192
CCLXXVII.—Writ of *Fieri Facias*	193
CCLXXVIII.—Ditto ditto against Married Woman	194
CCLXXIX.—Ditto ditto for Costs	195
CCLXXX.—Præcipe for Writ of Possession	196
CCLXXXI.—Writ of Possession	196
CCLXXXII.—Præcipe for Writ of Possession and *Fieri Facias*	197
CCLXXXIII.—Writ of Possession and *Fieri Facias*	197
CCLXXXIV.—Writ of *Fieri Facias* by Executors of Plaintiff	199
CCLXXXV.—Notice of Renewal of Writ of *Fieri Facias*	200
CCLXXXVI.—Application for Stay of Execution	200
CCLXXXVII.—Præcipe for Writ of Delivery	201
CCLXXXVIII.—Writ of Delivery	201

CHAPTER XXII.

ATTACHMENT OF PERSONS AND DEBTS.

NO.		PAGE
CCLXXXIX.—Notice of Motion for Leave to Issue Writ of Attachment	...	203
CCXC.—Summons for Leave to Issue Writ of Attachment	...	204
CCXCI.—Order Giving Leave to Issue Writ of Attachment	...	204
CCXCII.—Præcipe for Writ of Attachment	...	205
CCXCIII.—Writ of Attachment	...	205
CCXCIV.—Summons for Examination of Judgment Debtor		206
CCXCV.—Order ditto ditto ditto		207
CCXCVI.—Ditto ditto touching Means	...	207
CCXCVII.—Affidavit in Support of Application for Garnishee Order	...	208
CCXCVIII.—Garnishee Order *Nisi*	...	209
CCXCIX.—Ditto ditto Absolute	...	210
CCC.—Order for Issue between Judgment Creditor and Garnishee	...	211
CCCI.—Issue between Judgment Creditor and Garnishee	...	212

CHAPTER XXIII.

CHARGING ORDERS.

CCCII.—Affidavit on Application for Charging Order	...	214
CCCIII.—Charging Order *Nisi*	...	215
CCCIV.—Ditto ditto Absolute	...	216
CCCV.—Affidavit as to Stock	...	216
CCCVI.—Notice as to Stock	...	217
CCCVII.—Summons to Discharge Notice as to Stock	...	218
CCCVIII.—Request for Withdrawal of Notice as to Stock		218

CHAPTER XXIV.

INTERPLEADER PROCEEDINGS.

NO.			PAGE
CCCLX.—Affidavit by Applicant for Interpleader Order ...			219
CCCX.—Interpleader Summons by Defendant			220
CCCXI.—Ditto ditto Sheriff			221
CCCXII.—Interpleader Order (No. 1), Barring Claimant...			221
CCCXIII.—Ditto	ditto	(No. 1A), that Sheriff Withdraw	222
CCCXIV.—Ditto	ditto	(No. 2), Substituting Claimant	222
CCCXV.—Ditto	ditto	(No. 3), for Sale and Trial of Issue	223
CCCXVI.—Ditto	ditto	(No. 4), for Payment into Court by Claimant and Trial of Issue (A.) ...	224
CCCXVII.—Ditto	ditto	(No. 5), for Payment into Court by Claimant and Trial of Issue (B.) ...	225
CCCXVIII.—Ditto	ditto	(No. 6), on Summary Decision by Consent	225
CCCXIX.—Ditto	ditto	(No. 7), for Sale and Payment of Execution Creditor and Claimant	226
CCCXX.—Ditto	ditto	(No. 8), Remitting to County Court	226
CCCXXI.—Notice to Sheriff of Claim by Claimant ...			227
CCCXXII.—Notice by Sheriff to Execution Creditor of Claim			228
CCCXXIII.—Notice by Execution Creditor to Sheriff Admitting or Disputing Claim			228

CHAPTER XXV.

ORDERS AS TO PROPERTY. INJUNCTIONS. RECEIVERS.

NO. PAGE
CCCXXIV.—Application for Order for Preservation or Interim Custody of Property, etc. 229
CCCXXV.—Ditto ditto Order for Sale of Perishable Goods 229
CCCXXVI.—Ditto ditto Inspection of Property ... 230
CCCXXVII.—Order for Interim Injunction 230
CCCXXVIII.—Interim Order for Appointment of Receiver ... 231
CCCXXIX.—Application for Delivery up of Property where Lien is Claimed 232
CCCXXX.— Ditto Order for Private Sale ... 232
CCCXXXI.—Order for Private Sale 233

CHAPTER XXVI.

APPEALS.

CCCXXXII.—Notice of Appeal from Master to Judge in Chambers ... 234
CCCXXXIII.—Ditto ditto Judge in Chambers 235
CCCXXXIV.—Ditto ditto Judge in Court ... 236
CCCXXXV.—Memorandum of Entry of Appeal 237
CCCXXXVI.—Notice of Cross Appeal by Respondent ... 237
CCCXXXVII.—Notice of Motion for Security for Costs ... 238
CCCXXXVIII.— Ditto for New Trial 238
CCCXXXIX.— Ditto on Appeal from County Court ... 239

CHAPTER XXVII.

PARTNERSHIP PROCEEDINGS.

NO.		PAGE
CCCXL.—Summons for Disclosure of Names of Partners		240
CCCXLI.—Order ditto ditto ditto		241
CCCXLII.—Demand for Names of Plaintiff Firm ...	...	241
CCCXLIII.—Declaration of ditto ditto ...	...	242
CCCXLIV.—Summons for Order to Charge Partnership Property	...	242
CCCCXLV.—Order Charging Partnership Property	...	243

CHAPTER XXVIII.

ARBITRATIONS AND REFERENCES.

CCCXLVI.—Submission to Arbitration	...	244
CCCXLVII.—Summons to Stay Proceedings where there is a Submission	...	245
CCCXLVIII.—Notice to Appoint Arbitrator	...	245
CCCXLIX.—Summons for Appointment of Arbitrator	...	246
CCCL.— Ditto Leave to Enforce Award	...	246
CCCLI.—Notice of Motion to Set Aside Award...	...	247
CCCLII.—Order of Reference under Section 13 of Arbitration Act, 1889	...	248
CCCLIII.—Order of Reference under Section 14 of Arbitration Act, 1889	...	248
CCCLIV.—Special Case by Referee or Arbitrator	...	249

CHAPTER XXIX.

PROCEEDINGS IN DISTRICT REGISTRIES.

CCCLV.—Title in District Registry Proceedings	...	250
CCCLVI.—Notice of Entry of Appearance in District Registry	...	251

TABLE OF CONTENTS.   xxiii

NO.		PAGE
CCCLVII.—Summons in District Registry	... ...	251
CCCLVIII.—Notice of Appeal from District Registrar to Judge	... ...	251
CCCLIX.—Notice of Removal from District Registry to London	... ...	252
CCCLX.—Certificate of Non-Delivery of Defence		252
CCCLXI.—Summons to Remove Action to District Registry		252
CCCLXII.—Ditto ditto from ditto		253
CCCLXIII.—Notice of Defendant's Address for Service in London	... ...	253

CHAPTER XXX.

Miscellaneous Forms.

CCCLXIV.—Affidavit on Registration of Bill of Sale	...	254
CCCLXV.— Ditto Entry of Satisfaction of Bill of Sale		255
CCCLXVI.—Summons for ditto ditto	...	256
CCCLXVII.—Affidavit on Renewal of Registration of Bill of Sale	... ...	256
CCCLXVIII.—Summons for Security of Costs	... ...	257
CCCLXIX.—Summons to Review Taxation of Costs	...	257
CCCLXX.—Order for Arrest under Debtors Act	... ...	257
CCCLXXI.—Summons to Set Aside Proceedings on the Ground of Irregularity	... ...	258

TABLE OF STAMPS 259

QUEEN'S BENCH FORMS.

LIST OF ABBREVIATIONS.

A.P.	Annual Practice.
App.	Appendix.
ed.	edition.
r.	rule.
O.	Order.
Y.S.C.P.	Yearly Supreme Court Practice. By M. MUIR MACKENZIE, S. G. LUSHINGTON, Barristers-at-Law, and J. C. Fox, Master of the Supreme Court. 1899. Price 20s. Net.

QUEEN'S BENCH FORMS.

CHAPTER I.

WRITS OF SUMMONS.

No. I.
Writ of Summons, General Form.
(O. 2, r. 3 ; Y. S. C. P. and A. P., App. A., Part I., No. 1.)

         18   ,   , No. .
IN THE HIGH COURT OF JUSTICE,
Queen's Bench Division.
 BETWEEN   plaintiff (*a*),
     and
           defendant (*a*).

VICTORIA, by the grace of God, of the United Kingdom of Great Britain and Ireland, Queen, Defender of the Faith, To   of   in the county of   .

We command you, that within eight days after the service of this writ upon you, inclusive of the day of such service, you do cause an appearance to be entered for you in an action at the suit of

AND TAKE NOTICE that in default of your so doing the plaintiff may proceed therein, and judgment may be given in your absence.

Witness HARDINGE STANLEY, EARL OF HALSBURY (*b*), Lord High Chancellor of Great Britain, the   day

C.F.   B

of   in the year of Our Lord One thousand eight hundred and   .

N.B.—This writ is to be served within twelve calendar months from the date thereof, or, if renewed, within six calendar months from the date of the last renewal, including the day of such date, and not afterwards.*

The defendant may appear hereto by entering an appearance either personally or by solicitor at the Central Office, Royal Courts of Justice, London.

The plaintiff's claim is for (c)   .

[And the sum of l. for costs ; and if the amount claimed is paid to the plaintiff or his solicitor within four days from the service hereof, further proceedings will be stayed (d)].

This writ was issued by   of   , whose address for service is (e)   , [agent for   of   in the county of   ] solicitor for the said plaintiff, who resides at   .

This writ was served by me at   on the defendant   on   day (f), the   day of   18   .

INDORSED the   day of   18   .
(Signed)   .
(Address)   .

(a) For descriptions of parties, see pp. 4—6.

(b) If the office of Lord Chancellor be vacant, substitute the name of the Lord Chief Justice of England (O. 2, r. 8).

(c) For forms of general indorsements, see pp. 6—9.

(d) This to be added where the claim, though not specially indorsed, is for a debt or liquidated demand only (O. 3, r. 7). But if the amount claimed be less than 20l., this indorsement must not be added, otherwise the writ will not be issued at the Central Office.

(e) Not more than three miles from the principal entrance of the central hall at the Royal Courts of Justice (O. 4, r. 1).

(f) The indorsement of service should give the day of the week. It must be made within three days at most after service (O. 9, r. 15).

GENERAL FORM—DISTRICT REGISTRY. 3

No. II.
Writ of Summons, Specially Indorsed.
(O. 2, r. 3 ; O. 3, r. 6 ; Y. S. C. P. and A. P., App. A., Part I., No. 2.)

[*Proceed as in No. I. as far as asterisk.*]

Appearance is to be entered at the Central Office, Royal Courts of Justice, London.

Statement of Claim :

The plaintiff's claim is (*a*)   .

Particulars :

Place of trial (*b*)   .
(Signed)   .

And the sum of   *l.* (*c*) [*or*, such sum as may be allowed on taxation], for costs. If the amount claimed is paid to the plaintiff or his solicitor or agent within four days from the service hereof, further proceedings will be stayed.

This writ was issued, etc. [*Conclude as in No. I.*]

(*a*) For forms of special indorsements, see pp. 14—34˙
(*b*) Unless otherwise stated, will be Middlesex (O. 20, r. 5 ; O. 36, r. 1).
(*c*) O. 3, r. 7, and notes.

No. III.
Writ of Summons, General Form. District Registry.
(O. 2, r. 3 ; O. 4, r. 3 ; O. 5, rr. 3, 4 ; Y. S. C. P. and A. P., App. A., Part I., No. 3.)

18   ,   , No. .

IN THE HIGH COURT OF JUSTICE,
  Queen's Bench Division,
    (Norwich) District Registry.

BETWEEN, etc. [*Proceed as in No. I. as far as asterisk.*]

A defendant who resides or carries on business within the above-named district must enter appearance at the office of the registrar of that district (a) (No. 12, Castle Meadow, Norwich).

A defendant who neither resides, nor carries on business within the said district may enter appearance either at the office of the said registrar or at the Central Office, Royal Courts of Justice, London.*

The plaintiff's claim is for, etc. [*Conclude as in No. I.*]

(a) The address of the office of the district registrar must be inserted. Note also that the address for service must be within the district.

No. IV.

Writ of Summons, Specially Indorsed. District Registry.

(O. 2, r. 3 ; O. 3, r. 6 ; Y. S. C. P. and A. P., App. A., Part I., No. 4.)

[*Procced as in No. III. as far as asterisk.*]

Statement of Claim :

The plaintiff's claim is, etc. [*Conclude as in No. II. (a).*]

(a) Note that the address for service must be within the district.

No. V.

Description of Parties.

[*On the face of the writ.*]

The forms given below are specimens of the manner in which it is usual and desirable to describe the parties to an action on the face of the writ. Some of them show the representative capacity of the parties, which, whether specified or not on the face of the writ, is by O. 3, r. 4, required to be shown on the indorsement (see p. 6). In the case of executors and administrators, it is superfluous to describe them as such on the face of the writ ; their own names suffice.

A plaintiff must be described by his full name. In the case of a defendant whose full name is not known, his initials may be inserted, thus : " J. S. Moore, defendant." (For form of appearance by a defendant so sued, see p. 46.)

DESCRIPTION OF PARTIES.

(A.) Albert White, an infant, by Henry James Dobson, his next friend. Infant.
Thomas Henry Wilson, an infant, by Robert Wilson, his father and next friend.

(B.) John Smithson and Ada Mary Smithson, his wife. Husband and wife.

(C.) Jane Jackson, a married woman [*or*, widow, *or*, spinster]. Woman.

It is unnecessary to describe a married woman as "wife of A. B.," or to state that she is suing or being sued in respect of her separate estate.

(D.) (i.) *So found by inquisition.*—Richard Hansford, committee of the estate of Frederick Joseph Fleet, a person of unsound mind so found by inquisition, and the said Frederick Joseph Fleet by the said Richard Hansford, his committee. Lunatic.

(ii.) *Not so found.*—Frederick Joseph Fleet, a person of unsound mind not so found by inquisition, by Richard Hansford, his next friend.

(E.) Dodd, Weyman and Fox. Firm.
Brown, Margetson & Co. O. 48A.,
B. Jenkins and Son. r. 1.

In actions by or against a firm, the names of the partners need not be set out.

(F.) John William Paul, the trustee of the property of Henry Rogers, a bankrupt. Bankrupt.

(G.) The North London Railway Company. Company.
The Electric Lighting Corporation, Limited.

(H.) The Mayor, Aldermen and Burgesses of the Borough of Great Yarmouth (acting by the Council as the Urban Sanitary Authority for the said Borough). Municipal corporation.

(I.) The County Council of Kent. Council.
The Parish Council of Marwood.

(J.) William Angus Drogo Montagu, Duke of Manchester. Peer.

Government department.
(K.) The Secretary of State for India in Council.

Friendly society.
(L.) William Henry Thompson and Norman Fisher, trustees of the New Union Friendly Society.

Public officer.
(M.) Thomas Judson, public officer of the General Financial Bank.

No. VI.
Indorsement of Representative Capacity of Parties.
(O. 3, r. 4.)

Executor or administrator.
(A.) The plaintiff's claim is as [*or*, against the defendant as] executor [*or*, administrator] of Philip James Arkwright, deceased, for—

Trustee.
(B.) The plaintiff's claim is as [*or*, against the defendant as] trustee under the will of Edward Jamieson, for—

Lord Campbell's Act.
(C.) The plaintiff's claim is on behalf of herself and her children for—

Public officer.
(D.) The plaintiff's claim is as [*or*, against the defendant as] public officer of the New Colonial Banking Corporation.

For other forms, see Yearly Supreme Court Practice and the Annual Practice, App. A., Part III., Section VII.

General Indorsements.
(O. 2, r. 1 ; O. 3, rr. 1—3.)

I.—*Money Claims where no Special Indorsement.*

A large number of forms are given in the Yearly Supreme Court Practice and the Annual Practice, App. A., Part III., Section II. (*q.v.*). Since, however, it is usual to specially indorse the writ in actions for a debt or liquidated demand, arising in the cases enumerated in O. 3, r. 6, general indorsements for money claims are of comparatively infrequent occurrence. Accordingly only a few miscellaneous forms are given below.

DAMAGES AND OTHER CLAIMS.

No. VII.

(A.) The plaintiff's claim is 70*l.* for arrears of rent Rent. of No. 16, King Street, Marylebone.

(B.) The plaintiff's claim is 63*l.*, whereof 48*l.* is for Salary arrears of salary, and 15*l.* for commission earned by and commission. the plaintiff as a traveller.

(C.) The plaintiff's claim is 107*l.* 16*s.* for work done Work and money paid to the use of the defendant by the done and plaintiff as a builder. money paid.

(D.) The plaintiff's claim is 150*l.* for a return of Money money obtained from the plaintiff by fraud, or obtained alternatively for money lent. by fraud or lent.

(E.) The plaintiff's claim is 82*l.* 3*s.* 9*d.*, being as to 77*l.* 3*s.* 9*d.* thereof for the price of goods sold, and as Goods to 5*l.* thereof for the carriage of the said goods by sold and carriage. railway.

II.—Damages and other Claims.

A large variety of forms of general indorsement will be found in the Yearly Supreme Court Practice and the Annual Practice, App. A., Part III., Section IV. (*q.v.*). Although these concise forms, the use of which is prescribed by O. 3, r. 3, will be found sufficient in many cases, yet in numerous instances it will in practice be found desirable, or even necessary, to employ forms somewhat more explicit. Still it must be borne in mind that O. 3, r. 2, provides that in these indorsements "it shall not be essential to set forth the precise ground of complaint, or the precise remedy or relief to which the plaintiff considers himself entitled"; and by O. 20, r. 4, "whenever a statement of claim is delivered the plaintiff may therein alter, modify, or extend (*a*) his claim without any amendment of the indorsement of the writ." The risk of indorsements "other or more prolix than the forms . . . prescribed" (O. 2, r. 2), occasioning extra costs, to be borne by the party using them, may in practice be regarded as infinitesimal.

A few forms only are given below. They are intended to serve as specimens of the degree of preciseness which appears to be desirable in certain cases. A comparison of them with the corresponding forms in the Yearly Supreme Court Practice and the Annual Practice will, it is hoped, assist the practitioner in deciding how to frame his indorsement.

(*a*) As to the limits to which this permission extends, see the note to O. 20, r. 4.

WRITS OF SUMMONS.

No. VIII.

Assault, etc.
(A.) The plaintiffs' claim is for damages for assault and false imprisonment of the plaintiff, Sarah Ann Jones, who is the wife of the plaintiff Henry Jones, and for slander of the plaintiff Henry Jones.

Claims by or against husband and wife may be joined with claims by or against either of them separately (O. 18, r. 4).

Contract.
(B.) The plaintiff's claim is for damages for breach of contract to accept and pay for boiler plates.

(C.) The plaintiff's claim is for damages for breach of contract to employ the plaintiff as clerk.

(D.) The plaintiff's claim is for damages for breach of contract to do certain building work upon the plaintiff's premises at No. 4, Albany Grove, Peckham.

Detention.
(E.) The plaintiff's claim is for the return of a piano and certain household furniture, the property of the plaintiff, or their value, and damages for their detention.

Dismissal.
(F.) The plaintiff's claim is for damages for wrongful dismissal from the defendant's employment as traveller, and for arrears of salary and for commission.

Ejectment.
(G.) The plaintiff's claim is to recover possession of the house and premises known as Oakleigh, Grove Road, Shortlands, in the county of Kent, and for damages for breach of covenant to keep the said house in repair.

Fraudulent misrepresentation.
(H.) The plaintiff's claim is for damages for fraudulent misrepresentations on the sale of the defendant's business of a greengrocer.

Libel and injunction.
(I.) The plaintiff's claim is for damages for libel contained in a book called "The London Investor's Guide," and for an injunction to restrain the defendants, their servants and agents from publishing, selling or circulating the said book.

Negligence.
(J.) The plaintiffs' claim is for damages for injuries to the plaintiffs by reason of the negligent driving of the defendants or their servants.

DAMAGES AND OTHER CLAIMS.

(K.) The plaintiff's claim is for damages for injuries to the plaintiff while a passenger on the defendants' tramway by the negligence of the defendants' servants.

(L.) The plaintiff's claim is for damages for injury to the plaintiff by the negligence of the defendants or their servants in digging a trench upon the highway known as George Street, Marylebone, and leaving the same unfenced.

(M.) The plaintiff's claim is for damages for breach of covenant to keep in repair the house known as No. 45, Beauchamp Avenue, Leicester. Repairs.

(N.) The plaintiff's claim is for damages for wrongfully entering the plaintiff's meadow known as Borrett's Acre, in the parish of Fleet, in the county of Essex, and depositing rubbish there, and for an injunction to restrain the defendant, his servants, or agents from entering the said meadow and from interfering with the plaintiff's use and enjoyment thereof. Trespass and injunction.

Indorsements for Trial without Pleadings.

As to this, see p. 95.

CHAPTER II.

SPECIAL INDORSEMENTS.

(O. 3, r. 6; Y. S. C. P. and A. P., App. C., Sect. IV.)

The cases in which a writ may be specially indorsed with a statement of the plaintiff's claim are set out in O. 3, r. 6, in the following words :—" In all actions where the plaintiff seeks only to recover a debt or liquidated demand in money payable by the defendant, with or without interest, arising (A) upon a contract express or implied (as, for instance, on a bill of exchange, promissory note, or cheque, or other simple contract debt); or (B) on a bond or contract under seal for payment of a liquidated amount of money; or (C) on a statute where the sum sought to be recovered is a fixed sum of money or in the nature of a debt other than a penalty; or (D) on a guaranty, whether under seal or not, where the claim against the principal is in respect of a debt or liquidated demand only; or (E) on a trust; or (F) in actions for the recovery of land, with or without a claim for rent or mesne profits, by a landlord against a tenant whose term has expired or has been duly determined by notice to quit, or against persons claiming under such tenant."

A special indorsement is deemed to be a statement of claim (O. 20, r. 1 (a)).

Particulars.—In the Yearly Supreme Court Practice and the Annual Practice (App. C., Section IV., Nos. 1—12, and Section VII., No. 1), specimen forms are given, and by O. 3, r. 6, it is laid down that special indorsements " shall be to the effect of such of the forms in Appendix C., Section IV., as shall be applicable to the case." The indorsement should give sufficiently specific particulars to bring to the mind of the defendant knowledge as to what the plaintiff's claim is (*Bickers* v. *Speight*, 22 Q. B. D. 7). The defendant is entitled to have sufficient particulars to enable him to satisfy his mind whether he ought to pay or resist (*Walker* v. *Hicks*, 3 Q. B. D. 8; *Smith* v. *Wilson*, 5 C. P. D. 25; *Bickers* v. *Speight*, 22 Q. B. D. 7). An indorsement which would have been a sufficient special indorsement within the meaning of the Common Law Procedure Act, 1852 (15 & 16 Vict. c. 76), to entitle the plaintiff to judgment under s. 27, in default of appearance, is a special indorsement within the meaning of O. 3, r. 6, and O. 14 (*Bickers* v. *Speight*, 22 Q. B. D. 7; *Aston* v. *Hurwitz*, 41 L. T. (N.S.) 521).

A special indorsement should include definite particulars of parties, dates and items, and care must be taken not to omit any other material allegations (*e.g.*, notice of dishonour, notice to quit, etc.).

Where the particulars of debt exceed three folios, and are not set out in full in the indorsement, such fact must be stated in the indorsement and reference made to particulars either previously delivered in the form of an account or otherwise, or delivered with the specially indorsed writ (O. 19, r. 6. See *post*, Nos. X., XV., XVI., XXXIX., XL., XLI., and CXLIX.

Interest.—(i.) To date of writ. This may be included in a special indorsement, (A) where the right to it is given by statute, *e.g.*, the Bills of Exchange Act, 1882 (45 & 46 Vict. c. 61, ss. 9 (3), 57); the Judgments Act (1 & 2 Vict. c. 110, s. 17); and (B) where there is an express agreement to pay interest. Such agreement must be sufficiently alleged in the indorsement. (See *post*, Nos. XIX., XXII.—XXXIII.)

(ii.) To payment or judgment. A claim for this

INTEREST. 13

may be added in the case (A) above, but it is doubtful whether it ought to be included in case (B). See Odgers on Pleading, 3rd ed., p. 49 ; also *post*, Nos. XXIII.—XXV., XXX., XXXII., XXXIII.

As to specially indorsed writs generally, see the notes to O. 3, r. 6, in the Yearly Supreme Court Practice and the Annual Practice.

The forms which follow are those which, it is thought, will be found most generally useful. The short marginal descriptions are alphabetical.

No. IX.
Money Due on an Account stated.

Account stated.
The plaintiff's claim is for money found to be due from the defendant to the plaintiff on an account stated between them.

  1897.   Particulars: £ s. d.
4th December. Balance admitted by letter of defendant of this date to be due to plaintiff for the carriage of goods - £58 9 6

Place of trial, Surrey.
      (Signed) NICHOLSON and WEBSTER.
See also Nos. XV. and XL., *post*.

No. X.
Work done under a Building Contract.

Building contract.
The plaintiff's claim is for work and labour done, and materials supplied under a building contract, dated 3rd March, 1891, and for extras.

  1892.   Particulars: £ s. d.
12th September. To balance due on completion of the said contract, according to the certificate of Mr. John Johnson, defendant's architect, of this date - 150 0 0
     To extras, ordered by defendant, full particulars of which have been delivered to the defendant, and exceed three folios (*a*) - - 38 17 0

      Amount due - £188 17 0

Place of trial, Durham.
      (Signed)

(*a*) See No. CXLIX.

ALLOTMENT MONEY AND CALLS UPON SHARES. 15

No. XI.
Carriage of Goods by Railway.

The plaintiffs' claim is for money payable by the defendant to the plaintiffs for the carriage of the defendant's goods by the plaintiffs' railway, at the defendant's request. *Carriage of goods.*

Particulars:
1895. £ s. d.
3rd July. Carriage of 480 tons of machinery
 from London to Leicester, at
 2s. 6d. per ton - - - £60 0 0
Place of trial, Middlesex.
 (Signed) .

No. XII.
Commission on Sale of Houses.

The plaintiff's claim is for balance of commission due to the plaintiff from the defendant on the sale of the houses, Nos. 1, 3, 5, 7 and 9, South Road, Ipswich, by the plaintiff for the defendant at his request. *Commission.*

1896. Particulars : £ s. d.
7th June. Agreed commission at 5 per
 cent. on 3,500l., the proceeds of sale of the said
 houses - - - - 175 0 0
8th October. By cash - - - - 20 0 0

 Balance due - £155 0 0

Place of trial of trial, Suffolk. (Signed) .
See also No. XXXIX.

No. XIII.
Allotment Money and Calls upon Shares in Company.

The plaintiff's claim is for money due from the defendant, as a member of the plaintiff company, to the plaintiffs (being a company incorporated under the *Company.*

Companies Acts) for allotment money of five shillings per share on 200 shares in the said company allotted to the defendant as such member at his request, and for two calls of two shillings and sixpence each upon the said 200 shares, of which the defendant is a holder, whereby an action has accrued to the plaintiffs.

	Particulars :	£	s.	d.
1896. 12th September.	Allotment of 200 shares to defendant at 5s. per share	50	0	0
1897. 1st March.	First call at 2s. 6d. per share	25	0	0
1st July.	Second call at 2s. 6d. per share	25	0	0
	Amount due	£100	0	0

Place of trial, Middlesex. (Signed)   .

See Yearly Supreme Court Practice and the Annual Practice, App. C., Sect. IV., No. 9.

No. XIV.

Carriage of Goods by Sea.

Freight.

The plaintiff's claim is for money payable by the defendant to the plaintiff for freight for the conveyance by the plaintiff for the defendant at his request, of goods in the steamship "Puffin," from Poti to London, as per bill of lading.

	Particulars :	£	s.	d.
1894. 5th September.	Amount of freight on 3,000 quarters of wheat, at 10d. per quarter	£125	0	0

Place of trial, Middlesex.
(Signed)   .

No. XV.
Goods Sold and Delivered and Account Stated.

The plaintiff's claim is for the price of goods sold and delivered. *Goods sold and delivered*

		£	s.	d.
1896.	Particulars:			
1st February to 31st June.	To groceries supplied between these dates, full particulars of which, exceeding three folios (b), were delivered to defendant on or about 4th July, 1896	53	17	4
12th July.	To 3 lbs. fresh butter at 1s. 4d.	0	4	0
12th July.	To 2½ lbs. of best Indian tea at 3s.	0	7	6
14th July.	To 2 tins of biscuits	0	3	9
Credit.		54	12	7
1896.				
27th July.	By cash £5 0 0			
21st August.	,, £10 0 0			
		15	0	0
	Balance due	£39	12	7

The plaintiff also claims the said sum of 39l. 12s. 7d. upon an account stated.

		£	s.	d.
1896.	Particulars:			
29th October.	Amount found to be due from defendant to plaintiff, verbally admitted by defendant on this date	£39	12	7

Place of trial, Middlesex.

(Signed) GIBSON and FIELD.

(a) See No. CXLIX.

SPECIAL INDORSEMENTS.

No. XVI.
Guarantee for the Price of Goods Sold.

Guarantee.

The plaintiff's claim is against the defendant for the price of goods sold and delivered by the plaintiff to James Henry Wilson, under the following guarantee:

3rd January, 1896.

Mr. Arthur Stonehouse.
Dear Sir,
   In consideration of your supplying leather goods to the order of Mr. J. H. Wilson, of 12, King Street, I will be responsible for payment up to the amount of 80*l*.

Yours faithfully,
T. H. CUMMINGS.

1896.   Particulars: £ *s. d.*
5th January to 5th April. To goods supplied between these dates to Mr. J. H. Wilson, full particulars of which, exceeding three folios (*a*), as delivered herewith - £73 12 4
Place of trial, City of Bristol.
(Signed) .

(*a*) See No. CXLIX.

No. XVII.
Hire of Furniture.

Hire.

The plaintiff's claim is for money due to the plaintiff from the defendant for the hire of certain household furniture let on hire to the defendant, under an agreement dated 12th May, 1896.

1896.   Particulars: £ *s. d.*
15th September to } Hire of furniture for
 15th July 1897 } ten months at 5*l*.
       per month   -   - £50 0 0
Place of trial, Middlesex.
(Signed) .

No. XVIII.

Foreign Judgment.

The plaintiff's claim is against the defendant upon a judgment of the District Court of Tiflis, in the Empire of Russia, which judgment is still in force and unsatisfied.

Judgment.

Particulars:

1893.   £   s.   d.

8th June. Amount adjudged by a final judgment of the said Court on this date to be due from defendant to plaintiff and ordered by the said Court to be paid by defendant to plaintiff, 10,534 roubles, 76¼ copeks, the equivalent of which in English money is - - - - - £1,053   9   6

Place of trial, Middlesex.

(Signed) .

In the case of an action on a judgment of an English inferior court, an allegation that the original cause of action was within the jurisdiction of such court is necessary (*Read* v. *Pope*, 1 C. M. & R. 302; *Williams* v. *Jones*, 13 M. & W. 628). But, since in an action on a judgment of a foreign court jurisdiction is presumed until the contrary appears (*Robertson* v. *Struth*, 5 Q. B. 941; *Henderson* v. *Henderson*, 6 Q. B. 288), such an allegation is unnecessary.

The statute 1 & 2 Vict. c. 110, s. 17, does not appear to authorise a claim for interest upon a foreign judgment.

SPECIAL INDORSEMENTS.

No. XIX.

Money Lent and Interest.

Loan. The plaintiff's claim is for money lent to the defendant by the plaintiff, and for interest thereon as agreed.

		£	s.	d.
1893.	Particulars:			
2nd March.	To money lent	150	0	0
1894.				
2nd June.	To money lent	100	0	0
	To interest on the said sums of 150*l*. and 100*l*. at the agreed rate of 5 per cent. from 2nd December, 1895, to the date hereof	27	3	6
	Amount due	£277	3	6

Place of trial, Sussex.

(Signed)   .

No. XX.

Return of Deposit.

Money paid. The plaintiff's claim is against the defendant for the return of money paid by the plaintiff to the defendant, the consideration for which has failed.

		£	s.	d.
1896.	Particulars:			
1st June.	To amount of deposit on the sale by contract of this date of a house and land known as "Woodleigh," Little Ormeston, in the county of Cambridgeshire, to which the defendant failed to make out a good title	£125	0	0

Place of trial, Cambridgeshire.

(Signed)   .

No. XXI.

Money Received by Agent for Sale of Goods.

The plaintiff's claim is for money had and received by the defendant to the use of the plaintiffs. Money received.

Particulars:

	£ s. d.
1893.	
25th March. To amount received by defendant to this date, as agent for the sale of plaintiff's goods - -	93 17 3
Less agreed commission at 10 per cent. - - -	9 7 9
Amount due - -	£84 9 6

Place of trial, Middlesex.

(Signed) JENKINSON, PARR AND CO.

No. XXII.

Inland Bill of Exchange. Indorsee against Acceptor.

The plaintiff's claim is against the defendant, as acceptor of a bill of exchange for 200*l.*, dated 8th May, 1892, drawn by William Smith, payable three months after date to the order of Thomas Jackson, indorsed by the said Thomas Jackson to the plaintiff, and dishonoured on presentation. NEGOTI-
ABLE
INSTRU-
MENTS.
Indorsee
against
acceptor
of bill.

Particulars:

	£ s. d.
1895.	
11th August. Principal - - - -	200 0 0
Interest to date - - -	0 12 6
Amount due - -	£200 12 6

Place of trial, Liverpool.

(Signed) .

See also next Form.

No XXIII.

Inland Bill of Exchange. Indorsee against Acceptor.

NEGOTIABLE INSTRUMENTS.

Indorsee against acceptor of bill.

The plaintiff's claim is 20*l*. 17*s*. 8*d*. principal, noting and interest on the defendant's dishonoured acceptance.

Particulars:

	£	s.	d.
1891.			
21st November. To amount of bill of exchange, dated 18th June 1891, due this day, accepted by the defendant in favour of Chudleigh Brothers, and by them indorsed to the plaintiffs for full value and consideration -	20	10	0
To noting and interest thereon to date - -	0	7	8
Total - -	£20	17	8

The plaintiffs also claim interest on 20*l*. 10*s*. of the above sum at 5*l*. per cent. from the date hereof until payment or judgment.

Place of trial,

(Signed)

See *Lawrence* v. *Willcocks*, [1892] 1 Q. B. 696, where the Court of Appeal approved the above form.

No. XXIV.

Inland Bill of Exchange. Indorsee against Acceptor, Drawer and two Indorsers.

Indorsee against acceptor, drawer, and two indorsers of bill.

The plaintiff's claim is against the defendant James Thomas Harrison, as acceptor, the defendant Henry Cox, as drawer, and the defendants, Robert Williamson and Stephen George Haynes, as several indorsers of a bill of exchange for 120*l*., dated 2nd October, 1897, payable six months after date to the order of the defendant Henry Cox, indorsed by him to the defendant Robert Williamson, indorsed by the defendant Robert Williamson, to the defendant, Stephen George Haynes, and indorsed by the defendant Stephen George Haynes, to the plaintiff of the dishonour of which on presentation the defendants, Henry Cox, Robert Williamson, and Stephen George Haynes, had notice.

NEGOTI-
ABLE
INSTRU-
MENTS.

Particulars:

1898.   £   s. d.
5th April. Principal   -   -   -   - 120 0   0
           Interest to date -   -   -   8 5   0

           Amount due   -   - £128 5   0

The plaintiff also claims interest on the said sum of 120l. from the date hereof until payment or judgment.

Place of trial, Lancashire, West Derby Division.

(Signed) .

No. XXV.

Inland Bill of Exchange. Drawer against Acceptor.

The plaintiff's claim is against the defendant as acceptor of a bill of exchange for 100l., dated 9th April, 1896, drawn by the plaintiff, payable three months after date to John Gooch Kershaw or order, which said bill was delivered by the plaintiff to John Gooch Kershaw, and was dishonoured on presentation, and returned by the said John Gooch Kershaw to the plaintiff.

Drawer
against
acceptor
of bill.

Particulars:

1896.   £   s. d.
12th July. Principal   -   -   -   -   100 0   0
           Interest to date of writ - -   0 12 6
           Expenses of noting   -   -   0   3 0

           Amount due -   -   - £100 15 6

NEGOTIABLE INSTRUMENTS.

The plaintiff also claims interest on the said sum of 100*l.* until payment or judgment.
Place of trial, Derbyshire.
(Signed)

No. XXVI.

Inland Bill of Exchange. Payee against Acceptor.

Payee against acceptor of bill.

The plaintiff's claim is against the defendant as acceptor of a bill of exchange for 150*l.*, dated 3rd December, 1894, drawn by Charles Ernest Stokes and Co. upon the defendant, payable to the plaintiff three months after date, and delivered by the said Charles Ernest Stokes and Co. to the plaintiff, which was dishonoured on presentation.

Particulars:

1895.		£	s.	d.
6th March. Principal	- - - -	150	0	0
Interest	- - - -	0	2	9
Amount due	- -	£150	2	9

Place of trial, London.
(Signed)

No. XXVII.

Inland Bill of Exchange. Indorsee against Drawer in Default of Acceptance.

Indorsee against drawer in default of acceptance of bill.

The plaintiff's claim is against the defendant as drawer of a bill of exchange for 250*l.*, dated 17th August, 1897, drawn upon Murphy and Son, payable three months after date to the order of Walter Barnes, and indorsed by the said Walter Barnes to the plaintiff, which said bill was on 18th August, 1897, duly presented to the said Murphy and Son for acceptance,

FOREIGN BILL OF EXCHANGE.

and was dishonoured by non-acceptance, notice whereof was given to the defendant.

NEGOTIABLE INSTRUMENTS.

Particulars:

	£	s.	d.
Principal due on the said bill - -	250	0	0

Place of trial, City of Bristol.

(Signed) .

No. XXVIII.

Foreign Bill of Exchange. Drawer against Acceptor.

The plaintiff's claim is against the defendant as acceptor of the first of three parts of a foreign bill of exchange for 2,500 francs, dated the 12th day of November, 1893, drawn by the plaintiff at Bordeaux, in France, upon the defendant, payable to the plaintiff in London three months after date, which on presentation was dishonoured and duly protested for non-payment.

Drawer against acceptor of foreign bill.

Particulars:

1894.		£	s.	d.
15th February.	Principal, 2,500 francs, which is equivalent in English money to -	100	0	0
	Interest to date of writ -	0	10	6
	Notarial expenses - -	1	11	6
	Amount due - -	£102	2	0

Place of trial, Middlesex.

(Signed) .

SPECIAL INDORSEMENTS.

Negotiable Instruments.

No. XXIX.

Foreign Bill of Exchange. Indorsee against Drawer and Acceptor.

Indorsee against drawer and acceptor of foreign bill.

The plaintiff's claim is against the defendants, Hurst and Petersen, as acceptors, and against the defendants, Charles Oakley and Sons, as drawers of a foreign bill of exchange for 400*l.*, dated 1st January, 1897, payable in London six months after date to the order of the defendants, Charles Oakley and Sons, and indorsed by them to the plaintiff, which said bill was dishonoured on presentation and duly protested for non-payment, notice of which facts has been given to the defendants, Charles Oakley and Sons.

Particulars:

1897.		£	s.	d.
4th July. Principal	- - - -	400	0	0
Interest	- - - - -	1	4	0
Expenses consequent on dishonour	- - - -	2	2	0
Amount due -	- -	£403	6	0

Place of trial, London.

(Signed) .

No. XXX.

Cheque. Payee against Drawer.

Payee against drawer of cheque.

The plaintiff's claim is against the defendant as drawer of a cheque for 62*l.* 15*s.*, dated 18th November, 1896, drawn upon the London and County Banking Company, Limited (Chatham branch), payable to the plaintiff and delivered by the defendant to the plaintiff, which was dishonoured on presentation, notice whereof was given to the defendant.

Particulars:

	£	s.	d.
Principal	62	15	0
Interest	0	4	8
Amount due	£62	19	8

The plaintiff also claims interest on the said sum of 62l. 15s. until payment or judgment.
Place of trial, Sussex.
(Signed)

No. XXXI.

Cheque. Indorsee against Drawer and Indorser, with Waiver of Notice of Dishonour by Drawer.

The plaintiff's claim is against the defendant Frederick Gregson, as drawer, and the defendant Herbert Munro, as indorser, of a cheque for 171l. 10s., dated 17th March, 1898, drawn upon the Imperial Bank of China in favour of the defendant Herbert Munro, or order, and indorsed by the defendant Herbert Munro, to the plaintiff, which was duly presented for payment and dishonoured on 23rd March, 1898. Notice of such dishonour was given to the defendant Herbert Munro, but was waived by the defendant Frederick Gregson, by a promise to pay the said cheque contained in a letter to the plaintiff, dated 12th April, 1898.

Particulars:

	£	s.	d.
Principal	171	10	0
Interest	0	8	4
Bank charges	0	5	6
Amount due	£172	3	10

Place of trial, Middlesex.
(Signed)

No. XXXII.

Promissory Note. Payee against Maker.

Negotiable Instruments.

Payee against maker of note.

The plaintiff's claim is against the defendant as maker of a promissory note for 250*l.*, dated 1st January, 1892, payable four months after date, which was dishonoured on presentation.

Particulars:

1892.		£	*s.*	*d.*
4th May. Principal	- - - -	250	0	0
Interest -	- - - -	10	0	0
Amount due	- - -	£260	0	0

The plaintiff also claims interest at 5 per cent. on 250*l.* of the above sum until payment or judgment.

Place of trial, Essex.

(Signed) .

No. XXXIII.

Promissory Note. Indorsee against Indorser.

Indorsee against indorser of note.

The plaintiff's claim is against the defendant as indorser of two several promissory notes for 350*l.*, dated 30th April, 1896, and 7th May, 1896, respectively, both payable twenty-eight days after date to the defendant or order, and indorsed by him to the plaintiff, which said notes were dishonoured on presentation, notice whereof was given to the defendant.

1896.	Particulars:	£	*s.*	*d.*
31st May. Principal due on note dated				
30th April	- - -	350	0	0
Interest	- - - -	0	17	6
7th June. Principal due on note dated				
7th May	- - - -	350	0	0
Interest	- - - -	0	13	0
Amount due	- - -	£701	10	6

The plaintiff also claims interest at 5 per cent. upon 700l. of the above sum until payment or judgment.
Place of trial, Aylesbury.
(Signed)

No. XXXIV.
Recovery of Land.

The plaintiff is entitled to the possession of a farm and premises called Church Farm, in the parish of St. James, in the county of Surrey, which was let by the plaintiff to the defendant for the term of three years from the 29th of September, 1879, which term has expired [*or*, as tenant from year to year from the 29th of September, 1875, which said tenancy was duly determined by notice to quit, expiring on the 29th of September, 1881].

The plaintiff claims possession and 50l. for mesne profits.

Place of trial, Surrey.
(Signed)

See Yearly Supreme Court Practice and the Annual Practice, App. C., Sect. VII., No. 1.

Recovery of land.

No. XXXV.
Recovery of Land. Assignee of Reversion against Assignee of Term who has Paid Rent.

The plaintiff is entitled to the possession of a house and premises, known as No. 69, Waterloo Road, Brighton, in the county of Sussex, which were demised by one John Owen to William John Hudson for the term of seven years by a lease, dated 29th September, 1890, and of which the defendant became tenant as assignee of the said William John Hudson by deed, dated 12th March, 1892. The reversion of the said lease was assigned by the said John Owen to the plaintiff by deed, dated 15th September, 1895, notice in writing whereof was given to the defendant on 16th September, 1895, and the defendant has since

Recovery of land.

paid rent to the plaintiff in accordance with the terms of the said lease. The said term expired on 29th September, 1897.

The plaintiff claims possession and 35*l.* for mesne profits.

Place of trial, Sussex.

(Signed)

In an action for the recovery of land by a landlord against a tenant, the writ can be specially indorsed only when the plaintiff was party to the lease or agreement under which the hereditaments have been held, or when the defendant has paid rent to the plaintiff, thereby acknowledging his title, or where the defendant is otherwise estopped from denying the plaintiff's title (*Casey* v. *Hellyer*, 17 Q. B. D. 97). "The rule . . . was intended to include only the most simple cases between landlord and tenant where it is unnecessary to prove any devolution of title, at least, on the part of the plaintiff . . . or where the defendant has attorned to the plaintiff by payment of rent, or is otherwise estopped from denying the plaintiff's title" (*ibid.*, per ESHER, M.R.). "The rule mentions 'persons claiming under such tenant,' but it does not refer to persons claiming under the landlord" (*ibid.*, per LOPES, L.J.).

No. XXXVI.

Rent under a Yearly Tenancy.

Rent.

The plaintiff's claim is for rent of the house and premises, No. 64, Baker Street, Islington, of which the defendant was tenant to the plaintiff, under an agreement in writing, dated 3rd July, 1889, at the yearly rent of 80*l.*, payable quarterly upon the usual quarter days.

Particulars:

	£	s.	d.
Three quarters' rent from 25th March to 25th December, 1897	60	0	0

Place of trial, Middlesex.

(Signed)

No. XXXVII.
Rent under a Covenant in a Lease.

The plaintiff's claim is for rent due under a covenant Rent contained in a lease, dated 17th May, 1887, and made under a between George Robinson of the one part and the covenant. defendant of the other part, whereby the defendant covenanted to pay in respect of premises known as The Grange, Whitworth, in the county of Durham, the yearly rent of 175*l*. by equal quarterly payments on the usual quarter days, during the continuance of the term of 21 years, from 25th March, 1887, granted to him by the said lease. The reversion of the said lease was assigned by the said George Robinson to the plaintiff by deed, dated 5th April, 1894, notice whereof was given to the defendant by letter, dated 6th April, 1894.

Particulars:

	£	s.	d.
Two quarters' rent from 25th March to 29th September, 1896	87	10	0

Place of trial, Durham.

(Signed) .

No. XXXVIII.
Rent of Furnished Apartments.

The plaintiff's claim is for arrears of rent of furnished Rent of apartments at No. 6, Marine Terrace, Lowestoft, of lodgings. which the defendant was tenant under a weekly tenancy.

1896. Particulars:

	£	s.	d.
4th May to 10th August. 14 weeks at 3*l*. 13*s*. 6*d*. per week as agreed	51	9	0

Place of trial, Suffolk. (Signed) .

No. XXXIX.

Salary and Commission of Traveller.

Salary and commission.

The plaintiff's claim is under an agreement in writing, dated 14th March, 1895, for arrears of salary as a traveller, and for commission on sales effected by the plaintiff for the defendants, and for money paid by the plaintiff to the use of the defendants at their request.

Particulars:

		£	s.	d.
1897. 14th January to 14th September.	Eight months' salary at the agreed rate of 8*l*. 8*s*. per month - - - -	67	4	0
Ditto.	Commission on goods to the value of 250*l*. sold by the plaintiff between these dates, full particulars whereof, exceeding three folios (*a*), have been delivered to the defendants, at 7½ per cent as agreed - -	18	15	0
Ditto.	Expenses, full particulars whereof, exceeding three folios (*a*), are delivered herewith - - -	23	17	6
	Amount due -	£109	16	6

Place of trial, London.

(Signed)

(*a*) See No. CXLIX.

No. XL.
Board, Lodging and Tuition.

The plaintiff's claim is for money due from the School defendant to the plaintiff for the board, lodging, and bill. tuition of the three sons of the defendant.

		£	s.	d.
1897. 21st December.	Particulars: To board, lodging and tuition fees for two terms ending at this date at the agreed rate of 21l. per term for each boy - - -	126	0	0
Ditto.	To extras, full particulars of which, exceeding three folios (a), have been delivered to the defendant - - -	17	6	0
	Amount due -	£143	6	0

The plaintiff also claims the said sum of 143l. 6s. upon an account stated.

Place of trial, York.   (Signed)

(a) See No. CXLIX.

No. XLI.
Solicitors' Bill of Costs.

The plaintiffs' claim is for work and labour done Solicitors' and services rendered, and payments made by the costs. plaintiffs for the defendant at his request as solicitors for the defendant.

		£	s.	d.
1898. 1st February.	Particulars: To amount of plaintiffs' bill of costs, full particulars whereof, exceeding three folios (a), were delivered to defendant on this date, duly signed as required by statute - - - -	87	15	6

Place of trial, Norfolk.   (Signed)

(a) See No. CXLIX.

C.F.   D

No. XLII.
Charges for Warehousing Furniture.

Warehouse rent.

The plaintiffs' claim is for warehousing certain household furniture and effects, the property of the defendant, at his request.

Particulars:

1895.   £ s. d.

8th January to 10th September. Warehouse rent, 35 weeks at 1*l.* per week, according to an agreement between the plaintiff and the defendant contained in letters, dated 18th, 19th, and 21st December, 1894 - 35 0 0

Place of trial, Gloucestershire

(Signed)

CHAPTER III.

SERVICE OUT OF THE JURISDICTION, SUBSTIUTED SERVICE AND RENEWAL OF WRIT.

No. XLIII.

Writ for Service out of the Jurisdiction, or where Notice in Lieu of Service is to be Given out of the Jurisdiction.

(O. 2, r. 5 ; Y. S. C. P. and A. P., App. A., Part I., No. 5.)

1897. T. No. 641.

IN THE HIGH COURT OF JUSTICE,
Queen's Bench Division.

BETWEEN Henry Thompson and
Sons - - - - plaintiffs,
and
Pierre Coquelin - - defendant.

VICTORIA, by the grace of God, etc.
To Pierre Coquelin, of No. 24, Rue St. Sulpice, Bordeaux, in the Republic of France.
We command you, Pierre Coquelin, that within (*a*) days after service of [notice of] (*b*) this writ on you, inclusive of the day of such service, you do cause an appearance to be entered for you in the Queen's Bench Division of our High Court of Justice, in an action at the suit of Henry Thompson and Sons. And take notice that in default of your so doing the plaintiff may proceed therein, and judgment may be given in your absence. Witness, etc. [*Proceed as in No. I, using the same*

36 SERVICE OUT OF THE JURISDICTION, ETC.

memoranda and indorsements. Add the indorsement following :]

N.B.—This writ is to be used where the defendant, or all the defendants, or one or more defendant or defendants is or are out of the jurisdiction. When the defendant to be served is not a British subject, and is not in British dominions, notice of the writ, and not the writ itself, is to be served upon him.

(*a*) The number of days directed by the order must be inserted.

(*b*) The words in brackets must be added when the defendant is neither a British subject nor in British dominions. O. 11, r. 6. See indorsement " N.B." above.

For forms of specially indorsed writs, and writs from district registries, for service out of the jurisdiction, or where notice in lieu of service is to be given out of the jurisdiction, see Yearly Supreme Court Practice and the Annual Practice., App. A., Part I., Nos. 6, 7, and 8.

No. XLIV.

Affidavit in support of application for Leave to Issue Writ (or Notice) for Service out of the Jurisdiction.

(O. 2, r. 4 ; O. 11, rr. 1, 4.)

IN THE HIGH COURT OF JUSTICE,
  Queen's Bench Division.
In the matter of the Judicature Acts, 1873—1884.
In the matter of an intended action
  BETWEEN Henry Thompson and
      Sons - - - - plaintiffs,
         and
      Pierre Coquelin - - defendant.

I, Charles Morton, of 12, King's Road, Brixton, in the County of London, manager to the above-named plaintiffs, make oath and say as follows :

1. The above-named defendant, Pierre Coquelin, is a wine grower, who resides and carries on business at No. 24, Rue St. Sulpice, Bordeaux, in the Republic

AFFIDAVIT FOR WRIT OUT OF JURISDICTION. 37

of France, a place outside the jurisdiction of this Honourable Court, and the above-named plaintiffs are wine merchants carrying on business at 196, Leadenhall Street, in the City of London.

2. On or about the 13th day of January, 1897, it was agreed between the plaintiffs and the defendant, that the defendant should sell and deliver to the plaintiffs, at the port of London, certain wines for the price of 215*l*. The defendant has refused to carry out the said contract, and has broken the same by failing to deliver the said wines or any of them to the plaintiffs as agreed, whereby the plaintiffs have suffered damage by loss of profit to the amount of not less than 90*l*.

3. I am advised and believe that the said breach constitutes a good cause of action by the plaintiffs against the defendant, and that such cause of action arose within the jurisdiction of this Honourable Court.

4. The defendant is [not] a British subject.

5. I am informed and believe that the approximate time occupied in course of post from London to Bordeaux is 22 hours.

6. The plaintiffs are desirous of commencing an action against the defendant for damages for the said breach of contract.

SWORN, etc.

Filed on behalf of the plaintiffs.

The above is a form adapted to a particular case. For the essentials of these affidavits, see the note to O. 2, r. 4, in the Yearly Supreme Court Practice and the Annual Practice.

See also Table of Time for Appearance after Service out of the Jurisdiction, Yearly Supreme Court Practice, and the Annual Practice, Part III.

No. XLV.

Order giving Leave to Issue and Serve out of the Jurisdiction.

(O. 2, r. 4; O. 11; Y. S. C. P. and A. P., App. K., No. 20.)

IN THE HIGH COURT OF JUSTICE,
Queen's Bench Division.
The Hon. Mr. Justice   , Judge in Chambers.
In the matter of the Judicature Acts, 1873—1875, and in the matter of an intended action

BETWEEN Henry Thompson and
     Sons - - - - plaintiffs,
    and
   Pierre Coquelin - - defendant.

UPON reading the affidavit of Charles Morton, filed herein the 16th day of June, 1897,

IT IS ORDERED that the intended plaintiffs be at liberty to issue a writ of summons against the intended defendant.

AND IT IS FURTHER ORDERED that the said intended plaintiffs be at liberty to serve [notice of] the said writ at Bordeaux or elsewhere in the Republic of France, and that the time for appearance to the said writ by the said intended defendant be within 14 days after the service of the said [notice of the said] writ.

DATED the 18th day of June, 1897.

No. XLVI.
Notice of Writ in lieu of Service to be Given out of the Jurisdiction.
(O. 2, r. 5; O. 11, r. 6; Y. S. C. P. and A. P., App. A., Part I., No. 9.)

IN THE HIGH COURT OF JUSTICE   1897. T. No. 641.
Queen's Bench Division.
BETWEEN Henry Thompson and
         Sons - - - - plaintiffs,
       and
       Pierre Coquelin - - defendant.

To Pierre Coquelin, of No. 24, Rue St. Sulpice, Bordeaux, in the Republic of France.

TAKE NOTICE that Henry Thompson and Sons, of 196, Leadenhall Street, in the City of London, have commenced an action against you, Pierre Coquelin, in the Queen's Bench Division of Her Majesty's High Court of Justice, in England, by writ of that Court, dated the 18th day of June, A.D. 1897; which writ is indorsed as follows:

[*Copy all the indorsements of the writ.*]
and you are required within 14 days after the receipt of this notice, inclusive of the day of such receipt, to defend the said action, by causing an appearance to be entered for you in the said Court to the said action; and in default of your so doing, the said Henry Thompson and Sons may proceed therein, and judgment may be given in your absence.

You may appear to the said writ by entering an appearance personally or by your solicitor at the Central Office, Royal Courts of Justice, London.

         (Signed)   HURST AND JACKSON,
            of 217, Leadenhall Street, in the City of
            London, solicitors for the said Henry
            Thompson and Sons.
In the High Court of Justice,
Queen's Bench Division.

For corresponding district registry form, see Yearly Supreme Court Practice and the Annual Practice, App. A., Part I., No. 10.

No. XLVII.

Affidavit in support of Application for Order for Substituted Service.

(O. 10.)

1898. S. No. 210.

IN THE HIGH COURT OF JUSTICE,
Queen's Bench Division.

BETWEEN Henry George Stevenson - plaintiff,
and
William Budden - - defendant.

I, Albert Jones, of 16, Duke Street, Islington, in the County of London, clerk to Messrs. Allen and Bates, 72, Crutched Friars, in the City of London, solicitors for the above-named plaintiff, make oath and say as follows:

1. On the 14th day of July, 1896, I issued out of the central office of the Supreme Court of Judicature a writ of summons in this action, the same being duly sealed by the proper officer. A copy of the said writ is now produced and shown to me marked " A."

2. The above-named defendant is a grocer and resides and carries on business at No. 51, Prince's Street, Southwark.

3. On the said 14th day of July, 1896, at the hour of 5.15 in the afternoon, I attended at No. 51, Prince's Street, Southwark, aforesaid, for the purpose of serving the said defendant with a true copy of the said writ. On enquiring for the said defendant I was informed by a woman, who stated that she was the wife of the said defendant, that the said defendant was not at home. In answer to my further inquiries, the said woman stated that the said defendant would certainly be at home at all times between the hours of 9 and 11 o'clock on the following morning. I thereupon informed her that I had called in order to serve the said defendant with a copy of the writ of summons in this action at the suit of the above-named plaintiff, and I asked her to inform him that I should call again the next morning at

AFFIDAVIT FOR SUBSTITUTED SERVICE. 41

the hour of 10 o'clock for the same purpose; whereupon she replied that she would inform the said defendant of my intention to call as aforesaid.

4. Accordingly, on the 15th day of July, 1896, at the hour of 10 o'clock in the morning, I attended again at No. 51, Prince's Street, Southwark, aforesaid. I there saw the said woman, who informed me that the said defendant had been unexpectedly compelled to go to Brixton on business, and would not return until late in the evening. In answer to my inquiries, she further stated that the said defendant had refused to tell her the nature of his business in Brixton, or the address to which he was going. I then stated to her that I had come in accordance with the appointment made the previous day for the purpose of serving the said defendant with a copy of the writ herein, and that I should attend again on the following morning at the hour of ten o'clock for the same purpose.

5. I accordingly attended again at No. 51, Prince's Street, Southwark, aforesaid, on the following day, the 16th day of July, 1896, at the hour of 10 o'clock in the morning, as appointed, and there saw the said woman, who stated, in answer to my inquiry, that the said defendant had just gone out for a few minutes. I said that I should there await his return, which I proceeded to do. At the expiration of about 20 minutes, the said woman informed me that it was useless for me to wait, and that the defendant had gone away for two months. I thereupon stated again to her the purpose of my attendance, and handed to her a copy of the said writ of summons herein, requesting her to give the same to the said defendant as soon as he returned, which she promised to do.

6. I have endeavoured, as hereinbefore set out, to serve the said defendant with a true copy of the said writ, but have been unable to do so; and I verily believe that he is wilfully evading service thereof, and that prompt personal service is impossible.

7. In my belief, a copy of the said writ, if sent by prepaid letter post to the said defendant at No. 51,

42   SERVICE OUT OF THE JURISDICTION, ETC.

Prince's Street, Southwark, aforesaid, would come to his knowledge.
SWORN, etc.
Filed on behalf of the plaintiff.

For the essentials of these affidavits, see the note to O. 10 in the Yearly Supreme Court Practice and the Annual Practice.

No. XLVIII.
Order for Substituted Service.
(O. 10 ; Y. S. C. P. and A. P., App. K., No. 21.)
[*Heading as in No. XLVII.*]

UPON reading the affidavit of Albert Jones, filed the 22nd day of July, 1896,

IT IS ORDERED that service of a copy of this order, and of a copy of the writ of summons in this action, by sending the same by a prepaid post letter, addressed to the defendant at No. 51, Prince's Street, Southwark, shall be good and sufficient service of the writ.

DATED the 24th day of July, 1896.

No. XLIX.
Affidavit on Application for Renewal of Writ.
(O. 8, r. 1.)

1893. C. No. 2169.

IN THE HIGH COURT OF JUSTICE,
   Queen's Bench Division.
BETWEEN Henry Joseph Perrin - plaintiff,
   and
   William Jephson - - defendant.

I, James Sidney Groves, of 46, New Road, Highbury, in the County of Middlesex, managing clerk to Messrs. Sale, Burney and Jackson, of 6, Fore Court, in the City of London, solicitors for the above-named plaintiff, make oath and say as follows:

1. The original writ in this action, which I have seen and which appears to have been regularly issued out of

AFFIDAVIT FOR RENEWAL OF WRIT. 43

the central office of the Supreme Court of Judicature, bears date the 7th day of October, 1892. A copy thereof is now produced and shown to me marked " A."

2. On the 8th day of October, 1892, I instructed one John Hemming, a clerk in the employment of Messrs. Sale, Burney and Jackson, to attend at the residence of the above-named defendant, at 12, John Street, Lambeth, in order to serve the said defendant with a true copy of the said writ.

3. Subsequently I was informed by the said John Hemming that he had attended at the defendant's said residence on eight several occasions, between the 8th and 27th days of October, 1892, at divers hours of the day, but that he had been unable to see the defendant, who was stated to be absent from home, or to obtain any information as to the date of his return.

4. On or about the 10th day of November, 1892, I ascertained from the defendant's son that the defendant had left home on the 1st day of October, 1892, and was travelling in Russia, and that the date of his return was uncertain, but that he was likely to return at any time; and further, that the whereabouts of the defendant in Russia was not known to him and could not be accurately ascertained.

5. I have on divers dates between the said 10th day of November and the present time, the last of such dates being the 29th day of September, 1893, caused inquiries to be made at the defendant's said residence, and to the best of my knowledge, information and belief, the defendant has not yet returned from Russia.

Sworn, etc.

Filed on behalf of the plaintiff.

No. L.

Memorandum or Præcipe for Renewed Writ.

(O. 8, r. 1 ; Y. S. C. P. and A. P., App. A., Part I., No. 18 ;
App. G., No. 20.)

[*Heading as in No. XLIX.*]

SEAL in pursuance of order dated the 5th day of October, 1893, a renewed writ of summons in this action indorsed as follows :

[*Copy all the indorsements of the original writ.*]

DATED the 6th day of October, 1893.

(Signed) SALE, BURNEY and JACKSON,
of 6, Fore Court, in the City of
London, solicitors for the plaintiff.

CHAPTER IV.

APPEARANCE AND PROCEEDINGS IN DEFAULT THEREOF.

No. LI.

Entry of Appearance.—General Form.

(O. 12, rr. 8, 10, 13; Y. S. C. P. and A. P., App. A., Part II., No. 1.)

1896. L. No. 247.

IN THE HIGH COURT OF JUSTICE,
Queen's Bench Division.

BETWEEN Henry Lucas - - - plaintiff,
and
George Greville Murton - defendant.

ENTER an appearance for George Greville Murton in this action.

DATED the 13th day of March, 1896.

(Signed) WATSON and MILLS,
of (a) 16, Great Russell Street, Bloomsbury, in the County of London,* [Agents for William Hartley and Co., of 12, New Road, Leicester,] solicitors for the defendant.

(a) If this address be beyond three miles from the Royal Courts of Justice, an address for service within three miles thereof must be given, by inserting at * " whose address for service is," etc.

No. LII.

Notice of Appearance.

(O. 12, r. 9 ; Y. S. C. P. and A. P., App. A., Part II., No. 2.)

[*Heading as in writ.*]

TAKE NOTICE, that we have this day entered an appearance at the Central Office, Royal Courts of Justice, for the defendant, George Greville Murton, to the writ of summons in this action.

[The said defendant requires delivery of a statement of claim] (*a*).

DATED the 13th day of March, 1896.

(Signed) [*As in No. LI., except that the additional address for service, if any, apparently need not be inserted.*]

To Messrs. FOAKES and GURNEY,
solicitors for the plaintiff.

(*a*) This is be added if required. See also O. 20, r. 1.

No. LIII.

Entry of Appearance by Defendant Incompletely Described in Writ.

[*Heading as in writ.*]

ENTER an appearance for John Stephen Moore, sued as J. S. Moore (*a*) in this action.

DATED the 9th day of July, 1898.

(Signed) [*As in No. LI.*]

(*a*) See p. 4.

No. LIV.

Entry of Appearance by Partners Sued in Firm Name.

(O. 48A, r. 5.)

1894. P. No. 1066.

IN THE HIGH COURT OF JUSTICE,
Queen's Bench Division.

BETWEEN James Poole - - - plaintiff,
and
H. Turnbull and Co. - defendants.

ENTER an appearance for John William Turnbull, Henry East and Maurice Dugdale, trading as H. Turnbull and Co., the defendants in this action.

DATED, etc. [*Conclude as in No. LI.*]

No. LV

Entry of Appearance under Protest by Person Served as a Partner.

(O. 48A, r. 7.)

[*Heading as in writ.*]

ENTER an appearance for David Cohen, a person served as a partner, but who denies that he is a partner in the firm of Abrahams and Co., the defendants in this action.

DATED, etc. [*As usual.*]

No. LVI.

Entry of Appearance by Third Party.

(O. 16, r. 49 ; Y. S. C. P. and A. P., App. A., Part II., No. 5.)

[*Heading as in writ.*]

ENTER an appearance for Charles Wilson to the notice issued in this action on the 7th day of February, 1896,

APPEARANCE AND DEFAULT THEREOF.

by the defendant, Norman Percy Gough, under the Rules of the Supreme Court, 1883, Order 16, Rule 49.

DATED the 15th day of February, 1896.
(Signed) WALTER B. RICHARDS,
of 10, Pancras Lane, in the City of London (a), [Agent for, etc.,] solicitor for the said Charles Wilson.

(a) See No. LI.

No. LVII.

Entry of Appearance by Third Person to Counterclaim.

(O. 21, rr. 11, 13 ; Y. S. C. P. and A. P., App. A., Part II., No. 7.)

1895. C. No. 966.

IN THE HIGH COURT OF JUSTICE,
Queen's Bench Division.

BETWEEN Henry Graves Cuthbertson- plaintiff,
and
Isaac Goldsmid - - defendant
by original action ;
AND BETWEEN the said Isaac Goldsmid - plaintiff,
and
the said Henry Graves Cuthbertson, and Stanley Peters - - - - defendants
by counterclaim.

ENTER an appearance for Stanley Peters to the counterclaim of the above-named defendant, Isaac Goldsmid, in this action.

DATED the 12th day of November, 1894.
(Signed) DALE and HOUSTON,
of 41, Moorgate Street, in the City of London (a), [Agent for, etc.,] solicitors for the said Stanley Peters.

(a) See No. LI.

No. LVIII.

Entry of Appearance by Landlord Named in the Writ.

(O. 12, r. 26.)

1893. N. No. 641.

IN THE HIGH COURT OF JUSTICE,
Queen's Bench Division.

BETWEEN Edward Noakes - - plaintiff,
and
G. G. Towers and Arthur
Atkins - - - defendants.

ENTER an appearance for the defendant Arthur Atkins, as landlord of the defendant G. G. Towers, in this action.

DATED, etc. [*as usual*].

No. LIX.

Entry of Appearance Limiting Defence.

(O. 12, r. 28; Y. S. C. P. and A. P., App. A., Part II., No. 4.)

[*Heading as in writ.*]

ENTER an appearance for the defendant James Williamson in this action. The said defendant limits his defence to part only of the property mentioned in the writ of summons, namely, to the close called "The Big Field."

DATED, etc. [*as usual*].

No. LX.

Notice Limiting Defence.

(O. 12, rr. 28, 29 ; Y. S. C. P. and A. P., App. A., Part II., No. 3.)

[*Heading as in writ.*]

TAKE NOTICE that the above-named defendant, James Williamson, limits his defence to part only of the property mentioned in the writ of summons, namely, to the close called "The Big Field."

DATED, etc. [*as usual*].
   To Messrs. OGILVY and BUDD,
     the plaintiff's solicitors.

No. LXI.

Affidavit in Support of Application to Appear by Party not Named as Defendant.

(O. 12, r. 25.)

[*Heading as in writ.*]

I, Joseph Newman, of Parkhurst, Low Road, Chislehurst, in the County of Kent, tea merchant, make oath and say as follows :

1. This is an action brought to recover possession of a certain house and land, known as Oak Dene, situate in Windlesham Grove, Croydon, in the County of Surrey.

2. I am in possession of the said house and land by the above-named defendant, Charles Winter Hazell, as my tenant.

SWORN, etc.

No. LXII.

Order giving Party not Named as Defendant leave to Appeal.

(O. 12, r. 15.)

[*Heading as in writ.*]

UPON reading the affidavit of Joseph Newman, filed the 2nd day of December, 1897,

IT IS ORDERED that the said Joseph Newman be at liberty to appear and to defend this action, as landlord of the above-named Charles Winter Hazell, the defendant named in the writ.

DATED the 4th day of December, 1897.

No. LXIII.

Entry of Appearance by Leave by Party not Named as Defendant.

(O. 12, rr. 26, 27.)

[*Heading as in writ.*]

ENTER an appearance for Joseph Newman, as landlord of the above-named Charles Winter Hazell, pursuant to order of Master , dated the 4th day of December, 1897.

DATED, etc. [*as usual*].

No. LXIV.

Notice of Appearance by Party not Named as Defendant.

(O. 12, r. 27.)

[*Heading as in writ.*]

TAKE NOTICE that pursuant to order of Master , dated the 4th day of December, 1897, Joseph Newman, as landlord of the above-named Charles Winter Hazell, has this day appeared to this action [and that the said Joseph Newman requires delivery of a statement of claim].

DATED the 5th day of December, 1897.

(Signed) JONES AND GILL, of 17, High Street, Bloomsbury, in the County of London (*a*) [Agents for, etc.], solicitors for the said Joseph Newman.

To Messrs. PERRY and WILSON,
solicitors for the plaintiff.

(*a*) See No. LI.

No. LXV.

Entry of Appearance by Party Served with Order to Continue Action.

(O. 17, r. 5; Y. S. C. P. and A. P., App. A., Part II., No. 6.)

[*Heading as in writ.*]

ENTER an appearance for Frederick John Hadley, who, as executor of the above-named William Allen, deceased, has been served with an order, dated the 1st day of December, 1892, to carry on and prosecute the proceedings in this action.

DATED, etc. [*as usual*]

No. LXVI.
Affidavit of Personal Service of Writ.
(O. 13, r. 2 ; O. 67, r. 9 ; O. 9, r. 15.)

1894. L. No. 667.

IN THE HIGH COURT OF JUSTICE,
Queen's Bench Division.

BETWEEN Thomas Lamb - - - plaintiff,
and
Phillip Bertram Hodgson - defendant.

I, SAMUEL FINCH, of 17, Albert Road, Camberwell, in the County of London, clerk to Messrs. Hyde and Simpson, of 12, Old Inn, Fleet Street, in the City of London, solicitors for the plaintiffs herein, make oath and say as follows:

1. I did on the 30th day of May, 1894, at No. 37, Luxmore Road, Enfield, in the County of Middlesex, personally serve Philip Bertram Hodgson, the above-named defendant, with a true copy of the writ of summons in this action, which appeared to me to have been regularly issued out of the Central Office of the Supreme Court of Judicature, against the above-named defendant at the suit of the above-named plaintiff, and which was dated the 29th day of May, 1894.

2. At the time of the said service, the said writ and the copy thereof were subscribed and indorsed in the manner and form prescribed by the Rules of the Supreme Court.

3. I did on the 31st day of May, 1894 (a), indorse on the said writ the day of the month and the week of the said service on the said defendant.

SWORN, etc.
Filed on behalf of the plaintiff.

(a) The date of service must be indorsed within three days of service (O. 9, r. 15).

No. LXVII.

Affidavit of Substituted Service of Writ.

(O. 13, r. 2; O. 67, r. 9; O. 9, r. 15.)

[*Heading and commencement as in No. LXVI.*]

1. I did, on the 8th day of July, 1894, serve the above-named defendant with a true copy of the writ of summons in this action, and a true copy of the order of Master   for substituted service herein, by posting the same at the post office in Fleet Street, in the East Central district of London, in a prepaid letter or envelope addressed to the said defendant at No. 37, Luxmore Road, Enfield, pursuant to the said order.

2. The said writ of summons appeared to me to have been regularly issued out of the Central Office of the Supreme Court against the above-named defendant at the suit of the above-named plaintiff, and was dated the 29th day of May, 1894.

3. [*As in paragraph 3 of No. LXVI.*]

SWORN, etc.
Filed on behalf of the plaintiff.

No. LXVIII.

Affidavit of Service of Writ on Company.

(O. 13, r. 2; O. 67, r. 9; O. 9, r. 15.)

1897. D. No. 247.

IN THE HIGH COURT OF JUSTICE,
Queen's Bench Division.

BETWEEN Henry Davidson - - plaintiff,
and
The Patent Fibre Company,
Limited - - - defendants.

I, etc. [*as usual*].

1. I did, on the 22nd day of March, 1897, serve the above-named defendants, The Patent Fibre Company,

Limited (a), with a true copy of the writ of summons in this action, which appeared to me to have been regularly issued out of the Central Office of the Supreme Court of Judicature against the above-named defendants at the suit of the above-named plaintiff, which was dated the 22nd day of March, 1897, by leaving the same [or, by sending the same by post in a prepaid letter or envelope addressed to the company] at No. 217, Queen Victoria Street, London, E.C., which is the registered office of the said defendant company.

2. [*As in paragraph 2 of No. LXVI.*]

3. [*As in paragraph 3 of No. LXVI.*]

SWORN, etc.

Filed on behalf of the plaintiff.

(a) As to service on a registered company, see the Companies Act, 1862 (25 & 26 Vict. c. 89), s. 62.

No. LXIX.

Affidavit of Service of Writ on a Partner on behalf of the Firm.

(O. 13, r. 2 ; O. 67, r. 9 ; O. 9, r. 15 ; O. 48A, r. 3.)

[*Heading and commencement as in No. LXX.*]

1. I did, on the 9th day of August, 1896, at No. 12, Old Broad Street, in the City of London, personally serve Roger Jamieson, a partner in the above-named defendant firm, with a true copy, etc.

[*Continue as in No. LXVI, with necessary variations.*]

No. LXX.
Affidavit of Service of Writ upon Person in Control of Partnership Business.
(O. 13, r. 2 ; O. 67, r. 9 ; O. 9, r. 15 ; O. 48A, r. 3.)

1892. T. No. 1016.

IN THE HIGH COURT OF JUSTICE,
Queen's Bench Division.

BETWEEN Walter Yates Tomlin - plaintiff,
and
Moore and Fisher - defendants.

I, etc. [as usual].

1. I did, on the 28th day of October, 1892, at 71, Fish Street, in the City of London, the principal place of business of the above-named defendant firm, personally serve [Henry Fletcher] (a) the person having at the time of such service the management of the partnership business there, with a true copy of the writ of summons in this action, which appeared to me to have been regularly issued out of the Central Office of the Supreme Court of Judicature against the above-named defendant firm, at the suit of the above-named plaintiff, and which was dated the 28th day of October, 1892.

2. [As in No. LXVI.]

3. I did, on the said 28th day of October, 1892, indorse on the said writ the day of the month and the week of the said service on the said [Henry Fletcher, or,] (a) person having at the time of such service the management of the said partnership business.

4. I did at the same time deliver to the [said Henry Fletcher, or,] (a) person so served as aforesaid a notice (b) in writing that the said writ of summons was served upon him as the person having the control or management of the partnership business of the said defendant firm.

SWORN, etc.
Filed on behalf of the plaintiff.

(a) The name of the person served should, if known, be inserted.
(b) See No. LXXI.

No. LXXI.

Notice of Service upon Person in Control of Partnership Business.

(O. 48A, r. 4.)

[*Heading as in No. LXX.*]

TAKE NOTICE that the writ served herewith is served upon you as the person having the control or management of the partnership business of Moore and Fisher.
    (Signed) DODDS and MURRAY, of 24, Longacre, in the County of London [whose address for service is, etc.] (*a*) [agents for, etc.] solicitors for the plaintiff.

To Mr. HENRY FLETCHER (*b*).

(*a*) See No. LI.
(*b*) Insert the name, if known.

No. LXXII.

Notice of Service on Partnership where Capacity of Party Served is Uncertain.

(O. 48A, r. 4.)

[*Heading as in No. LXX.*]

TAKE NOTICE that the writ served herewith is served upon you as a partner in the defendant firm of Moore and Fisher, and also as the person in control of the business.

    (Signed) [*As in No. LXXI.*]

No. LXXIII.

Affidavit of Service of Notice of Writ.

(O. 13, r. 2 ; O. 67, r. 9 ; O. 9, r. 15 ; O. 11, r. 6.)

[*Heading as in writ.*]

I, etc. [*as usual.*]

1. I did on the 15th day of November, 1896, at 13, Langasse, Wiesbaden, in the Empire of Germany, personally serve the above-named defendant with a notice of the writ of summons in this action, a true duplicate of which notice is hereunto annexed, marked " A."

2. I did on the 15th day of November, 1896, indorse on the said copy notice hereunto annexed, the day of the month and the week of the said service on the said defendant.

SWORN, etc.
Filed on behalf of the plaintiff.

No. LXXIV.

Judgment in Default of Appearance. Liquidated Demand.

(O. 13, r. 3 ; Y. S. C. P. and A. P., App. F., No. 1.)

1896. P. No. 1286.

IN THE HIGH COURT OF JUSTICE,
   Queen's Bench Division.

BETWEEN Martin Prothero - - plaintiff,
             and
      William Lumsden - - defendant.

The 27th day of October, 1896.

The defendant not having appeared to the writ of summons herein, it is this day adjudged that the plaintiff recover against the said defendant, 280*l.*, and costs, to be taxed.

No. LXXV.

Judgment in Default of Appearance. Liquidated Demand. Several Defendants.

(O. 13, r. 4.)

[*Heading as in writ.*]

The 20th day of March, 1896.

The defendant [s], George Stewart Baker [and Herbert Morris], not having appeared to the writ of summons herein, it is this day adjudged that the plaintiff recover against the said defendant [s], the sum of 150*l*., and costs, to be taxed.

No. LXXVI.

Interlocutory Judgment in Default of Appearance. Unliquidated Demand.

(O. 13, r. 5; Y. S. C. P. and A. P., App. F., No. 2.)

[*Heading as in writ.*]

The 3rd day of April, 1891.

No appearance having been entered [by the defendant, Robert Hughes] to the writ of summons herein,

It is hereby adjudged that the plaintiff recover against the [said] defendant [the value of the goods and (*or*, or)] (*a*) damages to be assessed.

(*a*) *Or*, the goods in the said writ mentioned, or their value and damages to be assessed.

No. LXXVII.

Præcipe of Inquiry.

(O. 13 r. 5 ; Y. S. C. P. and A. P., App. G., No. 12.)

[*Heading as in writ.*]

Seal a writ of enquiry directed to the Sheriff of Middlesex to assess the damages in this action.

Judgment dated the 3rd day of April, 1891.

DATED the 5th day of April, 1891.

(Signed) MELVILLE and GIBBS, of 217, Tottenham Court Road, in the County of London, solicitors for the plaintiff.

No. LXXVIII.

Writ of Inquiry for Assessment of Damages.

(O. 13, r. 5 ; Y. S. C. P. and A. P., App. J., No. 8.)

[*Heading as in writ.*]

VICTORIA, by the Grace of God, of the United Kingdom of Great Britain, and Ireland, Queen, Defender of the Faith, To the Sheriff of Middlesex, greeting :

WHEREAS it has been adjudged that the plaintiff recover against the defendant [the goods in the writ of summons herein mentioned, or their value, and] damages to be assessed.

Therefore We command you, that by the oaths of twelve good and lawful men of your bailiwick you enquire [what is the value of the said goods, and] what damages the plaintiff is entitled to recover under the said judgment, and that forthwith thereafter you send the inquisition which you shall take thereupon to our said

Court, under your seal, and the seals of those by whose oaths you take the inquisition, together with this writ.

WITNESS, Hardinge Stanley, Earl of Halsbury, Lord High Chancellor of Great Britain, the thirty-first day of May, in the year of Our Lord, One thousand eight hundred and ninety-seven.

This writ was issued by Osborne and Morgan, of 93, Cheapside, in the City of London, whose address for service is the same, solicitors for the said plaintiff, who resides, at Denehurst, Victoria Road, Streatham, in the County of Surrey.

The defendant is a silk mercer, and resides at No. 71, Oak Road, Cricklewood, in your bailiwick.

No. LXXIX.

Final Judgment in Default of Appearance after Assessment of Damages

(O. 13, r. 5 ; Y. S. C. P. and A. P., App. F., No. 4.)

[*Heading as in writ.*]

22nd January, 1895.

The plaintiff having on the 25th day of October, 1894, obtained interlocutory judgment herein against the defendant in default of appearance, and a writ of enquiry dated the 30th day of October, 1894, having been issued, directed to the Sheriff (*a*) of Suffolk, to assess the damages which the plaintiff was entitled to recover, and the said sheriff having by his return dated the 15th day of January, 1895, returned that the said damages have been assessed at 75*l*., it is adjudged that the plaintiff recover 75*l*., and costs, to be taxed.

(*a*) For corresponding form where the damages have been assessed by an Official Referee, see Yearly Supreme Court Practice and the Annual Practice, App. F., No. 4A.

No. LXXX.

Judgment in Default of Appearance. Recovery of Land.

(O. 13, r. 8 ; Y. S. C. P. and A. P., App. F., Nos. 1 & 3.)

[*Heading as in writ.*]

The 7th day of February, 1898.

No appearance having been entered herein it is this day adjudged that the plaintiff recover possession of the land in the writ of summons herein mentioned and described as Marsh Close, in the Parish of Standon, in the County of Sussex.

The above judgment carries no costs. (See note to O. 13, r. 8.)

No. LXXXI.

Judgment in Default of Appearance. Recovery of Land, Rent and Damages.

(O. 13, r. 9.)

[*Heading as in writ.*]

The 6th day of August, 1893.

No appearance having been entered herein, it is this day adjudged that the plaintiff recover possession of the land in the writ of summons herein mentioned and described as No. 2, High Street, St. Albans, in the County of Hertford, and 30*l.* in the said writ claimed for arrears of rent, and   *l.* for costs, and also damages to be assessed.

As to the costs carried by the above judgment, which is final as to the land and arrears of rent, and interlocutory as to the damages, see note to O. 13, r. 9.

No. LXXXII.

Judgment in Default of Appearance against Married Woman (a).

(O. 13, r. 3 ; Y. S. C. P. and A. P., App. F., No. 1A.)

[*Heading as in writ.*]

The defendant [Marian Wilson] (b), not having appeared to the writ of summons herein, it is this day adjudged that the plaintiff recover against the defendant [Marian Wilson] (b) 130l. and 4l. 14s. costs [or, costs to be taxed], such sum and costs [so far as regards the defendant, Marian Wilson] (b) to be payable out of her separate property (c) as hereinafter mentioned, and not otherwise.

And it is ordered that execution hereon against the said defendant [Marian Wilson] (b), be limited to her separate property not subject to any restriction against anticipation (unless by reason of Section 19 of the Married Women's Property Act, 1882, the property shall be liable to execution notwithstanding such restriction).

(a) This form was settled by the Court of Appeal in *Scott* v. *Morley*, 20 Q. B. D. at p. 132.

(b) These bracketed words may apparently be omitted where the married woman is sole defendant.

(c) If the judgment be for an antenuptial debt, proceed thus : " whether subject to any restriction against anticipation or not, and not otherwise, and execution hereon is limited to such separate property."

CHAPTER V.

PROCEEDINGS UNDER ORDER XIV.

No. LXXXIII.

Summons for Leave to Enter Final Judgment under Order XIV.

(O. 14, rr. 1, 2.)

[*Heading as in writ.*]

LET all parties concerned attend the Master in Chambers, Central Office, Royal Courts of Justice, London, on Tuesday, the 16th day of February, 1897 (*a*), at 11 o'clock in the forenoon, on the hearing of an application on the part of the plaintiff that he be at liberty to sign final judgment in this action for the amount indorsed on the writ of summons, with interest, if any, and costs.

And that the costs of this application be costs in the cause.

DATED the 10th day of February, 1897.

This summons was taken out by Saunders and Wills, of 113, Aldersgate Street, in the City of London, solicitors for the plaintiff.

To the defendant, and to
    Messrs. JOHNSON and WATTS,
        his solicitors.

(*a*) There must be four clear days, exclusive of Sunday (O. 64, r. 2), between the date of service of a summons under O. 14, and the return day. In the above case the summons will accordingly be served on February 10th.

No. LXXXIV.

Affidavit of Plaintiff on Summons under Order XIV.

(O. 14, r. 1.)

[*Heading as in writ.*]

I, JOHN HERBERT HOPKINS, of No. 12, Cross Street, Dalston, in the County of London, Butcher, the above-named plaintiff, make oath and say as follows:

1. The defendant is justly and truly indebted to me in the sum of 39*l.* 12*s.* 7*d.*, for the price of goods sold and delivered by me to the defendant, and was so indebted at the beginning of this action. The particulars of the said claim appear by the indorsement on the writ of summons in this action.

2. I verily believe that there is no defence to this action.

SWORN, etc.

Filed on behalf of the plaintiff.

The essentials of an affidavit on summons for judgment under O. 14 (which must necessarily vary with the circumstances of each case) are as follows:

(1.) It must be made either by the plaintiff, or by some other person who can swear positively to the facts. A manager, or other responsible person, who is acquainted with the circumstances, may accordingly make it.

(2.) It must verify the cause of action. This means that it must state shortly the nature of the claim, and the facts on which it is founded. It may refer to the indorsement of the writ for the particulars of claim. A good working rule, which will cover a large number of cases, is to follow the indorsement as nearly as possible.

(3.) It must state that, in the belief of the deponent, there is no defence to the action.

No. LXXXV.
Affidavit of Defendant on Summons under Order XIV.
(O. 14, r. 3.)

[*Heading as in writ.*]

I, GEORGE BASSETT, of 16, Finsbury Circus, in the City of London, commission agent, the above-named defendant, make oath and say as follows :

1. I have read what purports to be a copy of the plaintiff's affidavit sworn herein on the 5th day of July, 1898, and in reply thereto I deny that I am indebted to the plaintiff in the amount alleged, or in any other sum.

2. I am advised and believe that I have on the merits a good defence to this action for the reasons hereinafter set out.

[*Continue according to circumstances.*]

Affidavits in opposition to applications for leave to sign summary judgment must, of necessity, vary very widely. It can only be said that the facts on which the defendant relies, as constituting his defence, must be clearly and concisely set out in consecutive paragraphs. If there is a set-off or counterclaim, the affidavit should disclose it with a reasonable amount of detail. Also " the affidavit shall state whether the defence alleged goes to the whole or to part only, and (if so) to what part, of the plaintiff's claim " (O. 14, r. 3 (*b*)).

No. LXXXVI.
Affidavit of Service of Summons and Affidavit under Order XIV.

[*Heading as in writ.*]

I, etc. [*as usual.*]

1. I did on the 13th day of May, 1897, before the hour of six o'clock in the afternoon, serve Messrs. Hobson and Biggs, solicitors for the above-named defendant, [*or* Arthur James Hazell, the above-named defendant, who appeared in person], in this action with a true copy of the summons now produced and shown to me marked " A," by leaving it at No. 22, New Broad Street, in the City of London, being the address for service, with their clerk there.

ORDER GIVING LEAVE TO DEFEND. 67

2. I did also at the same time leave with the said clerk a true copy of the affidavit of Joseph Ferguson, the above-named plaintiff, [and exhibits therein referred to], to be used in support of such summons.

SWORN, etc.

Filed on behalf of the plaintiff.

No. LXXXVII.

Order Empowering Plaintiff to Sign Final Judgment.
(No. 1.)

(O. 14, r. 1 ; Y. S. C. P., and A. P., App. K., No. 6.)

[*Heading as in writ.*]

UPON hearing the solicitors on both sides, and upon reading the affidavit of the plaintiff, filed the 2nd day of June, 1895, and the affidavit of the defendant, filed the 7th day of June, 1895,

IT IS ORDERED that the plaintiff may sign final judgment in this action for the amount indorsed on the writ, with interest, if any [*or*, possession of the land in the indorsement of the writ described as Croft Farm, Haslemere, in the County of Surrey], and costs to be taxed.

DATED the 9th day of June, 1895.

No. LXXXVIII.

Order Giving Defendant Unconditional Leave to Defend.
(No. 2.)

(O. 14, r. 6 ; Y. S. C. P., and A. P., App. K., No. 7.)

[*Heading as in writ.*]

UPON hearing the solicitors on both sides, and upon reading the affidavit of John William Hughes, filed on behalf of the plaintiff the 12th day of November, 1895, and the affidavit of the defendant, filed the 16th day of November, 1895,

IT IS ORDERED that the defendant be at liberty to defend this action, and that the costs of this application be costs in the cause.

DATED the 18th day of November, 1895.

No. LXXXIX.

Order Giving Defendant Conditional Leave to Defend.
(No. 3.)

(O. 14, r. 6 ; Y. S. C. P., and A. P., App. K., No. 8.)

[*Heading as in writ.*]

UPON hearing counsel on both sides, and upon reading, etc. [*as in preceding forms*],

IT IS ORDERED that if the defendant pay into court within a week from the date of this order the sum of 95*l.*, he be at liberty to defend this action, but that if that sum be not so paid, the plaintiff be at liberty to sign final judgment for the amount indorsed on the writ of summons, with interest, if any, and costs, and that in either event the costs of this application be costs in the cause.

DATED, etc.

No. XC.

Order Giving Defendant Conditional Leave to Defend as to Part of Claim. (No. 4.)

(O. 14, r. 4 ; Y. S. C. P., and A. P., App. K., No. 9.)

[*Commence as in preceding forms.*]

IT IS ORDERED that if the defendant pay into court within a week from the date of this order the sum of 250*l.*, he be at liberty to defend this action as to the whole of the plaintiff's claim.

And it is ordered that if that sum be not so paid, the plaintiff be at liberty to sign judgment for that sum, and the defendant be at liberty to defend this action as to the residue of the plaintiff's claim, and that the costs of this application be costs in the cause.

DATED, etc.

No. XCI.

Order Giving Defendant Unconditional Leave to Defend as to Part of Claim. (No. 5.)

(O. 14, rr. 4, 6 ; Y. S. C. P., and A. P., App. K., No. 9A.)

[*Commence as in preceding forms.*]

IT IS ORDERED that if the defendant do not pay to the plaintiff's solicitor within a week from the date of this order, the sum of 40*l*., the plaintiff be at liberty to sign judgment for the same.

And it is further ordered that the defendant be at liberty to defend this action as to the residue of the plaintiff's claim, and that the costs of this application be costs in the action.

DATED, etc.

No. XCII.

Order against a Married Woman and Others. (No. 6.)

(Y. S. C. P., and A. P., App. K., No. 9B.)

[*Commence as in preceding forms.*]

IT IS ORDERED that the plaintiff be at liberty to sign final judgment in this action for the amount indorsed on the writ, with interest (if any) and costs to be taxed, and that as regards the defendant, Jane Emily Bagshaw, such sum and costs be payable out of her separate property as hereinafter mentioned and not otherwise, and it is ordered that as regards the said defendant, Jane Emily Bagshaw, execution on such judgment be limited to her separate estate, not subject to any restriction against anticipation (unless by reason of section 19 of the Married Women's Property Act, 1882, the property shall be liable to such execution notwithstanding such restriction).

DATED, etc.

No. XCIII.

Order in Action on Bill of Costs. (No. 7.)

(Y. S. C. P. and A. P., App. K., No. 9c.)

[*Commence as in preceding forms.*]

IT IS ORDERED that the bill of costs on which this action is brought be referred to the Master to be taxed, pursuant to the statute 6 & 7 Vict. c. 73, and that the plaintiff give credit at the time of taxation for all sums of money received by him from or on account of the defendant, and that the plaintiff be at liberty to sign judgment for the amount, if any, found due to him by the Master's allocatur on the said taxation, and costs of action to be taxed.

DATED, etc.

No. XCIV.

Order Permitting One or More of Several Defendants to Defend.

(O. 14, r. 5.)

[*Commence as in preceding forms.*]

IT IS ORDERED that the plaintiff may sign final judgment in this action against the defendant, Harold Smith, for the amount indorsed on the writ, with interest, if any, and costs to be taxed.

And it is further ordered that the defendant [s], Archibald Henry James [and George Purvis Jackson] be at liberty to defend this action, and that, as regards the said defendant [s] Archibald Henry James [and George Purvis Jackson] the costs of this application be costs in the cause.

DATED, etc.

No. XCV.
Order under Order XIV. with Directions.
(O. 14, r. 8.)

[*Commence as in preceding forms.*]

IT IS ORDERED that the defendant be at liberty to defend this action, and that the costs of this application be costs in the cause.

And the following directions are hereby given:

[*Continue as in No. CXLIII.*]

No. XCVI.
Order for Entry of Action in the Short Cause List.
(O. 14, r. 8.)

[*Commence as in preceding forms.*]

IT IS ORDERED that the defendant be at liberty to defend this action, and that the action be forthwith set down for trial and entered in the Short Cause List, and that the costs of this application be referred to the Judge at the trial.

DATED, etc.

No. XCVII.
Order Remitting Action to the County Court.

[*Commence as in preceding forms.*]

IT IS ORDERED that the defendant be at liberty to defend this action, and that the action be remitted for trial before the Westminster County Court of Middlesex, and that the costs of this application be costs in the cause.

DATED, etc.

No. XCVIII.

Order Dismissing Application.

(O. 14, r. 9 (*b*).)

[*Commence as in preceding forms.*]

IT IS ORDERED that the application of the plaintiff be dismissed with costs to be taxed and paid by the plaintiff to the defendant.

DATED, etc.

No. XCIX.

Notice of Appeal to Judge from Order of Master.

(O. 54, r. 21.)

[*Heading as in writ.*]

TAKE NOTICE that the above-named plaintiff intends to appeal against the decision of Master   , given on the 12th day of December, 1893, ordering that the defendant be at liberty to defend this action, and that the costs of the application be costs in the cause.

And further take notice that you are required to attend before the Judge in Chambers, at the Central Office, Royal Courts of Justice, Strand, London, on Tuesday, the 17th day of December, 1893, at 11 o'clock in the forenoon, on the hearing of an application by the said plaintiff that the said order may be set aside and that the plaintiff may be at liberty to sign final judgment in this action for the amount indorsed on the writ of summons, with interest, if any, and costs, and that the costs of this

NOTICE OF APPEAL TO JUDGE.

appeal and of the application to the Master may be paid by the defendant to the plaintiff.

[And further take notice that it is the intention of the plaintiff to attend by counsel.]

DATED the 13th day of December, 1893.

    (Signed) SOTHEBY AND WILKINS,
      of 16, Bear Street, Bloomsbury,
      in the County of London, solicitors
      for the plaintiff.

To the defendant, and to
  Messrs. FORD and GRUNDY,
    his solicitors.

As to appeal from order of district registrar, see O. 35, r. 9, and No. CCCLVIII., *post*.

CHAPTER VI.

ALTERATION OR ADDITION OF PARTIES.
No. C.
Summons to Add a Defendant (*a*).

(O. 16, rr. 11, 12 ; O. 54, r. 10.)

1896. S. No. 987.

IN THE HIGH COURT OF JUSTICE,
Queen's Bench Division.

BETWEEN Thomas Winter Simmons - plaintiff,
and
Jacob Walker - - - defendant.

LET all parties concerned attend the Master [*or* Judge] in Chambers, Central Office, Royal Courts of Justice, Strand, London, on Thursday, the 8th day of February, 1896, at 11 o'clock in the forenoon, on the hearing of an application on the part of * the plaintiff for an order that George Albert Wilkinson be added as a defendant (*b*) herein, and that the writ of summons and all subsequent proceedings be amended accordingly.†

DATED the 5th day of February, 1896.

This summons was taken out by MASON and GREEN, of 17, Basinghall Street, in the City of London [Agents for, etc.], solicitors for the plaintiff.

To the defendant and to
Messrs. LEE, HENRY and STONE,
his solicitors.

[This summons will be attended by counsel.]

(*a*) The whole of the above summons, with the exception of that part between * and †, may be regarded as purely

ALTERATION OR ADDITION OF PARTIES. 75

formal, and with the substitution of appropriate names, dates, etc., will serve as a general form for all summonses at chambers in the Queen's Bench Division, except summonses for directions under O. 30. (See Yearly Supreme Court Practice and the Annual Practice, App. K., No. 1.) As such it is referred to in subsequent forms.

(*b*) It must be noted, however, that in cases to which O. 30 applies, the above application will, in common with other interlocutory applications, be made on the summons for directions (see No. CXLII.) or on application for further directions (see No. CXLVI.)

No. CI.

Order adding Defendant (*a*).

(O. 16, rr. 11, 12; O. 54, r. 29.)

1896. S. No. 987.

IN THE HIGH COURT OF JUSTICE,
Queen's Bench Division.
Master   [*or* The Honourable
Mr. Justice   ], in Chambers.

BETWEEN Thomas Winter Simmons - plaintiff,
and
Jacob Walker - - - defendant.

UPON hearing the solicitors on both sides [and upon reading the affidavit of the plaintiff filed the 5th day of February, 1896, and the affidavit of, etc.], *

IT IS ORDERED that George Albert Wilkinson be added as a defendant herein, and that the writ of summons and all subsequent proceedings be amended accordingly, and that the said George Albert Wilkinson be served as provided by Order 16, Rule 13, of the Rules of the Supreme Court. AND IT IS FURTHER ORDERED that the costs of this application be the defendant's in any event (*b*).† [Fit for counsel.]

DATED the 8th day of February, 1898.

(*a*) See note (*a*) to No. C. The formal parts of the above, with the necessary modifications, may be used as a general form for

ALTERATION OR ADDITION OF PARTIES.

orders at Queen's Bench Chambers. (See Yearly Supreme Court Practice and the Annual Practice, App. K., No. 2.)

(*b*) Since O. 30 applies now to the majority of cases, the above order, as well as other orders on interlocutory applications, will generally be included in a general order for directions (see No. CXLIII.), or an order for further directions (see No. CXLVII.).

No. CII.

Summons to Strike Out a Party.

(O. 16, rr. 11, 12.)

[*Formal parts as in No. C.*]

the defendant for an order that the name of the plaintiff, Bertram Steel, be struck out of the proceedings herein.

See No. C., note (*b*).

No. CIII.

Order Striking Out a Party.

(O. 16, rr, 11, 12.)

[*Formal parts as in No. CI.*]

IT IS ORDERED that the name of the plaintiff, Bertram Steel, be struck out of the proceedings herein, and that the costs of this application be costs in the cause.

See No. CI., note (*b*).

No. CIV.

Consent of Added Plaintiff, or Next Friend of Plaintiff.

(O. 16, r. 11.)

[*Heading as in writ.*]

I, THOMAS HENRY JENNINGS, of 12, New Grove, Peckham, S.E., Chartered Accountant, hereby consent to be added as plaintiff [*or*, as next friend of the above-named plaintiff] herein.

DATED the 6th day of January, 1896.

(Signed) T. H. JENNINGS.

No. CV.

Authority to Solicitor to Use Name of Next Friend.

(O. 16, r. 20.)

[*Heading as in writ.*]

I HEREBY authorise you to use my name as next friend of the plaintiff herein.

(Signed) MARTIN SCOTT, of 121, Cadogan Gardens, London, W.

To Messrs. C. and L. WILLIAMSON,
of 12, Fetter Lane, E.C.

No. CVI.

Notice of Application for Appointment of Guardian for Defendant Infant or Person of Unsound Mind.

(O. 13, r. 1.)

[*Heading as in writ.*]

TAKE NOTICE that the above-named plaintiff intends to apply to the Master, sitting at Chambers, at the Royal Courts of Justice, Strand, London, on Friday, the 27th day of April, 1894, for an order that Mr. Henry Montagu Butler, a solicitor of the Supreme Court, or some other proper person may be assigned guardian of the above-named defendant, an infant [*or*, a person of unsound mind not so found by inquisition], by whom he may appear and defend this action.

DATED the 19th day of April, 1894

(Signed) ROBERT STEVENS, of 201, Queen Victoria Street, in the City of London, plaintiff's solicitor.

To   (*a*)

(*a*) As to the person, or (in the case of an infant not residing under the care of his father or guardian) persons, on whom this notice must be served, see O. 13, r. 1.

No. CVII.

Affidavit on Application for Appointment of Guardian.

O. 13. r 1.)

[*Heading and commencement as in No. LXVI.*]

1. I did, on the 8th day of April, 1894, at No. 43, Emsworth Gardens, Kensington, in the County of Middlesex, serve the above-named defendant, Percy Manson, with a true copy of the writ of summons in this action, which appeared to me to have been regularly issued out of the Central Office of the Supreme Court of Judicature, against the above-named defendant at the suit of the above-named plaintiff, and which was dated the 7th day of April, 1894, by delivering the same to and leaving the same with Philip Gregory Phipps, the guardian of the said defendant (*a*) [*or*, the person with whom the said defendant resides ; *or*, the person, under whose care the said defendant is].

2. [*As in No. LXVI.*]

3. [*As in No. LXVI.*]

4. I did, on the 19th day of April, 1894, serve the said Philip Gregory Phipps with a notice in writing of an intended application herein, a true copy of which notice

is now produced and shown to me marked "A." by delivering a true copy of the said notice to and leaving the same with the said Philip Gregory Phipps (*b*). [I did also on the 19th day of April, 1894, at No. 12, Avenue Terrace, Hampstead, in the County of Middlesex, serve Edward Manson, who is the father [*or* guardian] of the said defendant, with the said notice, by delivering another true copy of the said notice to and leaving the same with the said Edward Manson.]

5. The said Percy Manson is an infant under the age of 21 years [*or, in case of a person of unsound mind*: The said Percy Manson has not been found by inquisition to be of unsound mind, but I am informed by Henry Whitmore, of 93, Harley Street, in the County of Middlesex, Doctor of Medicine, and verily believe, that the said Percy Manson is in fact a person of unsound mind, and incapable of managing his affairs.]

SWORN, etc.

Filed on behalf of the plaintiff.

(*a*) As to what is sufficient service upon an infant, and upon a person of unsound mind, see O. 9, rr. 4, 5.

(*b*) See note to No. CVI. The bracketed sentence must be added in the case of an infant not residing with, or under the care of, his father or guardian.

No. CVIII.

Affidavit for Entry of Appearance as Guardian of Infant.

(O. 16, rr. 18, 19 ; Y. S. C. P., and A. P., App. A.,
Part II., No. 8.)

[*Heading and commencement as usual.*]

NOEL MARSTON KARSLAKE, of No. 16, Victoria Road, St. John's Wood, in the County of London, tea merchant, is a fit and proper person to act as guardian *ad litem* of the above-named infant defendant, and has no interest in the matters in question in this action adverse to that of

the said infant, and the consent of the said Noel Marston Karslake to act as such guardian is hereto annexed.
SWORN, etc.
Filed on behalf of the plaintiff.
For consent of guardian, see next form.

No. CIX.

Consent of Guardian.

(Y. S. C. P., and A. P., App. A., Part II., No. 8.)

[*Heading as in writ.*]

I, NOEL MARSTON KARSLAKE, of No. 16, Victoria Road, St. John's Wood, in the County of London, tea merchant, consent to act as guardian *ad litem* for James Pedley, an infant defendant in this action, and I authorise Messrs. Morris and Benson, of 16, New Inn Square, in the County of London, to defend this action.

DATED the 2nd day of February, 1898.
(Signed) N. M. KARSLAKE.

No. CX.

Affidavit on Application for Leave to Sue in Forma Pauperis.

IN THE HIGH COURT OF JUSTICE,
Queen's Bench Division.
In the matter of the Judicature Acts, 1873—1884.
In the matter of an intended action
BETWEEN Charles Hodges - - plaintiff,
and
William White Sealy - defendant.

I, JAMES HERBERT HEDLEY, of No. 81, Bishopsgate Street Within, in the City of London, a solicitor of the Supreme Court, make oath and say as follows:

1. The case hereunto annexed, marked "A." contains, to the best of my knowledge, information and belief, a

full and true statement of all the material facts in the matters in question between the above-named intended plaintiff and the above-named intended defendant.

2. The said case was, on the 26th day of April, 1896, laid by me before counsel, and his opinion thereon is written at the end of the said case.

3. The said intended plaintiff is desirous of bringing an action *in formâ pauperis* against the said intended defendant in respect of the matters set out in the said case.

4. I am informed by the said intended plaintiff, and verily believe, that he is not worth 25*l*., save and except only his wearing apparel and the subject-matter of the said intended action.

SWORN, etc.

Filed on behalf of the plaintiff.

No. CXI.
Affidavit on Application for Leave to Issue Third Party Notice.

(O. 16, r. 48.)

[*Heading as in writ.*]

I, PHILIP DODDS, of 10, New Street Terrace, Richmond, in the County of Surrey, builder, the above-named defendant, make oath and say as follows:

1. This action is brought by the above-named plaintiff against me to recover damages for breach of covenant to keep a certain house and premises in repair.

2. On the 7th day of March last, I entered an appearance herein, and on the 18th day of March last, the plaintiff delivered his statement of claim. I have not yet delivered my defence.

3. The said house and premises were, by lease dated the 16th day of April, 1887, demised by the plaintiff to me for the term of 21 years. In the said lease I covenanted to keep the said house and premises in such repair as therein mentioned, during the continuance of the said term of 21 years.

82 ALTERATION OR ADDITION OF PARTIES.

4. By an assignment dated the 27th day of September, 1891, I assigned to one William Percival the remainder of the said term from the 29th day of September, 1891, and the said William Percival covenanted to indemnify me against liability for breaches of the covenants in the said lease during such remainder of the said term.

5. The breach of covenant, in respect of which the plaintiff is suing, has occurred since the date of the said assignment by me to the said William Percival, and I am advised and believe that I have a good claim for indemnity in respect thereof against the said William Percival.

6. I am accordingly desirous of issuing a third party notice against the said William Percival.

SWORN, etc.

Filed on behalf of the defendant.

An affidavit in support of an application for leave to issue a third party notice should state :
(1) The nature of the plaintiff's claim ;
(2) The steps already taken in the action, and that the defence has not been delivered ;
(3) The nature of defendant's claim to contribution or indemnity, showing a clear *primâ facie* right thereto.

See the note to O. 16, r. 48, in the Yearly Supreme Court Practice and the Annual Practice. The affidavit must necessarily vary with the facts of each case.

No. CXII.

Third Party Notice.

(O. 16, r. 48 ; Y. S. C. P., and A. P., App. B., No. 1.)

1894. T. No. 759.

IN THE HIGH COURT OF JUSTICE,
  Queen's Bench Division.

BETWEEN John Henry Tomlinson - plaintiff,
         and
         Philip Dodds - - - defendant.

Notice filed the 23rd day of March, 1894.

To Mr. William Percival.

TAKE notice that this action has been brought by the plaintiff against the defendant to recover damages for breach of covenant to keep in repair the house and premises known as No. 12, Suffolk Street, Greenwich, in the County of Kent.

The defendant claims to be indemnified by you against liability under the said covenant, on the ground that in deed of assignment dated 27th day of September, 1891, and made between the defendant of the one part and you of the other part, you covenanted so to indemnify him.

And take notice, that if you wish to dispute the plaintiff's claim against the defendant Philip Dodds, or your liability to the defendant Philip Dodds, you must cause an appearance to be entered for you within eight days after service of this notice.

In default of your so appearing, you will be deemed to admit the validity of any judgment obtained against the defendant Philip Dodds, and your own liability to contribute or indemnify to the extent herein claimed, which may be summarily enforced against you pursuant to the Rules of the Supreme Court, 1883, Order 16, Part 6.

(Signed) SMITH and JAMES, of 101, High Holborn, in the County of London, Solicitors for the defendant, Philip Dodds.

Appearance to be entered at the Central Office, Royal Courts of Justice, Strand, London.

For forms applicable in certain other cases, see Yearly Supreme Court Practice and the Annual Practice, App. B., No. 1.
For form of entry of appearance by third party, see No. LVI.

No. CXIII.

Order Giving Leave to Issue Third Party Notice.

(O. 16, r. 48; Y. S. C. P., and A. P., App. K., No. 23.)

[*Formal parts as in No. CI.*]

IT IS ORDERED that the defendant, Philip Dodds, be at liberty to issue a notice claiming indemnity [*or*, contribution] over against William Percival, pursuant to the Rules of the Supreme Court, Order 16, Rule 48.

No. CXIV.
Summons by Third Party to Discharge Order.

[*Formal parts as in No. C.*]

William Percival that the order of Master in this action, dated the 22nd day of March, 1894, be discharged [*or,* varied by, etc.].

For form of order on the above summons, see Yearly Supreme Court Practice and the Annual Practice, App. K., No. 14.

No. CXV.
Judgment by Default against Third Party.
(O. 16, r. 50.)

[*Heading as in writ.*]

The 23rd day of April, 1894.

THE third party, William Percival, mentioned in the third party notice, dated the 23rd day of March, 1894, not having appeared to such third party notice, and the defendant having satisfied the judgment entered against him on the 12th day of April, 1894, as appears by an affidavit of George Keppel Smith, filed this day.

It is this day adjudged that the defendant recover against the said William Percival the sum of 83*l.*

No. CXVI.
Judgment against Third Party after Trial.
(O. 16, r. 51.)

[*Heading as in writ.*]

DATED and entered the 15th October, 1894.

THIS action having on the 14th and 15th days of October, 1894, been tried before the Honourable Mr. Justice   , and the said Mr. Justice   , on the

15th day of October, 1894, having ordered that judgment be entered for the defendant against William Percival for 83l.

It is this day adjudged that the defendant recover from the said William Percival 83l., and costs to be taxed.

The above costs have been taxed and allowed at 41l. 12s. 6d., as appears by a taxing officer's certificate, dated the 8th day of November, 1894.

No. CXVII.
Summons for Judgment against Third Party after Decision without Trial.
(O. 16, r. 51.)

[*Formal parts as in No. C.*]

the defendant for an order that he be at liberty to sign judgment against William Percival, the third party named in the third party notice issued herein on the 23rd day of March, 1894, for 83l., and for 41l. 12s. 6d., the costs of his defence herein, and for the costs of the third party proceedings herein to be taxed.

No. CXVIII.
Summons for Directions as to Third Party.
(O. 16, r. 52.)

[*Formal parts as in No. C.*]

the defendant to show cause why an order for directions should not be made in this action as follows:

That the question as to the liability of William Percival, the third party herein, to indemnify the defendant, be tried at the trial of the action.

No. CXIX.

Order for Directions as to Third Party.

(O. 16, rr. 52, 53.)

[*Formal parts as in No. CI.*]

The following directions are hereby given :

That the third party, William Percival, be at liberty to appear at the trial by counsel, and to call witnesses, and to cross-examine the witnesses of the plaintiff and of the defendant ;

And that, if the said William Percival intends to rely on any points not raised in the defence of the defendant herein, he do within 10 days deliver to the plaintiff particulars of such points ;

And that the said William Percival be bound by the result of the trial ;

And that the costs of this application be reserved for the Judge at the trial.

No. CXX.

Affidavit on Application for Order to Carry on Proceedings.

(O. 17, r. 4.)

[*Heading and commencement as usual.*]

1. This action was commenced by writ dated the 11th day of January, 1898. The above-named defendant entered an appearance on the 18th day of January, 1898, and the above-named plaintiff delivered a statement of claim on the 8th day of February, 1898. The said defendant delivered his defence on the 23rd day of February, 1898. No reply has yet been delivered.

2. The said plaintiff was adjudicated bankrupt on the 1st day of March, 1898, and on the 5th day of March, 1898, James Groves was duly appointed trustee of the property of the said plaintiff under his bankruptcy.

3. The said James Groves is desirous of continuing the action, as trustee of the estate of the said plaintiff, against the said defendant.

SWORN, etc.

Filed on behalf of the plaintiff.

The affidavit in support of an application for an order under O. 17, r. 4, should show :
(1) The stage at which the action has arrived ;
(2) The change or transmission of interest or liability ;
(3) The title, interest, or liability of the party by or against whom it is proposed to carry on the action.

See the note to O. 17, r. 4, in the Yearly Supreme Court Practice and the Annual Practice.

No. CXXI.

Order to Carry on Proceedings.

(O. 17, r. 4.)

[*Formal parts as in No. CI.*]

IT IS ORDERED that the proceedings in this action be carried on between James Groves, as trustee of the estate of the above-named plaintiff, and the above-named defendant.

For form of appearance by a person, not already a party, who is served with an order to carry on proceedings (O. 17, r. 5), see No. LXV.

No. CXXII.

Summons to Discharge Order to Carry on Proceedings.

(O. 17, rr. 6, 7.)

[*See No. CXIV, which may be adapted.*]

No. CXXIII.

Summons to Compel Representative of Deceased Party to Proceed.

(O. 17, r. 8.)

[*Formal parts as in No. C.*]

the defendant for an order that Robert Elwell, the executor of the above-named plaintiff, deceased, do proceed with this action, and that, if the said Robert Elwell do not within 14 days proceed therewith, the defendant be at liberty to sign judgment for his costs of defence, and that the costs of this application be the defendant's in any event.

No. CXXIV.

Certificate of Abatement.

(O. 17, r. 9.)

[*Heading as in writ.*]

I HEREBY CERTIFY that this cause has become abated by reason of the death of the plaintiff on the 16th day of April, 1893.

DATED the 30th day of April, 1893.

(Signed)   HOWELL AND WILLIAMS,
      of 16, Salisbury Square, in the City of London, solicitors for the plaintiff.

No. CXXV.

Certificate of Change of Interest.

(O. 17, r. 9.)

[*Heading as in writ.*]

I HEREBY CERTIFY that a change of interest has taken place in this action by reason of the above-named plaintiff on the 2nd day of December, 1895, having been adjudicated bankrupt, and Henry George Cogswell, the trustee of the estate of the said plaintiff, having on the 12th day of January, 1896, been ordered to carry on the proceedings herein as such trustee, pursuant to Order 17, Rule 4, of the Rules of the Supreme Court.

DATED, etc. [*conclude as in No. CXXIV.*]

CHAPTER VII.

JOINDER OF CAUSES OF ACTION, TRANSFERS, AND CONSOLIDATION.

No. CXXVI.

Summons to Disunite or Exclude Causes of Action.

(O. 18, rr. 1, 8, 9.)

[*Formal parts as in No. C.*]

the defendant, that the causes of action joined herein be tried separately [or alternatively that the plaintiffs elect within a week which plaintiff's claim be proceeded with, and that the writ of summons and statement of claim herein be amended by striking out all parts thereof relating to the claim of the other plaintiff.]

The above form is applicable to a case where separate causes of action by two plaintiffs against one defendant have been united in one action. (See *Sandes* v. *Wildsmith*, [1893] 1 Q. B. 771.) The summons must necessarily vary with the facts of each case. The order may readily be framed accordingly.

In some cases this application will be made on application for further directions (see No. CXLVI.).

No. CXXVII.

Summons to Transfer Action.

(O. 49, r. 3.)

[*Formal parts as in No. C.*]

the defendant, for an order that, subject to the consent of the President of the Chancery Division of the High Court of Justice being first obtained, this action be transferred to the said Division.

This application must be made to the Judge in Chambers (O. 54, r. 12).

No. CXXVIII.

Order Transferring Action.

(O. 49, rr. 3, 7.)

[*Formal parts as in No. CI.*]

IT IS ORDERED that, subject to the consent of the President of the Chancery Division of the High Court of Justice being first obtained, this action be transferred to the said Division and assigned to Mr. Justice , and that the costs of this application be costs in the cause.

No. CXXIX.

Summons to Consolidate.

(O. 49, r. 8.)

[*Formal parts as in No. C.*]

the defendants, that this action, and the action of Austen v. The New Essex Brewery Company, Limited, 1897, A., No. 1783, be consolidated and tried together.

See No. C., note (*b*), and O. 30.

No. CXXX.

Summons to Consolidate. (Another Form)

1897. C. No. 3952.

In the High Court of Justice,
Queen's Bench Division.

Between Thomas Cobb - - - plaintiff,
and
The New Essex Brewery
Company, Limited - defendants,

and

1897. A. No. 1783.

In the High Court of Justice,
Queen's Bench Division.

Between Mary Jane Austen - - plaintiff,
and
The New Essex Brewery
Company, Limited - defendants.

Let all parties, etc. [*as usual*].

the defendants, that these actions be consolidated and tried together.

See No. C., note (*b*), and O. 30.

No. CXXXI.

Order to Consolidate.

(O. 49, r. 8.)

[*Formal parts as usual.*]

It is ordered that these actions be consolidated and tried together, and that the costs of this application be costs in the cause.

See No. CI., note (*b*), and O. 30.

No. CXXXII.
Order Refusing to Consolidate.

[*Formal parts as usual.*]

IT IS ORDERED that this action, and the action of Austin v. The New Essex Brewery Company, Limited, be entered consecutively and tried in such manner as the presiding Judge shall think fit, and that the costs of this application be reserved for the Judge at the trial.

See No. CI., note (*b*), and O. 30.

No. CXXXIII.
Heading when Actions are Consolidated.

1897. C. No. 3952.

IN THE HIGH COURT OF JUSTICE,
Queen's Bench Division.
BETWEEN Thomas Cobb - - - plaintiff,
and
The New Essex Brewery
Company, Limited - defendants;

and

1897. A. No. 1783.

IN THE HIGH COURT OF JUSTICE,
Queen's Bench Division.
BETWEEN Mary Jane Austen - - plaintiff,
and
The New Essex Brewery
Company, Limited - defendants.

Consolidated by order of Master , dated the 16th day of February, 1898.

No. CXXXIV.

Order Staying Proceedings pending Trial of Test Action.

[*Formal parts as usual.*]

IT IS ORDERED that all further proceedings be stayed in all the above-mentioned actions, except the action of Bateson v. Horledge, 1896, B. No. 1709, and that the said action of Bateson v. Horledge be treated as a test action, the defendants in all the other actions undertaking to be bound and concluded by the verdict in the said test action, provided such verdict shall be to the satisfaction of the judge who may try the same, and that the costs of this application be costs in the said test action.

As to staying proceedings in one or more of several actions, see the notes to O. 49, r. 8, in the Yearly Supreme Court Practice and the Annual Practice.

CHAPTER VIII.

TRIAL WITHOUT PLEADINGS.

No. CXXXV.
Indorsement for Trial without Pleadings—Contract.
(O. 18A, r. 1.)

THE plaintiff's claim is for 52*l*. 10*s*. damages for defendant's breach of contract to accept and pay for goods. On March 28th, 1896, the defendant agreed to purchase from the plaintiff 30 gross patent sail-hooks, to be manufactured by the plaintiff, at 1*l*. 15*s*. per gross. The plaintiff has manufactured the said hooks as agreed, but the defendant by letter, dated September 29th, 1896 refused, and still refuses, to accept and pay for the same.

If the defendant appears, the plaintiff intends to proceed to trial without pleadings.

The indorsement of the plaintiff's claim on the writ "shall contain a statement sufficient to give notice of the nature of his claim or of the relief or remedy required in the action, and shall state that if the defendant appears the plaintiff intends to proceed to trial without pleadings" (O. 18A, r. 1). The indorsement (which is not a pleading) should be fuller than a general indorsement. In practice it will be found desirable to be as explicit as in a special indorsement; otherwise particulars may be ordered under Rule 3.

It would appear that the place of trial need not be named on the writ in the case of an indorsement for trial without pleadings.

This form of indorsement should not be used, unless there can be no reasonable doubt as to the issues between the parties.

No. CXXXVI.

Indorsement for Trial without Pleadings—Tort.

THE plaintiff's claim is for 100*l*. damages for trespass by the defendant in wrongfully entering upon the plaintiff's lands at Marsham Farm, Oxton, in the County of Dorset, on divers occasions between the 8th and 18th days of June, 1895, and breaking down the plaintiff's fences.

If the defendant appears, the plaintiff intends to proceed to trial without pleadings.

See note to No. CXXXV.

No. CXXXVII.

Notice of Trial without Pleadings.

(O. 18A, r. 2; Y. S. C. P., and A. P., App. B., No. 16A.)

[*Heading as in writ.*]

TAKE NOTICE of the trial of this action without pleadings in Middlesex for the 15th day of July next.

    (Signed) JOHNSON and EDWARDS,
     of 113, Newington Causeway,
      in the County of London,
       plaintiff's solicitors.

DATED the 23rd day of June, 1896.

To Messrs. TAGG and NEWBURY,
 of 11, Copthall Gardens,
 in the City of London,
 defendant's solicitors.

No. CXXXVIII.

Summons for Statement of Claim.

(O. 18A, r. 3.)

[*Formal parts as in No. C.*]

the defendant, for an order that the plaintiff deliver a statement of claim herein.

NOTICE OF SPECIAL DEFENCE.   97

No. CXXXIX.

Order on Summons for Statement of Claim. (No. 1.)

(O. 18A, r. 3.)

[*Formal parts as in No. CI.*]

The following directions are hereby given, and it is ordered:

That the plaintiff shall within twenty-one days deliver a statement of claim, and that defence and reply be delivered as usual.

That the action be tried at Leicester.

That the action be tried without a jury.

No. CXL.

Order on Summons for Statement of Claim. (No. 2.)

(O. 18A, r. 3.)

[*Formal parts as in No. CI.*]

IT IS ORDERED that this action shall proceed to trial without pleadings [and that the defendant shall within ten days deliver particulars of his defence].

No. CXLI.

Notice of Special Defence.

(O. 18A, r. 5.)

[*Heading as in writ.*]

TAKE NOTICE that the defendant at the trial intends to rely upon the matters hereunder set out:

1. At the time of the alleged contract the defendant was an infant, under the age of twenty-one years.

2. The defendant was induced to enter into the said contract by the fraud of the plaintiff. Particulars are as follows: The plaintiff stated to the defendant at an interview on April 21st, 1891, that the business was doing a turnover of 45*l*. per week, whereas in truth and in fact the turnover was less than 20*l*. per week, as the plaintiff well knew.

3. The defendant counterclaims 150*l*. for money lent to the plaintiff between April 30th and June 16th, 1891, or dates which the defendant is unable further to specify.

DATED the 8th day of March, 1895.
     (Signed) HANBURY and GIBBS, of 61,
       Finsbury Circus, in the City of
       London, defendant's solicitors.
To Mr. GODFREY MILES,
 of 217, Bedford Row, W.C.,
  plaintiff's solicitor.

CHAPTER IX.

THE SUMMONS FOR DIRECTIONS.

No. CXLII.

Summons for Directions.

(O. 30, r. 1 ; Y. S. C. P., and A. P., App. K., No. 3A.)

[*Heading as in writ.*]

LET all parties concerned attend Master   , in chambers at the Central Office, Royal Courts of Justice, Strand, London, on Wednesday, the 16th day of February, 1898 (*a*), at eleven o'clock in the forenoon, on the hearing of an application on the part of the plaintiff to show cause why an order should not be made in this action as follows:

Pleadings. [That there be [no] pleadings in this action.] (*b*).

Particulars. [*See No. CL.*]

Admissions.

Discovery. [That the defendant file an affidavit of documents in ten days.] [*See No. CLXXXV.*]

Interrogatories. [For leave to interrogate the defendant. Answers to be filed within ten days.] [*See No. CLXXIX.*]

Inspection of documents. [*See No. CLXXXIX.*]

Inspection of real or personal property. [*See No. CCCXXVI.*]

Commissions. [*See No. CCXXXVI.*]

Examination of witnesses. [*See No. CCXXXIV.*]

Place of trial. [*See No. CCXXI.*]
Mode of trial.
Any other interlocutory matter or thing.

DATED the 11th day of February, 1898 (*a*).

This summons was taken out by EVANS AND SIBLEY, of 61, Moorgate Street, in the City of London, solicitors for the plaintiff.

To the defendant, and to
Messrs. FORD and LEE,
his solicitors.

(*a*) The summons is returnable in not less than four days (O. 30, r. 1 (a)). Sunday is excluded (O. 64, r. 2), as is also the day of the issue of the summons, but the return day is included (O. 64, r. 12).

(*b*) The official form has the following note—"N.B. The applicant should specifically state in the summons what he applies for, and should strike out from the print what he does not apply for." This direction is not, however, always followed in practice, the summons being not unfrequently left blank.

No. CXLIII.

Order for Directions.

(O. 30, r. 2 ; Y. S. C. P., and A. P., App. K., No. 4B.)

[*Heading as in No. CI.*]

UPON hearing the solicitors on both sides, the following directions are hereby given, and it is ordered :

That there be [no] pleadings in the action.

That the plaintiff deliver to the defendant an account in writing of the particulars of the alleged misrepresentations and damage, and that, unless such particulars be delivered within ten days from the date of this order, all further proceedings be stayed until the delivery thereof, and that the defendant have ten days after the delivery of the said particulars to deliver his defence.

That the plaintiff and defendant do, respectively, within ten days from the date of this order, answer on affidavit stating what documents are or have been in their possession or power relating to the matters in question in this action.

That the plaintiff be at liberty to deliver to the defendant, and that the defendant be at liberty to deliver to the plaintiff, interrogatories in writing as approved by the Master, and that the said interrogatories be answered as prescribed by Order 31, Rules 8 and 26, of the Rules of the Supreme Court.

That the action be tried at Middlesex.

That the action be tried with a special jury.

DATED the 16th day of February, 1898.

No. CXLIV.

Summons for Directions—Commercial List.

(O. 30, r. 1 ; A. P., App. K., No. 4c.)

[*Heading as in writ.*]

LET all parties concerned attend the Judge in chambers, at the Central Office, Royal Courts of Justice, Strand, London, on Friday, the 8th day of July, 1898 (a), at 10.30 of the clock in the forenoon, on the hearing of an application on the part of the plaintiff for an order for directions, as follows :

That the action be transferred to the commercial list.

That points of claim be delivered by the plaintiff in seven days.

That points of defence be delivered by the defendant in seven days afterwards.

That lists of documents be exchanged between the parties in seven days, and inspection be given within three days afterwards.

That the action be tried with [out] a [special] jury.

That the date of trial be fixed for August 5th, 1898.

That the costs of this application be costs in the cause.

DATED the 4th day of July, 1898 (a).

This summons was taken out by, etc. [*as usual*].

(a) See note to No. CXLII.

No. CXLV.

Order for Directions. Commercial List.

(O. 30, r. 2 ; A. P., App. K., No. 4d.)

1896. C. No. 2709.

IN THE HIGH COURT OF JUSTICE,
Queen's Bench Division.
Mr. Justice   , in Chambers.

BETWEEN Arthur Cridland   -   -   plaintiff,
                      and
         The Midland Rubber Company, Limited   -   -   defendants.

UPON hearing Counsel on both sides,

IT IS ORDERED :

That the action be transferred to the commercial list.

That points of claim be delivered by the plaintiff in ten days.

That points of defence be delivered by the defendant in ten days afterwards.

That lists of documents be exchanged between the parties in seven days, and inspection be given in three days afterwards.

That the action be tried with [out] a [special] jury.

That the date of the trial be fixed for August 10th, 1898.

That the costs of this application be costs in the cause.

DATED the 8th day of July, 1898.

No. CXLVI.

Notice of Application for Further Directions.

(O. 30, r. 5.)

1896. S. No. 277.

IN THE HIGH COURT OF JUSTICE,
Queen's Bench Division.
Master   , Master in Chambers.

BETWEEN Alexander Burton Simpson   plaintiff,
and
Andrew Macfarlane Stuart   defendant.

TAKE NOTICE that the above-named plaintiff intends to apply to Master   , at the Central Office, Royal Courts of Justice, Strand, London, on Tuesday, the 9th day of August, 1898 (a), at 12 o'clock noon for further directions in this action as to—

1. Interrogatories. That the plaintiff be at liberty to administer to the defendant the interrogatories hereto annexed, to be answered by the defendant within ten days.

2. Examination of witnesses. That Robert Wilton, a witness on behalf of the plaintiff, be examined at Liverpool before an examiner of the Court.

DATED the 5th day of August, 1898 (a).
        (Signed) RICHARD JACKSON,
           of 180 James Street, Bedford Row,
           W.C., solicitor for the plaintiff.
To Messrs. WHEELER and DIXON,
    the solicitors for the defendant.

(a) The notice must be a two clear days' notice (O. 30, r. 5). See also O. 64, rr. 2, 12.

No. CXLVII.

Order for Further Directions.

(O. 30, rr. 5, 6.)

[*Heading as in No. CXLVI.*]

UPON hearing the solicitors on both sides [and upon reading the affidavit of Herbert James Knox filed herein the 5th day of August, 1898] the following further directions are hereby given, and it is ordered :

That Robert Wilton be examined at Liverpool before an examiner of the Court, and that the costs of this application be costs in the cause.

DATED the 9th day of August, 1898.

CHAPTER X.

PLEADINGS AND PROCEEDINGS IN CONNEXION THEREWITH.

Since pleadings, other than specially indorsed claims (as to which see Chapter II.), are as a rule settled by counsel, it has not been considered necessary in this book to give forms of statement of claim, defence, or reply. The following references to the forms in the Appendices in the Yearly Supreme Court Practice and the Annual Practice are, however, given for convenience.

Statement of Claim, General Form	- - - -	Y.S.C.P; A.P.; App.C. Sect.			I.
Special Indorsements (see also Chapter II., *ante*)	- -	„	„ „	„	IV.
Statements of Claim, Contract		„	„ „	„	V.
„ „ Tort	-	„	„ „	„	VI.
„ „ Recovery of Land		„	„ „	„	VII.
Defence (and Counterclaim), General Form	- - -	„	„ App.D.	„	I.
Defences to Specially Indorsed Claims	- - - -	„	„ „	„	IV.
General Defences	- - -	„	„ „	„	IV.
Defences, Contract	- - -	„	„ „	„	V.
„ Tort	- - -	„	„ „	„	VI.
„ Recovery of Land	-	„	„ „	„	VII.
„ including an objection in Point of Law		„	„ App.E.	„	III.
Counterclaims	- - -	„	„ App.D.	„	VIII.
Reply	- - - -	„	„ App.E.	„	I.
Example of a Statement of Claim, Defence and Reply		„	„ „	„	II.

Bullen and Leake's Precedents of Pleading, and Dr. Blake Odgers' Principles of Pleading may also be referred to.

No. CXLVIII.

Summons for Time.

(O. 64, rr. 7, 8 ; O. 65, r. 27 (24); Y. S. C. P., App. K., No. 4c.)

[*Formal parts as in No. C.*]

the plaintiff [*or*, defendant] for an order that the plaintiff [*or*, defendant] have fourteen days' further time to deliver his statement of claim [*or*, defence] in this action ; *or*

the plaintiff for an order that the plaintiff have seven days' further time to reply in this action.

The order on a summons for time need not be drawn up, unless the Master so directs (O. 52, r. 14).

In cases to which O. 30 applies, the above application will be made on application for further directions. (See No. C., note (*b*), and No. CXLVI.)

No. CXLIX.

Particulars Exceeding Three Folios.

(O. 19, r. 6.)

[*Heading as in writ.*]

The following are the particulars of the debt [*or*, expenses, *or*, damages] referred to in the indorsement on the writ of summons [*or*, in (paragraph 3 of) the statement of claim, *or*, defence] herein :—

	Particulars.	£	s.	d.
1896.				
17th May.	Commission on 1 ton copal, R. J. Clarke & Co., 1s. per cwt. - - -	1	0	0
12th July.	Commission on 10 cases (each 2 cwt.) kauri, Colthurst and Harding, 1s. per cwt.	1	0	0
31st August.	Commission on 4 tons 16 cwt. gum, W. J. Miller, 1s. per cwt. - - - -	4	16	0
15th September.	Travelling expenses to Hull charged against commission and debited erroneously to plaintiff -	1	6	4
9th October.	Travelling expenses to Bristol - - - -	0	18	0
	Etc., etc.			
	£			

Delivered the 18th day of May, 1897, by FORREST and HENDERSON, of No. 113, Fenchurch Street, in the City of London, solicitors for the plaintiff.

To the defendant, and to
Messrs. GOODING and SIM,
his solicitors.

As to particulars, delivered thus separately, see p. 12.

108 PLEADINGS, ETC.

No. CL.
Summons for Particulars.
(O. 19, r. 7.)

[*Formal parts as in No. C.*]

the defendant for an order that the plaintiff do within seven days deliver to the defendant [further and better] particulars of :

1. The alleged payments by the plaintiff during the years 1890 and 1891.

2. The contract alleged in paragraph 4 of the statement of claim, stating by whom, when and where the same was made, and whether verbal or in writing.

And that all further proceedings be stayed until the delivery of such particulars.

And that the defendant have ten days' further time to deliver defence after the delivery of the said particulars. And that the costs of this application be costs in the cause.

The delivery of particulars is now ordinarily dealt with on the hearing of the summons for directions (see Nos. CXLII—CXLV., *ante*), or on application for further directions (see No. CXLVI).

No. CLI.
Order for Particulars.
(O. 19, r. 7.)

[*Formal parts as in No. CI.*]

IT IS ORDERED that the plaintiff deliver to the defendant an account in writing with dates and items of the expenses alleged in the statement of claim, and that unless such particulars be delivered within seven days all further proceedings be stayed until after the delivery thereof, and that the defendant have ten days further time to deliver his defence after the delivery of the said particulars, and that the costs of the application be costs in the cause.

See also Yearly Supreme Court Practice and the Annual Practice, App. K., No. 12 ; also the note to Form No. CL, and No. CXLVII.

No. CLII.

Order for Particulars of Counterclaim.

(O, 19, r. 7; Y. S. C. P., App. K., No. 13A; A. P., App. K., No. 12A.)

[*Formal parts as in No. CI.*]

IT IS ORDERED that the defendant's solicitor or agent do within ten days deliver to the plaintiff's solicitor or agent particulars of the said defendant's set-off [and counterclaim], that in default the said defendant be precluded from giving evidence in support thereof on the trial of this action, and that the costs of this application be the plaintiff's costs in the cause.

See also No. CXLVII.

No. CLIII.

Particulars Delivered Pursuant to Order.

[*Heading as in writ.*]

The following are the particulars [of negligence] delivered pursuant to order of Master , dated the 18th day of May, 1897.

The negligence of the defendant consisted in:

1. Suffering the cart to be driven on the wrong side of the highway.

2. Not holding the reins, but fastening them to the shaft.

3. Driving a horse which the defendant well knew was liable to bolt.

DATED the 25th day of May, 1897.

      Yours, etc.,
    BROWN, WILLIAMS and SIMPSON,
     of 116, Bedford Row, W.C.,
      plaintiff's solicitors.

To Mr. W. H. BOWERS,
 defendant's solicitor.

No. CLIV.
Summons for Leave to Amend Pleading (a).
(O. 28, r. 1.)

[*Formal parts as in No. C.*]

the plaintiff for an order that the plaintiff be at liberty to amend his statement of claim by striking out paragraph 4 thereof, and the words " and the matters alleged in paragraph 4 hereof" in paragraph 7, and by substituting " 162*l*. 17*s*. 2*d*." in paragraph 10 for " 179*l*. 15*s*. 6*d*." (*b*)

(*a*) As to amendment generally, see the notes to O. 28, r. 1, in the Yearly Supreme Court Practice and the Annual Practice. As to when leave is unnecessary, see O. 28, rr. 2, 3. Amendments should be made in red ink. In cases of extensive amendments (as to which see O. 28, r. 8), the document must be printed in amended form. An amended document must be marked with the date on which the amendment is made, thus :—"Amended the 23rd day of November, 1896" ; and if the amendment is made by order, the date, etc., of the order must be added, thus :—"pursuant to order of Master   , dated the 21st day of November, 1896" (O. 28, r. 9). When an amended pleading is delivered, it should be marked, " Delivered, as amended, the 29th day of etc., by etc."

(*b*) In cases to which O. 30 applies, the application will be made on the summons for directions (see No. CXLII.), or on application for further directions (see No. CXLVI.).

No. CLV.
Order Giving Leave to Amend Pleading.
(O. 28, r. 1.)

[*Formal parts as in No. CI.*]

IT IS ORDERED that the defendant be at liberty to amend his defence by striking out paragraphs 2 and 3 thereof, and that the plaintiff have fourteen days after the delivery of such amended defence to reply thereto. And that the costs of the application be the plaintiff's in any event.

See also Yearly Supreme Court Practice and the Annual Practice, App. K., No. 10. The order need not be drawn up unless the Master so directs (O. 52, r. 14). See further, No. CLIV., note (*b*).

No. CLVI.

Summons to Disallow Amendment.

(O. 28, r. 4.)

[*Formal parts as in No. C.*]

the defendant for an order that the amendments made by the plaintiff in his statement of claim herein under Order 28, Rule 2, of the Rules of the Supreme Court, be disallowed.

The order may readily be framed from the terms of the summons as approved or varied by the Master. See No. CLIV., note (*b*).

No. CLVII.

Summons to Disallow Counterclaim.

(O. 19, r. 3 ; O. 21, r. 15.)

[*Formal parts as in No. C.*]

the plaintiff for an order that the defendant's counterclaim be disallowed or excluded [*or*, struck out] on the ground that it cannot be conveniently disposed of in this action.

The order may be framed from the terms of the summons. See No. CI., note (*b*), as to the above being made on application for further directions.

No. CLVIII.

Summons to Strike out Pleading.

(O. 19, r. 27.)

[*Formal parts as in No. C.*]

the defendant for an order that so much of the statement of claim herein as alleges concealment and nondisclosure of material facts on the part of the defendant be struck out on the ground that the same is unnecessary and scandalous, and tends to prejudice, embarrass or delay the fair trial of the action, and that the defendant have ten days further time to deliver his defence, and that the costs of and occasioned by this application be paid by the plaintiff to the defendant.

See note to No. CLIX. See also No. C., note (*b*).

No. CLIX.

Summons to Strike Out where No Reasonale Cause of Action.

(O. 25, r. 4.)

[*Formal parts as in No. C.*]

the defendant [*or*, plaintiff] for an order that the statement of claim [*or*, defence] herein be struck out on the ground that it discloses no reasonable cause of action [*or*, answer] and is frivolous and vexatious [and that the action be stayed or dismissed, and that the defendant be at liberty to sign judgment for his costs of defence and of this application to be taxed].

An application under O. 25, r. 4, may be combined with one under O. 19, r. 27 (see No. CLVIII). The application under O. 25, r. 4, may also be made by motion, and the notice of motion may include an application under O. 19, r. 27. See No. CLX., where both applications are combined. See also No. C., note (*b*), as to the applicability of the summons for directions to interlocutory applications.

No. CLX.

Notice of Motion to Strike Out or Dismiss.

(O. 25, r. 4.)

1898. C. No. 197.

IN THE HIGH COURT OF JUSTICE,
Queen's Bench Division.

BETWEEN George William Chalmers - plaintiff,
and
The North Nottingham Colliery Company, Limited - defendants.

TAKE NOTICE, that the Court will be moved on Thursday, the 19th day of May, 1898 (a), at 10.30 o'clock in the forenoon, or so soon thereafter as counsel can be heard, by [Mr.   , of] counsel on behalf of the defendants for an order that the statement of claim herein, or so much thereof as alleges wrongful dismissal of the plaintiff by the defendants be struck out, on the ground that the same is unnecessary and scandalous, and tends to prejudice, embarrass, or delay the fair trial of the action, and on the ground that the same discloses no reasonable cause of action, and is frivolous and vexatious, and an abuse of the process of the court, or alternatively that the action be stayed or dismissed, and that the defendant be at liberty to sign judgment for his costs of defence and of this application to be taxed.

DATED the 16th day of May, 1898 (a).

(Signed) CHARLES WILLIAM KNOX,
of 86, Whitefriars Street, E.C.,
defendants' solicitor.

To Messrs. HARPER and BIRD,
plaintiffs' solicitors.

(a) The notice must give two clear days between the date of service and the day named for the hearing (O. 52, r. 5).

No. CLXI.

Judgment Pursuant to Order Dismissing Action.

(O. 25, r. 4 ; O. 41, r. 7 ; Y. S. C. P., and A. P., App. F., No. 12.)

[*Heading as in writ.*]

The 26th day of October, 1897.

PURSUANT to an order of Master   , dated the 26th day of October, 1897, whereby it was ordered that this action be dismissed, and that the defendant be at liberty to sign judgment for his costs of defence to be taxed—

It is this day adjudged that the defendant recover against the plaintiff his costs of defence to be taxed.

The above costs have been taxed and allowed at 12*l*. 1*s*. 6*d*., as appears by a Taxing Officer's certificate dated the 11th day of November, 1897.

No. CLXII.

Notice of Counterclaim to Person not a Party.

(O. 21, r. 12 ; Y. S. C. P., and A. P., App. B., No. 2.)

[*Heading as in writ.*]

To the within-named Stanley Peters.

TAKE NOTICE that if you do not appear to the within counterclaim of the within-named Isaac Goldsmid within eight days from the service of this defence and counter-claim upon you, you will be liable to have judgment given against you in your absence.

Appearance to be entered at the Central Office, Royal Courts of Justice, Strand, London.

The above notice must be indorsed on the defence served upon the person not a party to the action. For form of appearance by person so served, and for title of the action thereafter, see No. LVII.

No. CLXIII.

Summons for Leave to Plead after Reply.

(O. 23, r. 2.)

[*Formal parts as in No. C.*]

the defendant for an order that the defendant be at liberty to deliver a rejoinder herein.

But see O. 30, r. 5, and No. CXLVI. ; also No. C., note (*b*).

No. CLXIV.

Summons for Leave to Deliver Further Defence.

(O. 24, r. 2.)

[*Formal parts as in No. C.*]

the defendant for an order that the defendant be at liberty to deliver a further defence herein in the form hereto annexed in respect of matters arising after the delivery of his defence herein.

But see O. 30, r. 5, and No. CXLVI.; also No. C., note (*b*).
The above application should be supported by an affidavit, stating that the new matter is true, and that it arose subsequent to the delivery of the defence. The following, or some similar form will suffice :

[*Formal parts as usual.*] The matters alleged in the form of further defence now produced and shown to me, marked "A," are true in substance and in fact, and the grounds of defence therein alleged arose [on or about the 13th day of May, 1898], after the delivery of the defence herein.

No. CLXV.

Confession of Defence.

(O. 24, r. 3 ; Y. S. C. P., and A. P., App B., No. 5.)

[*Heading as in writ.*]

THE plaintiff confesses the defence stated in the second paragraph of the defendant's [further] defence.

Delivered the 27th day of May, 1898, by JONES and BUDD, of 301, Piccadilly, in the County of London, plaintiff's solicitors.

No. CLXVI.

Judgment for Costs after Confesssion of Defence.

(O. 24, r. 3 ; Y. S. C. P., and A. P., App. F., No. 15.)

[*Heading as in writ.*]

The 28th day of May, 1898.

The defendant in his [further] defence herein having alleged a ground of defence which arose after the commencement of this action, and the plaintiff having on the 27th day of May, 1898, delivered a confession of that defence—

It is this day adjudged that the defendant recover against the plaintiff costs to be taxed.

The above costs have been taxed and allowed at 10*l*. 15*s*. 6*d*., as appears by a Taxing Officer's certificate dated the 8th day of June, 1898.

CHAPTER XI.

PROCEEDINGS IN DEFAULT OF PLEADING.

No. CLXVII.

Summons to Dismiss Action for Want of Prosecution.

(O. 27, r. 1.)

[*Formal parts as in No. C.*]

 the defendant for an order that this action be dismissed, for want of prosecution, with costs to be taxed and paid by the plaintiff to the defendant, and that the defendant be at liberty to sign judgment for his said costs.

The above form will also meet the case of defendant applying, under O. 30, r. 8, for an order to dismiss the action, where the plaintiff has not taken out a summons for directions, or for judgment under O. 14.

No. CLXVIII.

Order Dismissing Action for Want of Prosecution.

(O. 27, r. 1.)

[*Formal parts as in No. CI.*]

IT IS ORDERED that this action be dismissed, for want of prosecution, with costs to be taxed and paid by the plaintiff to the defendant, and that the defendant be at liberty to sign judgment for his said costs, and that the costs of this application be costs in the cause.

No. CLXIX.

Judgment on Dismissal of Action for Want of Prosecution.

(O. 27, r. 1.)

[Heading as in writ.]

The 8th day of March, 1896.

PURSUANT to the order of Master   , dated the 27th day of February, 1896, whereby it was ordered that this action should be dismissed, for want of prosecution, with costs, to be taxed and paid by the plaintiff to the defendant, and that the defendant should be at liberty to sign judgment for his said costs, and the said costs having been taxed and allowed at 4*l.* 6*s.* as appears by the certificate of the Taxing Master herein dated the 5th day of March, 1896—

It is this day adjudged that the defendant recover against the plaintiff 4*l.* 6*s.*, the amount of the said certificate, and 1*l.* 1*s.* for further costs of the judgment.

No. CLXX.

Judgment in default of Defence.   Liquidated Demand.

(O. 27, rr. 2, 3.)

[Heading as in writ.]

The 17th day of December, 1897.

THE defendant [Robert Giles] not having delivered any defence, it is this day adjudged that the plaintiff recover against the [said] defendant 122*l.* 3*s.* 4*d.* and costs to be taxed.

The above costs have been taxed and allowed at 8*l.* 16*s.*, as appears by a Taxing Officer's certificate, dated the 15th day of January, 1898.

The combined effect of O. 27, r. 2, and O. 30. r. 1 (b), is that it is not necessary for the plaintiff to apply for leave to enter final judgment in default of defence in the case of a liquidated demand.

No. CLXXI.

Judgment in Default of Defence. Unliquidated Demand.

(O. 27, r. 4.)

[*Heading as in writ.*]

The 8th day of February, 1898.

PURSUANT to order of Master   , dated the 26th day of January, 1898, whereby it was ordered that [unless the defendant should within ten days deliver a defence herein] the plaintiff should be at liberty to enter judgment against the defendant for damages to be assessed [and the defendant not having delivered any defence]—

It is this day adjudged that the plaintiff recover against the defendant damages to be assessed.

In view of the effect of O. 30, it is presumed that the above will be the form of interlocutory judgment.

For præcipe and writ of inquiry, see Nos. LXXVII. and LXXVIII.

For form of final judgment after assessment of damages, see No. LXXIX., substituting "defence" for "appearance."

No. CLXXII.

Judgment in Default of Defence. Recovery of Land.

(O. 27, r. 7.)

[*Heading as in writ.*]

The 28th day of June, 1898.

PURSUANT to order of Master   , dated the 18th day of June, 1898, whereby it was ordered that [unless the defendant should within seven days deliver a defence herein] the plaintiff should be at liberty to enter final judgment for the recovery of possession of the land named in the writ of summons herein [and the defendant not having delivered any defence]—

It is this day adjudged that the plaintiff recover possession of the land in the writ of summons herein mentioned and described as No. 11 New Street, Wandsworth, in the county of Surrey, and costs to be taxed.

No. CLXXIII.

Judgment for Part of Claim Unanswered by Defence.

(O. 27, r. 9.)

[*Heading as in writ.*]

The 23rd day of April, 1897.

PURSUANT to order of Master   , dated the 20th day of April, 1897, whereby it was ordered that the plaintiff should be at liberty to enter final [*or*, interlocutory] judgment for 38*l*. [*or*, damages to be assessed] in respect of the cause of action alleged in paragraph 5 of the statement of claim herein—

It is this day adjudged that the plaintiff recover against the defendant 38*l*. [*or*, damages to be assessed].

No. CLXXIV.

Notice of Motion for Judgment in Default of Defence.

(O. 27, r. 11.)

[*Heading as in writ.*]

TAKE NOTICE that the Court will be moved, on Wednesday, the 16th day of December, 1897, at 10.30 o'clock in the forenoon, or so soon thereafter as counsel can be heard by [Mr.   , of] counsel on behalf of the above-named plaintiff for an order that judgment be entered for the above-named plaintiff herein for 230*l*. and costs to be taxed, and that the costs of this application be costs in the cause.

    Yours, etc.,
        STANDING and LOWRIE,
           of 84 Craven Street, W.C., solicitors
            for the above-named plaintiff.

To the above-named defendant,
    and to Mr. E. Y. JOHNSON,
      his solicitor.

No. CLXXV.
Affidavit of Service of Notice of Motion.
(O. 27, r. 11.)

[*Formal parts as in No. LXVI.*]

I DID on Wednesday, the 3rd day of August, 1898, before the hour of 6 o'clock in the afternoon [personally] serve Messrs. Bates and Hollings, the solicitors in this action for the above-named defendant with a true copy of the notice of motion hereunto annexed [by delivering the same to and leaving the same with a clerk of the said Messrs. Bates and Hollings, at their place of business at Ashley House, No. 101, New Broad Street, in the City of London].

No. CLXXVI.
Affidavit of Default of Defence.
(O. 27, r. 11.)

[*Heading as in writ.*]

I, WILLIAM HENRY WOOD, clerk to Messrs. Roberts and Hay, of 19 Bolt Court, in the City of London, the solicitors for the plaintiff in this action, make oath and say as follows:

1. I have had and have the conduct and management of this action.

2. The writ of summons herein was issued on the 18th day of January, and appearance entered on the 26th day of January, 1898. Pursuant to order of Master , dated the 3rd day of February, 1898, whereby it was ordered that the plaintiff should, within ten days, deliver his statement of claim, and that the defendant should within seven days after such delivery deliver his defence, the plaintiff did on the 12th day of February, deliver his statement of claim. The defendant has made default in delivering his defence, no defence having been delivered as ordered or at all.

SWORN, etc.

Filed on behalf of the plaintiff.

122   PROCEEDINGS IN DEFAULT OF PLEADING.

No. CLXXVII.
Judgment on Motion.
(O. 27, r. 11.)

[*Heading as in writ.*]

The 18th day of January, 1898.

PURSUANT to the order of this Court herein, dated the 18th day of January, 1898, whereby it is ordered that judgment be entered for the plaintiff for 230*l*. and costs to be taxed—

It is this day adjudged that the plaintiff recover against the defendant 230*l*. and costs to be taxed.

The above costs have been taxed and allowed at 15*l*. 4*s*. 9*d*., as appears by a Taxing Officer's certificate, dated the 12th day of February, 1898.

See also Yearly Supreme Court Practice and the Annual Practice, App. F., No. 10.

No. CLXXVIII.
Summons to Set Aside Judgment by Default.
(O. 27, r. 15.)

[*Formal parts as in No. C.*]

the defendant, for an order that the judgment entered herein on the 17th day of May, 1897, be set aside.

If it is proposed to set aside the judgment for irregularity, the grounds must be stated in the summons (see O. 70, r. 3).

The above application must be supported by an affidavit showing the circumstances under which the default has arisen, and a substantial ground of defence.

CHAPTER XII.

DISCOVERY AND INSPECTION.
No. CLXXIX.
Application for Leave to Deliver Interrogatories.

(O. 31, rr. 1, 2.)

This must now be made, in cases to which O. 30 applies, under the original summons for directions (see No. CXLII.), or on an application for further directions (see No. CXLVI.). The material words will be in the following or some similar form :

THAT the plaintiff be at liberty to administer to the defendant the interrogatories hereto annexed [to be answered by the defendant within ten days].

No. CLXXX.
Interrogatories.

(O. 31, r. 4 ; Y. S. C. P., and A. P., App. B., No. 6.)

[*Heading as in writ.*]

INTERROGATORIES on behalf of the above-named defendant for the examination of the above-named plaintiff.
1. Did not, etc.
2. Has not, etc.
  Etc., etc., etc.
The above-named plaintiff is required to answer all the above interrogatories.

For forms of interrogatories applicable to particular cases, see Odgers on Pleading, 3rd ed., pp. 408—412 ; Chitty's Forms, 12th ed., pp. 289—292.

No. CLXXXI.

Interrogatories where More than One Plaintiff or Defendant.

(O. 31, r. 4; Y. S. C. P., and A. P., App. B., No. 6.)

[*Heading as in writ.*]

INTERROGATORIES on behalf of the above-named plaintiff [*or*, defendant, James Bowes] for the examination of the above-named defendants, Henry George Allison and William Strickland [*or*, plaintiff].

1. Did not, etc.
2. Has not, etc.
   Etc., etc., etc.

The defendant, Henry George Allison, is required to answer the interrogatories numbered 1 to 5 inclusive.

The defendant, William Strickland, is required to answer the interrogatories numbered 4 to 7 inclusive.

See note to No. CLXXX.

No. CLXXXII.

Application for Leave to Deliver Interrogatories to a Corporation.

(O. 31, r. 5.)

See No. CLXXIX. The material words will be as follows:

THAT the plaintiff be at liberty to administer to the defendant company [*or*, corporation] the interrogatories hereto annexed, to be answered by the secretary or other proper officer of the said company [*or*, corporation] [within ten days].

No. CLXXXIII.

Affidavit in Answer to Interrogatories, with Objections.

(O. 31, rr. 6, 9 ; Y. S. C. P., and A. P., App. B., No. 7.)

[*Heading as in writ.*]

THE ANSWER of the above-named defendant [Peter Young] to the interrogatories for his examination by the above-named plaintiff.

In answer to the said interrogatories, I, the above-named defendant, Peter Young, make oath and say as follows:

1. To the first of the said interrogatories, that etc.

2. To the second of the said interrogatories, that etc.

3. I object to answer the third of the said interrogatories on the ground that it is scandalous and irrelevant.

4. I object to answer the fourth of the said interrogatories on the ground that it is not put *bonâ fide* for the purpose of this action.

5. I object to answer the fifth of the said interrogatories on the ground that the matters inquired into are not sufficiently material at this stage of the action.

6. I object to answer the sixth of the said interrogatories on the ground that the same is a fishing interrogatory and not put *bonâ fide* for the purpose of this action.

SWORN, etc.

Filed on behalf of the defendant [Peter Young].

No. CLXXXIV.

Applications for Further Answer to Interrogatories.

(O. 31, r. 11.)

This will now be made, in cases to which O. 30 applies, under an application for further directions. (See No. CXLVI.) The material words will be as follows:

THAT the defendant be ordered within seven days to answer the interrogatories delivered for his examination numbered 2 and 5 respectively, and to answer further the interrogatory numbered 4.

For form of order, see No. CXLVII.

No. CLXXXV.

Application for Discovery of Documents.

(O. 31, r. 12.)

This must be made, in cases to which O. 30 applies, under the summons for directions (see No. CXLII). The form will be as follows:

THAT the defendant do, within ten days from the date of this order, answer on affidavit stating what documents are or have been in his possession or power relating to the matters in question in this action.

For form of order, see No. CXLIII.

No. CLXXXVI.

Affidavit as to Documents.

(O. 31, r. 13; Y. S. C. P., and A. P., App. B., No. 8.)

[*Heading as in writ.*]

I, the above-named defendant, Henry Owen Smith, make oath and say as follows:

1. I have in my possession or power the documents relating to the matters in question in this suit, set forth in the first and second parts of the [first] schedule hereto.

AFFIDAVIT AS TO DOCUMENTS. 127

2. I object to produce the said documents set forth in the second part of the said [first] schedule hereto.

3. That the grounds of my objection are that the said documents are privileged, being communications between my solicitors and myself, relating exclusively to my case, instructions to counsel, and his opinion thereon.

[4. I have had, but have not now, in my possession or power the documents relating to the matters in question in this suit set forth in the second schedule hereto.

5. The last-mentioned documents were last in my possession or power on the 17th day of September last.

6. That the said last-mentioned documents were handed by me on the 17th day of September last to one James Shipley, and to the best of my knowledge, information, and belief, they are now in his possession or power.]

7. According to the best of my knowledge, information, and belief, I have not now and never had in my possession, custody, or power, or in the possession, custody, or power of my solicitors or agents, solicitor or agent, or in the possession, custody, or power of any other persons or person on my behalf, any deed, account, book of account, voucher, receipt, letter, memorandum, paper, or writing, or any copy of or extract from any such document, or any other document whatsoever, relating to the matters in question in this suit, or any of them, or wherein any entry has been made relative to such matters, or any of them, other than and except the documents set forth in the said [first and second] schedule[s] hereto.

SWORN, etc.

Filed on behalf of the defendant.

The [First] Schedule above referred to.

First Part.

Lease of No. 16, New Street, Guildford, plaintiff to defendant, dated 4th April, 1890.

Letters from plaintiff to defendant, dated 9th, 17th, 21st, 23rd, and 28th June, and 4th, 6th, and 11th July, 1897.

Copy letters from defendant to plaintiff, dated 18th, 22nd, 25th, and 29th June, and 5th, 7th, and 12th July, 1897.

Receipts for rent, dated 12th January, and 8th April, 1897.

Letter from plaintiff's solicitors to defendant, dated 8th August, 1897.

Letters from plaintiff's solicitors to defendant's solicitors, dated 13th August, 25th and 27th September, and 5th October, 1897.

Copy letters from defendant's solicitors to plaintiff's solicitors, dated 12th August, 26th and 29th September, and 6th October, 1897.

Second Part.

Correspondence between defendant and his solicitors, instructions to counsel, opinion of counsel, and papers relating to the preparation of this case.

[The Second Schedule above referred to.

Notice of dilapidations, dated 12th June, 1897.

Book marked " Repairs Book."]

No. CLXXXVII.

Notice to Produce Documents for Inspection.

(O. 31, rr. 15, 16 ; Y. S. C. P., and A. P., App. B., No. 9.)

[*Heading as in writ.*]

TAKE NOTICE that the defendant requires you to produce for his inspection the following documents referred to in your statement of claim [*or*, affidavit, dated the 16th day of March, 1895] :

Two letters from defendant to plaintiff, dated 28th November and 4th December, 1894, respectively.

DATED the 20th day of March, 1895.

Moss and WIX,
solicitors to the defendant.

To Messrs. HENRY and WATSON,
solicitors for the plaintiff.

No. CLXXXVIII.

Notice to Inspect Documents.

(O. 31, r. 17; Y. S. C. P., and A. P., App. B., No. 10.)

[*Heading as in writ.*]

TAKE NOTICE that you can inspect the documents mentioned in your notice of the 20th day of March, A.D. 1895 [except the document last mentioned in that notice], at our office at No. 86, Essex Street, Strand, London, W.C., on Thursday next, the 25th instant (*a*), between the hours of 12 and 4 o'clock.

[And further take notice that the plaintiff objects to giving you inspection of the document last mentioned in the said notice, on the ground that the said document is privileged.]

DATED the 22nd day of March, 1895 (*b*).

HENRY and WATSON,
solicitors for the plaintiff.

To Messrs. Moss and WIX,
solicitors for the defendant.

(*a*) The time appointed for inspection must be within three days from the delivery of the above notice (O. 31, r. 17).

(*b*) The notice appointing the time for inspection must, if all the documents of which inspection is required are set forth in an affidavit of documents (O. 31, r. 13), be delivered within two days, or, in other cases, within four days, from the receipt of the notice requiring inspection (O. 31, r. 17).

No. CLXXXIX.

Application to Inspect Documents Not Mentioned in the Pleadings, etc.

(O. 31, r. 18 (2)).

This must be made, except in cases to which O. 30 does not apply, under an application for further directions (see No. CXLVI.). The material part will be in the following or some similar form :

THAT the defendant do at all seasonable times on reasonable notice produce, at the office of his solicitors, at Albany House, Cheapside, in the city of London, the following documents, viz., diaries of the defendant for the years 1892 and 1893 ; and that the plaintiff and his solicitor be at liberty to inspect and peruse the documents so produced, and to take copies thereof or extracts therefrom at his expense.

For form of order on application for further directions, see No. CXLVII. The order in the above case may readily be framed from the words of the application, as approved or varied by the Master.

For form of affidavit in support, see No. CXC. Such an affidavit is necessary (O. 31, r. 18 (2)).

No. CXC.

Affidavit in Support of Application to Inspect Documents.

(O. 31, r. 18 (2).)

[*Heading as usual.*]

I, HERBERT OLIVER PRENTICE, the above-named defendant, make oath and say as follows :

1. This is an application for inspection of the following documents :

> Lease of Church Farm, Manor Road, Overton, in the county of Sussex, James Wilson to Samuel Jenkinson, dated 12th November, 1860.
>
> Release of Church Farm aforesaid, George William Jenkinson to Mary Ann Turnbull and Philip Homan, dated 19th October, 1871.

AFFIDAVIT OF VERIFICATION OF COPIES. 131

2. The said documents are material to the matters in question in this action, and I am advised that I am entitled to inspect them. The said documents form part of the alleged title of the plaintiff to the lands the subject-matter of this action.

3. The said documents are, to the best of my knowledge, information, and belief, in the possession or power of the plaintiff.

SWORN, etc.

Filed on behalf of the defendant.

No. CXCI.

Affidavit of Verification of Copies of Business Books.

(O. 31, r. 19A (1).)

[*Heading as usual.*]

I, PERCY WITHERS SMYTHE, of 16, Cork Street, Brixton, in the county of London, clerk in the employment of the New City Banking Company, Limited, make oath and say as follows:

1. The paper writings now produced and shown to me, marked "P. W. S. 1," "P. W. S. 2," and "P. W. S. 3" respectively, are copies of certain entries in the business books of the New City Banking Company, Limited, whose registered office and place of business is situate at No. 331, Lombard Street, in the city of London.

2. On the 18th day of May instant, I examined each of the said paper writings with the original entries in the said books, whereof the said paper writings are copies, and I say that the said copies are true and accurate copies of the said entries, and in no way differ from the said entries.

3. There are not in the said original entries in the said books any erasures, interlineations, or alterations.

SWORN, etc.

Filed on behalf of the plaintiff.

CHAPTER XIII.

PAYMENT INTO COURT.

No. CXCII.
Application for Leave to Pay into Court after Defence Delivered.
(O. 22, r. 1.)

This must be made, except in cases to which Order 30 does not apply, on application for further directions. (See No. CXLVI.) The form will be as follows:

THAT the defendant be at liberty to pay into court the sum of 75l., in satisfaction of the plaintiff's claim herein.

The order (see No. CXLVII.), may readily be framed from the above. Where money is paid into Court under an order, the request for lodgment (see Form No. 11 in the Appendix to the Supreme Court Funds Rules, Yearly Supreme Court Practice, and the Annual Practice, Vol. II., Part III.) must state that the money is paid in " under order of Master   , dated, &c."

No. CXCIII.
Notice of Payment into Court.
(O. 22, r. 4 ; Y. S. C. P. and A. P., App. B., No. 3.)

[*Heading as in writ.*]

TAKE NOTICE that the defendant has paid into court 35l., and says that that sum is enough to satisfy the plaintiff's claim [for damages for assault, *or*, in respect of the matters alleged in paragraphs 5, 6 and 7 of the statement of claim].

DATED the 12th day of July, 1898.

       HENRY CHEESEMAN,
          defendant's solicitor.

To Messrs. Cox and WELLDON,
  the plaintiff's solicitors.

No. CXCIV.

Authority of Plaintiff for Money to be Paid out of Court.

(O. 22, r. 5 ; Y. S. C. P., and A. P., Part III., Supreme Court Funds Rules, Form No. 14 (a).)

1897. P. No. 1641.

Title of cause or matter: Price v. Hawkins.
Ledger credit: as above.
To the Assistant Paymaster-General.

I HEREBY request that payment of the sum of 25l. paid in in the above action may be made to Wilson Holmes, the solicitor to me, the plaintiff.

GEORGE PRICE,
18, King Street, Clapham, London, S.W.
7th November, 1897.

Witness, JOSEPH R. THOMPSON,
121, Clover Street, Clapham, S.W.,
Journeyman Tailor.

No. CXCV.

Notice of Acceptance of Money Paid into Court.

(O. 22, r. 7 ; Y. S. C. P., and A. P., App. B., No. 4.)

[*Heading as in writ.*]

TAKE NOTICE that the plaintiff accepts the sum of 42l., paid by you into court in satisfaction of the claim in respect of which it is paid in.

DATED the 18th day of January, 1896.
HARRIS and ELWORTHY,
plaintiff's solicitors.

To the defendant, and to
Messrs. CROAKE, JACKSON and FISHER,
his solicitors.

No. CXCVI.

Judgment for Costs after Acceptance of Money Paid into Court.

(O. 22, r. 7 ; Y. S. C. P., and A. P., App. F., No. 16.)

[*Heading as in writ.*]

The 17th day of May, 1898.

THE defendant having paid into Court the sum of 75*l*., in satisfaction of the plaintiff's claim, and the plaintiff having by his notice dated the 3rd day of May, 1898, accepted that sum in satisfaction of his entire cause of action, and the plaintiff's costs herein having been taxed, and the defendant not having paid the same within forty-eight hours after the said taxation—

It is this day adjudged that the plaintiff recover against the defendant costs to be taxed.

The above costs have been taxed and allowed at 9*l*. 17*s*., as appears by a Taxing Officer's certificate, dated the 13th day of May, 1898.

As to payment into court by a life assurance company under the Life Assurance Companies (Payment into Court) Act, 1896 (59 Vict. c. 8), see Order 54c, where the essentials of an affidavit accompanying such payment are given (r. 1).

CHAPTER XIV.

ADMISSIONS.
No. CXCVII.
Voluntary Notice of Admission of Facts.
(O. 32, r. 1.)

[*Heading as in writ.*]

TAKE NOTICE that the plaintiff in this cause, for the purposes of this cause only, hereby admits the several facts respectively hereunder specified [subject to the qualifications or limitations, if any, hereunder specified,] saving all just exceptions to the admissibility of such facts, or any of them, as evidence in this cause.

Provided that this admission is made for the purposes of this action only, and is not an admission to be used against the plaintiff or any other occasion, or by anyone other than the defendant.

DATED the 20th day of December, 1894.

WILLIAMS and JONES,
solicitors for the plaintiff.

To Messrs. STEELE and EVANS,
solicitors for the defendant.

Facts admitted:

1. That defendant, or his predecessors in title have occupied the lands the subject-matter of this action since March, 1873.

2. That defendant's father, Walter Pringle, in the year 1890, lent to the plaintiff sums of money amounting to 170*l.*

3. That neither the said sum of 170*l.*, nor any part thereof, has ever been repaid by the plaintiff.

See also No. CC.

No. CXCVIII.

Notice to Admit Documents.

(O. 32, r. 3 ; Y. S. C. P., and A. P., App. B., No. 11.)

[*Heading as in writ.*]

TAKE NOTICE that the plaintiff in this cause proposes to adduce in evidence the several documents hereunder specified, and that the same may be inspected by the defendant, his solicitor or agent, at my offices at 103, Cannon Street, in the City of London, on Monday, the 8th day of November, 1897, between the hours of 4 and 6 o'clock ; and the defendant is hereby required within forty-eight hours from the last-mentioned hour, to admit that such of the said documents as are specified to be originals were respectively written, signed, or executed, as they purport respectively to have been ; that such as are specified as copies are true copies; and such documents as are stated to have been served, sent, or delivered, were so served, sent, or delivered respectively ; saving all just exceptions to the admissibility of all such documents as evidence in this cause.

DATED the 4th day of November, 1897.

(Signed) BUDD and COLLIER,
solicitors for plaintiff.

To Mr. LESLIE JONES,
solicitor for defendant.

ORIGINALS.

Description of Documents.	Date.
Deed of Covenant between Henry James, first part, and Noel William Percival, second part.	1 January, 1848.
Indenture of Lease from Henry James to George Dixon.	1 February, 1848.
Letter—defendant to plaintiff - - -	8 March, 1893.
Bill of Exchange for 100*l.* at three months, drawn by William Delacour on, and accepted by George Dixon, indorsed by Alfred Stevenson.	2 August, 1892.

COPIES.

Description of Documents.	Date.	Original or duplicate, served, sent, or delivered, when, how, and by whom.
Register of baptism of Arthur Wilson Berry in the parish of Roehampton.	1 January, 1848	—
Letter — plaintiff to defendant.	6 March, 1893	Posted on date by clerk to plaintiff's solicitors.
The like	13 March, 1893	Ditto.
Notice to produce	4 November, 1897	Served by clerk to plaintiff's solicitors.

No. CXCIX.
Notice to Admit Facts.
(O. 32, rr. 4, 5 ; Y. S. C. P., and A. P., App. B., No. 12.)

[*Heading as in writ.*]

TAKE NOTICE that the plaintiff in this cause requires the defendant to admit, for the purposes of this cause only, the several facts respectively hereunder specified ; and the defendant is hereby required, within six days from the service of this notice, to admit the said several facts, saving all just exceptions to the admissibility of such facts as evidence in this cause.

DATED the 16th day of February, 1897.

JOSEPH JACOBS,
solicitor for the plaintiff.

To Messrs. MURRAY and PEARSON,
solicitors for the defendant.

The facts, the admission of which is required, are :
1. That John Smith died on the 1st of January, 1870.
2. That he died intestate.
3. That James Smith was his only lawful son.
4. That Julius Smith died on the 1st of April, 1876.
5. That Julius Smith never was married.

No. CC.

Admission of Facts Pursuant to Notice.

(O. 32, r. 5 ; Y. S. C. P., and A. P., App. B., No. 13.)

[*Heading as in writ.*]

THE defendant is this cause, for the purposes of this cause only, hereby admits the several facts respectively hereunder specified, subject to the qualifications or limitations, if any, hereunder specified, saving all just exceptions to the admissibility of such facts, or any of them, as evidence in this cause.

Provided that this admission is made for the purposes of this action only, and is not an admission to be used against the defendant on any other occasion, or by any one other than the plaintiff [or *party requiring the admission*].

Delivered the 20th day of February, 1897, by MURRAY and PEARSON, solicitors for the defendant.

To Mr. JOSEPH JACOBS,
   solicitor for the plaintiff.

Facts admitted.	Qualifications or Limitations, if any, subject to which they are admitted.
1. That John Smith died on the 1st of January, 1870.	1.
2. That he died intestate.	2.
3. That James Smith was his lawful son.	3. But not that he was his only lawful son.
4. That Julius Smith died.	4. But not that he died on the 1st of April, 1876.
5. That Julius Smith never was married.	5.

No. CCI.

Affidavit of Signature of Admissions.

(O. 32, r. 7.)

[*Heading as usual.*]

I, MARTIN ELGOOD, of 12, Cross Road, Bow, in the County of London, clerk to Messrs. James, Norton and Fairbairn, solicitors for the above-named defendant in this action, make oath, and say as follows:

1. The admissions now produced and shown to me, marked " A," are signed by Messrs. James, Norton and Fairbairn, the solicitors for the above-named defendant in this action, and the signature thereto, "James, Norton and Fairbairn" is in the handwriting of William Norton, one of the said firm.

[2. I saw the said William Norton, on the 18th day of March, instant, subscribe the said signature "James, Norton and Fairbairn," to the said admissions.]

SWORN, &c.
Filed on behalf of the defendant.

No. CCII.

Notice to Produce Documents.

(O. 32, r. 8; Y. S. C. P., and A. P., App. B., No. 14.)

[*Heading as in writ.*]

TAKE NOTICE that you are hereby required to produce and show to the Court on the trial of this action all books, papers, letters, copies of letters, and other writings and documents in your possession, custody or power, containing any entry, memorandum or minute relating to the matters in question in this action, and particularly—

Underlease of Penge House, Sydenham, plaintiff to defendant, dated 12th January, 1893.

Letters—plaintiff to defendant, dated 4th, 16th and 21st May, 1896.

Letters—plaintiff's solicitors to defendant, dated 16th June, 1896.

Letters—plaintiff's solicitors to defendant's solicitors, dated 25th and 28th June, 1896.

Cheques and counterfoil cheques during years 1894 and 1895.

Bankers' pass-book or books for the whole of the years 1894 and 1895.

Receipts for goods sold, dated 17th May, 1894, and 2nd January, 1896.

This notice to produce.

DATED the 17th day February, 1897.

    ELLIS and BURN, of 16, Clement's Row, in the City of London, [agents for, etc.], solicitors for the above-named plaintiff.

To the above-named defendant, and
To Messrs. FORDHAM and BRINSMEAD,
 his solicitors.

No. CCIII.

Affidavit of Service of Notice to Produce.

(O. 32, r. 8.)

[*Heading as usual.*]

I, JAMES ALFRED ALCROFT, of 17, James Street, Islington, clerk to Paul Rogers, solicitor for the above-named plaintiff in this action, make oath and say as follows:

1. I did on Wednesday, the 1st day of May last, between the hours of 4 and 5 o'clock in the afternoon, serve Messrs. Brown and Higginson, the solicitors for the above-named defendants in this action, with a notice to produce, whereof a true copy is hereto annexed, marked "A," by delivering the same to and leaving the same with a clerk of the said Messrs. Brown and Higginson, at their offices at No. 61, Great John Street, in the County of London, which is their address for service.

SWORN, etc.

Filed on behalf of the plaintiff.

CHAPTER XV.

SPECIAL FORMS OF TRIAL.

(For Forms relating to trial by an arbitrator or referee, see chapter xxviii., p. 244.)

No. CCIV.

Application to Set Down Points of Law.

(O. 25, r. 2.)

This application must be made, except in cases to which O. 30 does not apply, as an application for further directions (see No. CXLVI.). The material parts will be as follows:

That the following points of law raised by the defence herein may be forthwith set down for hearing and disposed of before the trial of the action:

1. Whether the documents referred to in paragraph 1 of the statement of claim constitute a contract enforceable at law by the plaintiff against the defendant.

2. Whether, by the terms on which the action Herbert Smith v. The Secretary of State for India in Council, 1893. S. No. 1162 was settled, the plaintiff is precluded from bringing the present action.

For form of order, see No. CXLVII., which may readily be adapted.

No. CCV.
Special Case by Consent.
(O. 34, r. 1.)

[*Heading as in writ.*]

SPECIAL CASE.

This is an action brought by the plaintiff against the defendant for damages for breach of contract, and the parties hereto have concurred pursuant, to Order XXXIV, Rule 1, of the Rules of the Supreme Court, in stating the questions of law arising herein for the opinion the court as follows :

1.
2. [*According to circumstances*] (*a*).
3.

Etc., etc., etc.

The questions for the opinion of the court are:

1.
2. } Whether [or not], etc.

[If the court shall be of opinion in the affirmative, then judgment shall be entered for the plaintiff for 162*l*. and costs to be taxed.

If the court shall be of opinion in the negative, then judgment shall be entered for the defendant for his costs to be taxed] (*b*).

DATED the 17th day of January, 1898.

PETERS and WICKHAM,
solicitors for the above-named plaintiff (*c*).

GEORGE PHILIPS,
solicitor for the above-named defendant (*c*).

(*a*) The special case must be divided into paragraphs numbered consecutively, and must state concisely such facts and documents as may be necessary to enable the court to decide the questions raised (O. 34, r. 1).

(*b*) This to be added where the parties have entered into such agreement in writing as is mentioned in O. 34, r. 6. For form of such agreement, see No. CCIX.

(*c*) By O. 34, r. 3, every special case must be signed by the parties, or their counsel or solicitors. If settled by counsel it must be signed by him. It must in all cases be printed and filed by the plaintiff.

No. CCVI.

Application for Special Case.

(O. 34, r. 2.)

This should now be made in cases to which O. 30 applies on the summons for directions (see No. CXLII.), or on application for further directions (see No. CXLVI.). The material parts will be as follows :

That the question of law arising herein, viz., whether or not the plaintiff's claim is barred by lapse of time, be raised for the opinion of the court by special case or in such other manner as the court may deem expedient, and that in the meantime all such further proceedings as the decision of such question of law may render unnecessary, be stayed.

The order (see No. CXLVII.) may readily be framed according to the terms imposed by the Master.

No. CCVII.

Application for Leave to Set Down Special Case where Person under Disability a Party.

(O. 34, r. 4.)

This should be made, except in cases to which O. 30 does not apply, by application for further directions (see No. CXLVI.), as follows :

That the special case herein be set down for argument.

The application must be supported by an affidavit by a competent witness that the statements in the special case affecting the person under disability are true. The persons to whom the rule applies are married women, who are not parties in respect of separate property or separate rights of action by or against them, infants, and persons of unsound mind not so found by inquisition.

No. CCVIII.
Memorandum of Entry of Special Case.
(O. 34, r. 5 ; Y. S. C. P., and A. P., App. G., No. 25.)

[*Heading as in writ.*]

Set down the Special Case dated the 23rd day of November, 1894 [of Mr.   the special [*or*, official] referee in this action], for hearing as a special case.

DATED the 8th day of December, 1894.

MILLER AND JUDSON, of 24, Conduit Street, Holborn, in the County of London, solicitors for the plaintiff.

No. CCIX.
Agreement as to Result of Special Case.
(O. 34, r. 6.)

[*Heading as in writ.*]

WE, the undersigned, as solicitors for and on behalf of the respective parties hereto, do hereby agree in respect to the special case herein, dated the 19th day of June, 1896 [*or*, the special case to be stated herein], as follows :

1. If the judgment of the court shall be given in the affirmative of the question of law raised therein, the defendant shall pay to the plaintiff the sum of 200*l*. [*or*, a sum of money to be ascertained by the court, or in such manner as the court shall direct], together with the plaintiff's costs of the action to be taxed.

2. If the judgment of the court shall be given in the negative of the said questions, the plaintiff shall pay to the defendant his costs of defence to be taxed.

DATED the 23rd day of June, 1896.

WILKINSON and Co.,
solicitors for the plaintiff.
HARVEY and ROBERTSON,
solicitors for the defendant.

ISSUE OF FACT. 145

No. CCX.

Judgment on Special Case.

(O. 34, r. 6.)

[*Heading as in writ.*]

The 29th day of March, 1897.

PURSUANT to the order of Mr. Justice , dated the 29th day of March, 1897, whereby it was ordered that judgment be entered for the plaintiff on the special case herein for 93l. with costs—

It is this day adjudged that the plaintiff recover against the defendant 93l. and costs to be taxed.

The above costs have been taxed and allowed at 43l. 11s. 4d., as appears by a Taxing Officer's certificate, dated the 17th day of April, 1897.

No. CCXI.

Issue of Fact.

(O. 34, r. 9 ; Y. S. C. P., and A. P., App. B., No. 15.)

[*Heading as in writ.*]

WHEREAS the plaintiff affirms and the defendant denies that certain wheat, sold by sample by the plaintiff to the defendant and bought by the defendant on the 22nd day of May, 1897, was up to sample ; and it has been ordered by Master , by order dated the 12th day of December, 1897, that the said question shall be tried at Middlesex by a judge without a jury: therefore let the same be tried accordingly.

C.F. L

No. CCXII.

Application for Trial of Issue of Fact.

(O. 34, r. 9.)

This must be made, except in cases to which O. 30 does not apply, on the summons for directions (see No. CXLII), or on application for further directions (see No. CXLVI). It will be in some such form as the following:

That the parties do proceed to the trial of the following questions of fact, viz., whether certain wheat sold by sample by the plaintiff to the defendant and bought by the defendant on the 22nd day of May, 1897, was up to sample, without formal pleadings.

It is open to the parties to fix a sum of money to be paid according to the result of the trial of the issue. An agreement to this effect, which may be embodied in the order on the above application, may be framed on the lines of No. CCIX.

CHAPTER XVI.

DISCONTINUANCE AND WITHDRAWAL.

No. CCXIII.

Notice of Discontinuance.

(O. 26, r. 1.)

[*Heading as in writ.*]

TAKE NOTICE that the plaintiff hereby wholly discontinues this action [*or*, withdraws so much of his claim in this action as relates to the alleged breach of warranty] [as against the defendant James Oldroyd] (*a*).

DATED the 2nd day of April, 1896.

        HAMBOROUGH and MARKHAM, of 16 St. Clement's Lane, in the City of London, solicitors for the plaintiff.

To the above-named defendant
   [James Oldroyd] (*a*), and
   to Messrs. FORBES and
   SMITH, his solicitors.

(*a*) This to be added where the action is not discontinued against all the defendants.

No. CCXIV.

Application by Plaintiff for Leave to Discontinue.

(O. 26, r. 1.)

This will be made, except in the cases to which O. 30 does not apply, on application for further directions (see No. CXLVI). It will be as follows:

That the plaintiff be at liberty wholly to discontinue this action [*or*, to withdraw so much of his claim in this action as relates to the premises known as No. 2, New Street, Shoreditch, in the County of London] [against the defendant, Robert Wilkinson] (*a*).

(*a*) See note to No. CCXIII.

No. CCXV.

Order Giving Plaintiff Leave to Discontinue.

(O. 26, r. 1.)

[*Formal parts as in No. CXLVII.*]

That the plaintiff be at liberty, on payment of the defendant's costs, wholly to discontinue this action [*or*, to withdraw, etc., *as in No. CCXIV.*], and that, if the said costs be not paid within four days after taxation thereof, the defendant be at liberty to enter judgment for the same.

JUDGMENT FOR DEFENDANT'S COSTS. 149

No. CCXVI.
Application by Defendant for Leave to Withdraw Defence.
(O. 26, r. 1.)

This will be made, except in cases to which O. 30 does not apply, on application for further directions (see No. CXLVI). It may be worded as follows :

That the defendant be at liberty to withdraw the whole of his defence [or, counterclaim] herein [or, such part of his defence [or, counterclaim] herein as relates to, etc.],

Or, That the whole of the defence [or, counterclaim] herein [or, such part of the defence [or, counterclaim] herein as relates to, etc.] be struck out.

For form of Order see No. CCXV, which may be adapted.

No. CCXVII.
Judgment for Defendant's Costs on Discontinuance after Notice.
(O. 26, r. 3 ; Y. S. C. P., and A. P., App. F., No. 14.)

[*Heading as in writ.*]

The 23rd day of November, 1897.

THE plaintiff having by a notice in writing, dated the 3rd day of November, 1897, wholly discontinued this action [or, withdrawn so much of his claim in this action as relates to, etc.] [against the defendant, James Nicholls] (a),

It is this day adjudged that the defendant [James Nicholls] (a) recover against the plaintiff costs to be taxed.

The above costs have been taxed and allowed at 14l. 12s., as appears by a Taxing Officer's certificate dated the 17th day of November, 1897.

(a) See note to No. CCXIII.

No. CCXVIII.

Judgment for Defendant's Costs on Discontinuance by Order.

(O. 26, r. 3 ; Y. S. C. P., and A. P., App. F., No. 12.)

[*Heading as in writ.*]

The 13th day of July, 1898.

PURSUANT to order of Master   , dated the 20th day of June, 1898, whereby it was ordered that this action be wholly discontinued [*or*, so much of this action as relates to, etc., be withdrawn] upon payment by the plaintiff of the defendant's costs to be taxed, and that, in default of such payment within four days after taxation, the defendant be at liberty to enter judgment for the same, and default having been made—

It is this day adjudged that the defendant recover against the plaintiff costs to be taxed.

The above costs have been taxed and allowed at 17*l.* 6*s.* 2*d.*, as appears by a Taxing Officer's certificate dated the 5th day of July, 1898.

No. CCXIX.

Consent for Withdrawal of Action after Entry for Trial.

(O. 26, r. 2.)

[*Heading as in writ.*]

WE, the undersigned, hereby consent to the withdrawal of this action, which was entered for trial on the 7th day of March last.

DATED the 17th day of April, 1896.

    ROBERT HASTINGS,
      the above-named plaintiff.
    STEPHEN WYNDHAM PERRY,
    JOSEPH GILLING,
      the above-named defendants.

CHAPTER XVII.

NOTICE OF AND ENTRY FOR TRIAL AND PROCEEDINGS IN CONNEXION THEREWITH.

No. CCXX.

Notice of Place of Trial.

(O. 36, r. 1.)

[*Heading as in writ.*]

TAKE NOTICE that the place of trial of this action is Middlesex.

DATED the 7th day of August, 1895.

      EDE AND SIMMONS,
       solicitors for the plaintiff.

To the defendant, and to
 Messrs. SMYTHE and Co.,
  his solicitors.

Except in actions commenced by specially indorsed writ, the venue will now generally be settled on the hearing of the summons for directions (see No. CXLII.).

No. CCXXI.

Application for Change of Venue.

(O. 36, r. 1.)

This will be made, except in cases to which O. 30 does not apply, on the original summons for directions (see No. CXLII.), or on application for further directions (see No. CXLVI.). It may be worded as follows :

That the place of trial be changed from Middlesex to Norfolk.

In general the application should be supported by an affidavit, showing that a preponderance of convenience or saving of expense will result from the proposed change.

No. CCXXII.

Notice of Trial.

(O. 36, r. 13.)

[*Heading as in writ.*]

TAKE NOTICE of trial of this action [*or*, the issues in this action ordered to be tried] by a judge with [out] a jury (*a*) in Middlesex [*or*, at the ensuing assizes to be holden at Lewes, in and for the county of Sussex] for the the 13th day of November (*b*) next.

DATED the 3rd day of November, 1894 (*b*).

GEORGE HARRISON,
plaintiff's solicitor.

To Messrs. FRISBY and WHEELER,
defendant's solicitors.

For form of notice of trial without pleadings, see No. CXXXVII.

(*a*) In the classes of actions specified in O. 36, r. 2, the notice of trial may state that the trial is to be by a judge with a jury. But since the mode of trial is now generally determined on the summons for directions (see No. CXLII.), the notice will commonly specify the mode of trial in all classes of actions, and applications subsequent to the notice of trial (see O. 36, rr. 6, 7) will seldom be made.

(*b*) The notice of trial must be a ten days' notice.

No. CCXXIII.

Notice of Trial with Jury by Defendant.

(O. 36, r. 2.)

[*Heading as in writ.*]

TAKE NOTICE that the defendant desires to have the issues of fact herein tried by a judge with a jury.

DATED the 17th day of March, 1896 (*a*).

WILLIAM HENRY Moss,
defendant's solicitor.

To Messrs. ABRAHAMS and Co.,
plaintiff's solicitors.

(*a*) This notice must be given by the defendant within four days from the service of the notice of trial, unless the time be extended by the court or a judge. But the above notice will now be rarely required (see note (*a*) to No. CCXXII).

No. CCXXIV.

Notice of Special Jury.

(O. 36, r. 7 (b), (c).)

[*Heading as in writ.*]

TAKE NOTICE that the plaintiff [*or*, defendant] intends to have the issues herein tried by a special jury.

DATED, etc. [*Conclude as in Nos. CCXXII. and CCXXIII.*]

See No. CCXXII, note (*a*).

No. CCXXV.

Application by Defendant to Dismiss in Default of Notice of Trial.

(O. 36, r. 12.)

This will be made, except in cases to which O. 30 does not apply, by application for further directions (see No. CXLVI.). It will be in the following form :

That the plaintiff having made default in giving notice of trial, this action be dismissed for want of prosecution, with costs to be taxed and paid by the plaintiff to the defendant, and that the defendant be at liberty to sign judgment for his said costs.

See also No. CLXVII. For form of order see Nos. CXLVII. and CLXVIII., and for form of judgment see No. CLXIX.

No. CCXXVI.

Consent to Countermand Notice of Trial.

(O. 36, r. 19.)

[*Heading as in writ.*]

WE, the undersigned, as solicitors for and on behalf of the respective parties hereto, do hereby consent to the notice of trial, given herein by the plaintiff on the 25th day of February last, being countermanded.

DATED the 1st day of March, 1897.
      Ross and PHIPSON,
        solicitors for the plaintiff,
      WILLIAM BODLEY,
        solicitor for the defendant.

No. CCXXVII.
Application for Leave to Countermand Notice of Trial.
(O. 36, r. 19.)

This will be made, except in cases to which O. 30 does not apply, on an application for further directions (see No. CXLVI.). The form will be as follows :

That the plaintiff be at liberty to countermand the notice of trial given herein on the 28th day of March last.

No. CCXXVIII.
Notice Countermanding Notice of Trial.
(O. 36, r. 19.)

[*Heading as in writ.*]

TAKE NOTICE that pursuant to the order of Master , dated the 12th day of August instant, I hereby countermand the notice of trial of this action, dated the 6th day of August instant.

DATED the 12th day of August, 1897.
     ROBERT MURRAY,
       solicitor for the plaintiff.
To Messrs. WALKER and JOHNSTONE,
 solicitors for the defendant.

No. CCXXIX.
Entry of Action for Trial.
(O. 36, r. 15, 20 ; Y. S. C. P., and A. P., App. G., No. 22.)

[*Heading as in writ.*]

Enter this action for trial.
DATED the 6th day of July, 1898.
     BERNARD and WILLIAMS,
      of 16, Rood Lane, in the
      City of London, solicitors
      for the plaintiff.

No. CCXXX.

Application for Postponement of Trial.

(O. 36, r. 34.)

Unless made in court, this application should be made, except in cases to which O. 30 does not apply, as an application for further directions (see No. CXLVI.). It will be as follows:

That the trial of this action be postponed until the 1st day of November next [*or*, until the Hilary Sittings, 1896] [on the ground of the absence of a material witness for the plaintiff].

This application should in general be supported by an affidavit setting out the grounds.

CHAPTER XVIII.

EVIDENCE.

No. CCXXXI.
Agreement to take Evidence by Affidavit.
(O. 37, r. 1.)

[*Heading as in writ.*]

WE, the undersigned, as solicitors for and on behalf of the respective parties hereto, do hereby agree that the evidence herein shall be taken by affidavit alone.

DATED the 3rd day of January, 1897.

    GILBERT and CARTER,
     solicitors for the plaintiff.
    CARPENTER and BARLOW,
     solicitors for the defendant
     James Ferguson.
    GEORGE WILSON ROGERS,
     solicitor for the defendant
     Jane Humphreys.

No. CCXXXII.
Application for Leave to Prove Particular Facts by Affidavit.
(O. 37, r. 1.)

This must, except in cases to which O. 30 does not apply, be made on the summons for directions (see No. CXLII.), or on application for further directions (see No. CXLVI.). It may be worded as follows :

That the due execution of the deeds constituting the plaintiff's title may be proved at the trial by affidavit.

The order may readily be framed to include any terms imposed by the Master.

No. CCXXXIII.

Notice of Intention to Read Evidence Taken in Another Cause.

(O. 37, r. 3.)

[*Heading as in writ.*]

TAKE NOTICE that it is the intention of the plaintiff at the trial of this action to read the evidence of James Bell and Ronald Murray taken in the action entitled "Hanbury v. Austin and Co., 1896, H. No. 1341," saving all just exceptions to the admissibility of such evidence.

DATED the 3rd day of May, 1898.

JOSEPH FELL,
solicitor for the plaintiff.

To the defendant, and to
Messrs. BUCK and DONALDSON,
his solicitors.

No. CCXXXIV.

Application for Examination of Witness before Examiner.

(O. 37, r. 5.)

This must, except in cases to which O. 30 does not apply, be included in the original summons for directions (see No. CXLII.), or made on application for further directions (see No. CXLVI.). It will run as follows:

That Stephen Wilson, a witness on behalf of the defendants be examined before an examiner of the Court.

The application should be supported by an affidavit showing the grounds, *e.g.*, that the witness is going abroad, or that, from age, illness, or infirmity, he is not likely to be able to attend at the trial. In the case of illness either an affidavit should be obtained from a doctor, or else a certificate verified by affidavit.

No. CCXXXV.

Order for Examination of Witness before Trial.

(O. 37, r. 5; Y. S. C. P., and A. P., App. K., No. 35.)

[*Formal parts as in No. CXLIII. or No. CXLVII.*]

That Stephen Wilson, a witness on behalf of the defendant, be examined *vivâ voce* (on oath or affirmation) before one of the examiners of the court [*or*, before a Master, *or*, before   , Esquire, special examiner,] the defendant's solicitor or agent giving to the plaintiff's solicitor or agent seven days notice in writing of the time and place where the examination is to take place.

And it is further ordered that the examination so taken be filed in the Central Office of the Supreme Court of Judicature, and that an office copy or copies thereof may be read and given in evidence on the trial of this cause, saving all just exceptions, without any further proof of the absence of the said witness than the affidavit of the solicitor or agent of the party using the same as to his belief, and that the costs of this application be costs in the action.

DATED the 16th day of May, 1898.

No. CCXXXVI.

Application for Commission.

(O. 37, r. 6.)

This must, except in cases to which O. 30 does not apply, be made either on the original summons for directions (see No. CXLII.), or on application for further directions (see No. CXLVI.). It may be worded thus:

That a commission do issue for the examination of witnesses at Philadelphia, in the United States of America, on behalf of the plaintiff, and that the trial of this action be stayed until the return of the said commission.

The application should be supported by an affidavit, and the Master must be satisfied :

(1.) That the application is made *bonâ fide*.
(2.) That the issue is one which the court ought to try.
(3.) That the witnesses can give material evidence.
(4.) That there is good reason why they cannot be examined in England.
(5.) That the examination will be effectual.

The affidavit should name at least one proposed witness. See further the note to O. 37, r. 5, in the Yearly Supreme Court Practice and the Annual Practice.

No. CCXXXVII.

Short Order for Commission.

(O. 37, r. 6. See Y. S. C. P., and A. P., App. K., No. 36.)

[*Formal parts as in No. CXLVII.*]

That the plaintiff be at liberty to issue a commission for the examination of witnesses on his behalf at Philadelphia, in the United States of America.

And it is further order that the trial of this action be stayed until the return of the said commission, the usual long order (*a*) to be drawn up, and unless agreed upon by the parties within one week, to be settled by the Master, and that the costs of this application be costs in the cause.

DATED the 7th day of June, 1898.

a) See next Form.

No. CCXXXVIII.

Long Order for Commission.

(O. 37, r. 6 ; Y. S. C. P., and A. P., App. K., No. 37.)

[*Commence as in No. CXLVII.*]

, and it is ordered as follows:

1. A commission may issue to   of   , and of   , commissioners named by and on behalf of the plaintiff, and to   of   , and   of   , commissioners named by and on behalf of the defendant, for the examination upon interrogatories and *vivâ voce* of witnesses on behalf of the said plaintiff and defendant respectively at Philadelphia in the United States of America before the said commissioners, or any two of them, so that one commissioner only on each side be present and act at the examination.

2. Both the said plaintiff and defendant shall be at liberty to examine upon interrogatories and *vivâ voce* upon the subject-matter thereof or arising out of the answers thereto such witnesses as may be produced on their behalf, with liberty to the other party to cross-examine the said witnesses upon cross-interrogatories and *vivâ voce*, the party producing the witness for examination being at liberty to re-examine him *vivâ voce*; and all such additional *vivâ voce* questions, whether on examination, cross-examination, or re-examination, shall be reduced into writing, and, with the answers thereto, returned with the said commission.

3. Within ten days from the date of this order the solicitors or agents of the said plaintiff and defendant shall exchange the interrogatories they propose to administer to their respective witnesses, and shall also, within seven days from the exchange of such interrogatories, exchange copies of the cross-interrogatories intended to be administered to the said witnesses.

4. Fourteen days previously to the sending out of the said commission, the solicitors of the said plaintiff shall give to the solicitors of the said defendant notice in

writing of the mail or other conveyance by which the commission is to be sent out.

5. Seven days previously to the examination of any witness on behalf of the said plaintiff or defendant respectively, notice in writing signed by any one of the commissioners of the party on whose behalf the witness is to be examined, and stating the time and place of the intended examination, and the names of the witnesses intended to be examined, shall be given to the commissioners of the other party by delivering the notice to them personally, or by leaving it at their usual place of abode or business, and if the commissioners of that party neglect to attend pursuant to the notice, then one of the commissioners of the party on whose behalf the notice is given shall be at liberty to proceed with and take the examination of the witness or witnesses *ex parte*, and adjourn any meeting or meetings, or continue the same, from day to day until all the witnesses intended to be examined by virtue of the notice have been examined, without giving any further or other notice of the subsequent meeting or meetings.

6. In the event of any witness on his examination, cross-examination, or re-examination producing any book, document, letter, paper, or writing, and refusing, for good cause to be stated in his deposition, to part with the original thereof, then a copy thereof, or extract therefrom, certified by the commissioners or commissioner present to be a true and correct copy or extract, shall be annexed to the witness's deposition.

7. Each witness to be examined under the commission shall be examined on oath, affirmation, or otherwise in accordance with his religion by or before the said commissioners or commissioner.

8. If any one or more of the witnesses do not understand the English language (the interrogatories, cross-interrogatories, and *vivâ voce* questions, if any, being previously translated into the language with which he or they is or are conversant), then the examination shall be taken in English through the medium of an interpreter or interpreters, to be nominated by the commissioners or commissioner, and to be previously sworn according

to his or their several religions by or before the said commissioners or commissioner truly to interpret the questions to be put to the witness or witnesses, and his and their answers thereto.

9. The depositions to be taken under and by virtue of the said commission shall be subscribed by the witness or witnesses, and by the commissioners or commissioner who shall have taken such depositions.

10. The interrogatories, cross-interrogatories, and depositions, together with any documents referred to therein, or certified copies thereof or extracts therefrom, shall be sent to the Senior Master of the Supreme Court of Judicature on or before the 1st day of November, 1898, or such further or other day as may be ordered, enclosed in a cover under the seal or seals of the said commissioners or commissioner, and office copies thereof may be given in evidence on the trial of this action by and on behalf of the said plaintiff and defendant respectively, saving all just exceptions, without any other proof of the absence from this country of the witness or witnesses therein named, than an affidavit of the solicitors or agents of the said plaintiff or defendant respectively, as to his belief of the said absence.

11. The trial of this cause is to be stayed until the return of the said commission.

12. The costs of this order, and of the commission to be issued in pursuance hereof, and of the interrogatories, cross-interrogatories, and depositions to be taken thereunder, together with any such document, copy, or extract as aforesaid, and official copies thereof, and all other costs incidental thereto, shall be costs in the action.

DATED the 13th day of June, 1898.

No. CCXXXIX.

Writ of Commission.

(O. 37, r. 6; Y. S. C. P., and A. P., App. J., No. 13.)

[*Heading as in writ.*]

VICTORIA, by the grace of God, etc., to   , of   , and   , of   , commissioners named by and on behalf of the plaintiff, and to   , of   , and   , of   , commissioners named by and on behalf of the defendant, greeting: Know ye that We in confidence of your prudence and fidelity have appointed you and by these presents give you power and authority to examine on interrogatories and *vivâ voce* as hereinafter mentioned witnesses on behalf of the said plaintiff and defendant respectively at Philadelphia, before you or any two of you, so that one commissioner only on each side be present and act at the examination. And we command you as follows:

1. Both the said plaintiff and the said defendant shall be at liberty to examine on interrogatories and *vivâ voce* on the subject-matter thereof or arising out of the answers thereto such witnesses as shall be produced on their behalf with liberty to the other party to cross-examine the said witnesses on cross-interrogatories and *vivâ voce*, the party producing any witness for examination being at liberty to re-examine him *vivâ voce*; and all such additional *vivâ voce* questions, whether on examination, cross-examination, or re-examination, shall be reduced into writing, and with the answers thereto shall be returned with the said commission.

2. Not less than seven days before the examination of any witness on behalf of either of the said parties, notice in writing, signed by any one of you, the commissioners of the party on whose behalf the witness is to be examined, and stating the time and place of the intended examination and the names of the witnesses to be examined, shall be given to the commissioners of the other party by delivering the notice to them, or by leaving it at their usual place of abode or business, and

if the commissioners or commissioner of that party neglect to attend pursuant to the notice, then one of you, the commissioners of the party on whose behalf the notice is given, shall be at liberty to proceed with and take the examination of the witness or witnesses *ex parte*, and adjourn any meeting or meetings, or continue the same from day to day until all the witnesses intended to be examined by virtue of the notice have been examined, without giving any further or other notice of the subsequent meeting or meetings.

3. In the event of any witness on his examination, cross-examination, or re-examination producing any book, document, letter, paper, or writing, and refusing for good cause to be stated in his deposition to part with the original thereof, then a copy thereof, or extract therefrom, certified by the commissioners or commissioner present and acting to be a true and correct copy or extract, shall be annexed to the witness's deposition.

4. Each witness to be examined under this commission shall be examined on oath, affirmation, or otherwise in accordance with his religion by or before the commissioners or commissioner present at the examination.

5. If any one or more of the witnesses do not understand the English language (the interrogatories, cross-interrogatories, and *vivâ voce* questions, if any, being previously translated into the language with which he or they is or are conversant), then the examination shall be taken in English through the medium of an interpreter or interpreters to be nominated by the commissioners or commissioner present at the examination, and to be previously sworn according to his or their several religions by or before the said commissioners or commissioner truly to interpret the questions to be put to the witness and his answers thereto.

6. The depositions to be taken under this commission shall be subscribed by the witness or witnesses, and by the commissioners or commissioner who shall have taken the depositions.

7. The interrogatories, cross-interrogatories, and depositions, together with any documents referred to therein,

or certified copies thereof or extracts therefrom, shall be sent to the Senior Master of the Supreme Court of Judicature on or before the 1st day of November, 1898, enclosed in a cover under the seals or seal of the commissioners or commissioner.

8. Before you or any of you, in any manner act in the execution hereof, you shall severally take the oath hereon indorsed on the Holy Evangelists or otherwise in such other manner as is sanctioned by the form of your several religions, and is considered by you respectively to be binding on your respective consciences. In the absence of any other commissioner a commissioner may himself take the oath.

And we give you or any one of you authority to administer such oath to the other or others of you.

WITNESS, etc.

The writ was issued, etc.

No. CCXL.

Order for Letter of Request for Commission.

(O. 37, r. 6A ; Y. S. C. P., and A. P., App. K., No. 37A.)

[*Formal parts as in No. CXLIII. or No. CXLVII.*]

That a letter of request do issue directed to the proper tribunal for the examination of the following witnesses, that is to say :
James Ferguson, of Seville, in the kingdom of Spain ;
Pedro Garcia, of Seville, in the kingdom of Spain.

And that the depositions taken pursuant thereto when received be filed at the central office, and be given in evidence on the trial of this action saving all just exceptions.

And that the trial of this action be stayed until the said depositions have been filed.

DATED the 16th day of November, 1897.

In cases to which O. 30 does not apply, the formal parts of the above will be as in No. CI.

No. CCXLI.

Request for Commission.

(O. 37, r. 6A; Y. S. C. P., and A. P., App. K., No. 37B.)

To the President and Judges of the Supreme Court of New Zealand (a).

WHEREAS an action is now pending in the Queen's Bench Division of the High Court of Justice in England, in which Frederick William Benson is plaintiff and Walter Jackson is defendant. And in the said action the plaintiff claims damages for non-delivery of meat (b).

And whereas it has been represented to the said Court that it is necessary, for the purposes of justice and for the due determination of the matters in dispute between the parties, that the following persons should be examined as witnesses upon oath touching such matters, that is to say:

George Robertson Duncan, of Dunedin, New Zealand, and Herbert Hodges, of Dunedin, New Zealand.

And it appearing that such witnesses are resident within the jurisdiction of your honourable Court.

Now I, Charles, Baron Russell of Killowen, as the President of the said Queen's Bench Division of the High Court of Justice, have the honour to request, and do hereby request, that for the reasons aforesaid and for the assistance of the High Court of Justice, you, as the President and Judges of the said Supreme Court of New Zealand, or some one or more of you, will be pleased to summon the said witnesses (and such other witnesses as the agents of the said plaintiff and defendant shall humbly request you in writing so to summon) to attend at such time and place as you shall appoint before some one or more of you, or such other person as, according to the procedure of your Court, is competent to take the examination of witnesses, and that you will cause such witnesses to be examined upon the interrogatories which accompany this letter of request (or *vivâ voce*) touching the said matters in question in the presence of the agents of the plaintiff and defendant, or such of them as shall, on due notice given, attend such examination.

And I further have the honour to request that you will be pleased to cause the answers of the said witnesses to be reduced into writing, and all books, letters, papers, and documents produced upon such examination to be duly marked for identification, and that you will be further pleased to authenticate such examination by the seal of your tribunal, or in such other way as is in accordance with your procedure, and to return the same, together with such request in writing, if any, for the examination of other witnesses through Her Majesty's Secretary of State for the Colonies (c), for transmission to the said High Court of Justice in England.

DATED the 8th day of June, 1897.

(a) The heading will necessarily vary according to the constitution of the foreign court.
(b) The indorsement on the writ should be followed.
(c) This will be the form in the case of a British colony. In the case of foreign countries substitute "foreign affairs" for "the colonies." In the case of India, the request is transmitted and returned direct; the words from "through Her Majesty's" to "transmission" must accordingly be omitted.

No. CCXLII.
Undertaking by Solicitors as to Costs of Request for Commission.
(O. 37, r. 6A ; Practice Master's Rules, 13A, A. P., Part III.)

[*Heading as in writ.*]

WE HEREBY undertake to be responsible for all expenses incurred by Her Majesty's Secretary of State for the Colonies [*or*, Foreign Affairs] in respect of the execution of the letter of request issued herein on the 8th day of June, 1897, and on receiving due notification of the amount of such expenses, we undertake to pay the same to the Senior Master.

     LINDOW and BRIGGS, of 71, Fenchurch
      Street, in the City of London,
      solicitors for the plaintiff.
DATED the 8th day of June, 1897.

No. CCXLIII.

Order for Appointment of Special Examiner to take Evidence Abroad.

(O. 37, r. 5 ; Y. S. C. P., App. K., No. 35B ;
A. P., App. K., No. 37c.)

[*Formal parts as in No. CXLIII. or No. CXLVII.*]

That   , Esquire, be appointed as special examiner for the purpose of taking the examination, cross-examination, and re-examination, *vivâ voce*, on oath or affirmation, of Joshua Turnbull and Alfred Croft Hayes, both of Madrid, in the kingdom of Spain, witnesses on the part of the plaintiff at Madrid aforesaid, the plaintiff's solicitors to give to the defendant's solicitors ten days' notice in writing of the date on which they propose to send out this order to Madrid for execution, and that seven days after the service of such notice the solicitors for the plaintiff and defendant respectively do exchange the names of their agents at Madrid, to whom notice relating to the examination of the said witnesses may be sent. And that four days (exclusive of Sunday) prior to the examination of any witness hereunder notice of such examination shall be given by the agent of the party on whose behalf such witness is to be examined to the agent of the other party (unless such notice be dispensed with). And that the deposition when so taken, together with any documents referred to therein, or certified copies of such documents, or of extracts therefrom, be transmitted by the examiner, under seal, to the Senior Master of the Supreme Court of Judicature, Royal Courts of Justice, London, on or before the 10th day of October next, or such further or other day as may be ordered, there to be filed in the proper office. And that either party be at liberty to read and give such depositions in evidence on the trial of this action, saving all just exceptions. And that the trial of this action be stayed until the filing of such depositions. And that the costs of and incident to this application and such examination be costs in the action.

DATED the 12th day of August, 1898.

No. CCXLIV.

Application for Inspection of Bankers' Books.

This application, under the Bankers' Books Evidence Act, 1879 (42 Vict. c. 11, ss. 7, 8) will, except in cases to which O. 30 does not apply, be made on application for further directions (see No. CXLVI). It will be as follows :

That the plaintiff be at liberty to inspect and take copies of all entries in the books of the London and Westminster Bank relating to the account of the defendant with the said bank.

The application may be made *ex parte*, and should be supported by an affidavit, as to the contents of which and the practice generally see the note to O. 37, r. 7, in the Yearly Supreme Court Practice and the Annual Practice.

No. CCXLV.

Præcipe of Subpœna.

(O. 37, r. 26 ; Y. S. C. P., and A. P., App. G., No. 21.)

[*Heading as in writ.*]

SEAL writ of subpœna *ad testificandum*, on behalf of the defendant, directed to Henry Rogers.

Returnable June 20th, 1897.

DATED the 12th day of June, 1897.

    HOWARD and SWEARS, of 104,
     Southampton Street, Strand,
     in the county of London,
     solicitors for the defendant.

No. CCXLVI.
Subpœna ad Testificandum. General Form.
(O. 37, r. 27 ; Y. S. C. P., and A. P., App. J., No. 1.)

[*Heading as in writ.*]

VICTORIA, by the grace of God of the United Kingdom of Great Britain and Ireland, Queen, Defender of the Faith, to William Rogers, John Henry Tuffill and Mary Ann Tuffill, greeting :* We command you to attend before , Esquire, at the Official Referee's Court, Portugal Street, London, W.C., on Thursday, the 27th day of October, 1898, at the hour of 10.30 o'clock in the forenoon, and so from day to day until the above cause is tried, to give evidence on behalf of the defendant.

Witness, HARDINGE STANLEY, EARL OF HALSBURY, Lord High Chancellor of Great Britain, the 24th day of October, in the year of Our Lord One thousand eight hundred and ninety-eight.

The above form will serve for trial before an official referee, etc. For High Court and Assize forms, see Nos. CCXLVII. and CCXLVIII. If used for examination before an examiner, for the words "the above cause is tried," substitute "your evidence shall have been taken." More than three names may be inserted (O. 37, r. 29).

No. CCXLVII.
Subpœna ad Testificandum. High Court.
(O. 37, r. 27 ; Y. S. C. P., and A. P., App. J., No. 6.)

[*Proceed as in No. CCXLVI. to *.*]

WE command you to attend at the Royal Courts of Justice, Strand, London, at the sittings of the Queen's Bench Division of our High Court of Justice, to be holden on Tuesday, the 10th day of May, 1898, at the hour of 10.30 o'clock in the forenoon, and so from day to day during the said sittings, until the above cause is tried, to give evidence on behalf of the plaintiff.

Witness, etc. [*as in No. CCXLVI*].

See note to No. CCXLVI.

No. CCXLVIII.

Subpœna ad Testificandum. Assizes.

(O. 37, r. 27 ; Y. S. C. P., and A. P., App. J., No. 4.)

[*Proceed as in No. CCXLVI. to* *.]

WE command you to attend before our justices assigned to take the assizes in and for the County of Norfolk, to be holden at Norwich, on Tuesday, the 1st day of November, 1898, at the hour of 11 o'clock in the forenoon, and so from day to day during the said assizes, until the above cause is tried, to give evidence on behalf of the defendant.

Witness, etc [*as in No. CCXLVI.*]

See note to No. CCXLVI.

No. CCXLIX.

Subpœna Duces Tecum.

(O. 37, r. 27 ; Y. S. C. P., and A. P., App. J., Nos. 3, 5, 7.)

This will be the same as Nos. CCXLVI., CCXLVII. or CCXLVIII. (according to circumstances), except that in all cases at the end of the body of the writ and before the teste must be added the words :

, and also to bring with you and produce at the time and place aforesaid [*specify documents to be produced*, *e.g.*,

Lease of No. 16, High Road, New Cross, in the County of London, dated 16th May, 1861.

Letters from the plaintiff to you, dated 16th March and 18th April, 1897.]

Not more than three names may be included in a subpœna *duces tecum*. (O 37, r. 30.)

No. CCL.

Writ of Habeas Corpus ad Testificandum.

(O. 37, r. 27; O. 36, r. 35; Y. S. C. P., and A. P., App. J., No. 2.)

[*Heading as in writ.*]

VICTORIA, by the Grace of God, of the United Kingdom of Great Britain and Ireland, Queen, Defender of the Faith, to the keeper of our prison at Reading, in the County of Berkshire.

We command you that you bring John Knutt, who it is said is detained in our prison under your custody, before   at   , on Tuesday, the 7th day of March, 1897, at the hour of 10.30 in the forenoon, and so from day to day until the above action is tried, to give evidence on behalf the plaintiff. And that immediately after the said John Knutt shall have so given his evidence, you safely conduct him to the prison from which he shall have been brought.

Witness, etc. [*as in No. CCXLVI*].

This writ was issued by WILLIAMS and GRAY, of 21, St. Swithin's Lane, London, solicitors for the plaintiff.

Compare the above form with No. CCXLVI. It may readily be adapted for the sittings of the High Court or for Assizes, by varying it in accordance with Nos. CCXLVII. and CCXLVIII.

The order for the writ to issue is obtained *ex parte* from the judge in chambers. The application should be supported by an affidavit, which should show :

(1.) That the prisoner is a material witness, and in what way his evidence is material ;

(2.) The place where he is imprisoned, and the cause of his imprisonment ;

(3.) That the applicant cannot safely proceed to trial without the prisoner's evidence ;

(4.) That (if such is the fact) the prisoner is ready and willing to give evidence.

No. CCLI.

Affidavit of Service of Subpœna.

(O. 37, rr. 32, 33.)

[*Commence as in No. LXVI.*]

1. I did, on the 28th day of May, 1897, serve Eleanor Mary Williamson, the person named in the subpœna hereinafter mentioned, with a subpœna issuing out of, and under the seal of the Central Office of the Supreme Court of Judicature, by delivering to and leaving with the said Eleanor Mary Williamson, at No. 11, High Street, Ipswich, in the County of Suffolk, a true copy of the said subpœna, and of the indorsement thereon, and I did at the same time show the said subpœna, so under seal as aforesaid, to the said Eleanor Mary Williamson.

2. By the said subpœna, the said Eleanor Mary Williamson was commanded to attend before the justices assigned to take the assizes in and for the County of Suffolk, to be holden at Ipswich, on Thursday, the 8th day of June, 1897, at the hour of 10.30 o'clock in the forenoon, and so from day to day during the said assizes, to give evidence on behalf of the plaintiff.

Sworn, etc.

Filed on behalf of the plaintiff.

No. CCLII.

Notice of Evidence in Mitigation of Damages.

(O. 36, r. 37.)

[*Heading as in writ.*]

TAKE notice that the defendant intends at the trial of this action to give in evidence the following matters with a view to mitigation of damages :

1. That on the 20th day of April, 1896, the defendant published in the *North London Herald*, the following apology :

[*Set out the apology in full.*]

2. That on the 16th day of March, 1896, and on divers other days prior to the publication by the defendant of the alleged libel of the plaintiff, the plaintiff slandered the defendant in the office of the defendant, and in the presence of his clerks, by accusing the defendant of immorality.

Etc., etc., etc.

DATED the 27th day of November, 1896.
    ROBERTS and MARGETTS,
     solicitors for the plaintiff.

To the defendant, and to
Mr. H. T. NOBLE, his solicitor.

176   EVIDENCE.

No. CCLIII.
Affidavit by One Deponent.
(O. 38.)

1897. C. No. 2306.

IN THE HIGH COURT OF JUSTICE,
Queen's Bench Division (a).

BETWEEN Robert Percy Hall [and
    others] (b) - - plaintiff[s],
    and
Benjamin Brown [and
    others] (b) - - defendant[s].

I, MAURICE HELMSLEY, of 71, Highclere Road, Streatham, in the County of Surrey (c), silk merchant (d), make oath and say as follows :

1. On the 15th day of etc. (e).
2. I did, etc.
3. I am, etc.
Etc., etc., etc.

SWORN at No. 61, Cannon Street,
  in the City of London, the
  13th day of September, 1898,
  Before me,
    WILLIAM TAYLOR,
  a Commissioner to administer
  oaths in the Supreme Court
  of Judicature.

M. HELMSLEY.

This affidavit is filed on behalf of the plaintiff.

(a.) By O. 38, r. 2 "every affidavit shall be intituled in the cause or matter in which it is sworn." But where the action has not been already commenced, the heading should be as follows :

IN THE HIGH COURT OF JUSTICE,
  Queen's Bench Division.
In the matter of the Judicature Acts, 1873—1884.
In the matter of an intended action
    BETWEEN, etc.

See No. XLIV.

(b) By O. 38, r. 2 "in every case in which there are more than one plaintiff or defendant, it shall be sufficient to state the full name of the first plaintiff or defendant respectively, and that there are other plaintiffs or defendants as the case may be ; and the costs occasioned by any unnecessary prolixity in any such title shall be disallowed by the taxing officer."

(c) By O. 38, r. 8 "every affidavit shall state the description and true place of abode of the deponent.'

(d) See note (c). For descriptions which have been held good and bad respectively, see Reference Table for Commissioners of Oaths, A. P., Part III. If the deponent is a party to the action, add after his description "the above-named plaintiff," or "one of the above-named defendants," or as the case may be.

(e) As to the contents of affidavits and their form generally, see O. 38, rr. 3, 7.

No. CCLIV.

Affidavit by Two or More Deponents.

(O. 38.)

[*Heading as in No. CCLIII.*] (a).

WE, Henry James Dobbs, of No. 2, Maida Road, Putney, in the County of Surrey, manufacturer [the above-named defendant], [and] Robert Higson, of 216, Strand, in the County of London, solicitor in this action for the above-named defendant [and George Price, of 17, Cross Lane, John Street, Brixton, in the County of London, clerk to the said Robert Higson], make oath and say as follows :

And first, I, the said Henry James Dobbs, for myself say,

1. I am, etc.
2. According to, etc.
3. The said, etc.

And next, I, the said Robert Higson, for myself say,

4. On or about, etc.
5. I did, etc.

[And next, I, the said George Price, for myself, say,
6. On the, etc.]

And lastly, we both [*or*, all] say,
7. There is not, etc.
8. The said, etc.

Sworn by both [*or*, all of] the above-named deponents (*b*) severally at etc. [*as in No. CCLIII.*].
} HENRY JAMES DOBBS.
ROBERT HIGSON.
[GEORGE PRICE.]

This affidavit is filed on behalf of the defendant.

(*a*) See the notes to No. CCLIII.

(*b*) The above is the form of jurat where all the deponents swear the affidavit at one time before the same officer. Where two or more deponents swear at different times, or before different officers, the names of the persons swearing on each occasion must be inserted in the jurats respectively, *e.g.* "sworn by the above-named Robert Higson," or "sworn by the above-named Robert Higson and George Price, severally."

CHAPTER XIX.

MOTION FOR JUDGMENT.

No. CCLV.

Notice of Motion for Judgment.

(O. 40, r. 1.)

See No. CLXXIV., which may be adapted to meet the circumstances of the case. For form of affidavit of service of notice of motion, see No. CLXXV.; and for form of judgment on motion, see No. CLXXVII. For the cases where judgment may be obtained otherwise than by notice of motion, see the note to O. 40, r. 1, in the Yearly Supreme Court Practice and the Annual Practice.

No. CCLVI.

Notice of Motion to Set Aside Judgment Directed (1).

(O. 40, r. 3.)

1896. S. No. 297.

IN THE COURT OF APPEAL.

BETWEEN Richard Stevenson - - plaintiff,
and
Alfred George Thomas - defendant.

TAKE NOTICE that this Honourable Court will be moved on Monday, the 6th day of December, 1897 (a), at 10.30 o'clock in the forenoon, or so soon thereafter as counsel can be heard, by [Mr.   , of] counsel for the defendant on his behalf, for an order * that the judgment directed to be entered herein by Mr. Justice   at the trial hereof with a jury before him, on the 15th day of November, 1897, be set aside, and that judgment be entered for the defendant, on the ground that the judgment directed to be entered is wrong by reason that the finding of the jury upon the questions submitted to them has not been properly entered †, and that the costs of this application be paid by the plaintiff to the defendant.

DATED the 22nd day of November, 1897 (*b*).

Yours, etc.,
BLAKESLEY and WILLCOX,
defendant's solicitors.

To the above-named plaintiff,
and to Messrs. HICKS
and Co., his solicitors.

(*a*) The notice of motion is a fourteen days notice. O. 39, r. 5, and note ; O. 39, r. 4.

(*b*) The notice must be served within eight days after the trial, if the trial has been in London or Middlesex ; if elsewhere, within seven days after the last day of sitting on the circuits for England and Wales during which the trial shall have taken place. Vacations are not reckoned in the computation of the time. O. 39, r. 4.

No. CCLVII.

Notice of Motion to Set Aside Judgment Directed (2).

(O. 40, r. 4.)

[*As is No. CCLVI. to* *]

that the judgment directed to be entered herein by Mr. Justice (*a*), at the trial hereof [with a jury] before him, on the 15th day of November, 1897, be set aside, and that judgment be entered for the defendant, on the ground that upon the finding [of the jury] as entered the judgment so directed is wrong.

[*As in No. CCLVI. from* †]

(*a*) The above form will, with the name of the referee substituted for that of the judge, and " In the High Court of Justice, Queen's Bench Division" for " In the Court of Appeal," be applicable to a motion under O. 40, r. 6.

LEAVE TO SET DOWN MOTION.

No. CCLVIII.

Notice of Motion for Judgment after Trial of Issues.

(O. 40, r. 7.)

· [*Heading as in writ.*]

TAKE NOTICE that the court will be moved on Tuesday, the 4th day of December next, at 10.30 o'clock in the forenoon, or so soon thereafter as counsel can be heard by counsel on behalf of the above-named plaintiff for an order that judgment be entered herein for the plaintiff for 230*l.* and costs to be taxed, and that the costs of this application be paid by the defendant to the plaintiff.

DATED, etc. [*as in No. CCLVI.*].

For form of judgment, see No. CLXXVII.

No. CCLIX.

Application for Leave to Set Down Motion for Judgment.

(O. 40, r. 8.)

This should apparently now be made, except in cases to which O. 30 does not apply, on application for further directions (see No. CXLVI.). It may be worded as follows:

That the plaintiff be at liberty forthwith to set down a motion for judgment herein without waiting for the trial or determination of the issues not already tried or determined.

CHAPTER XX.

JUDGMENTS.

See also Nos. LXXIV.—LXXVI., LXXIX.—LXXXII., CXV., CXVI., CLXI., CLXVI., CLXIX.—CLXXIII., CLXXVII., CXCVI., CCXVII., CCXVIII. ; and the index. Further forms will also be found in the Annual Practice, Part III. (Table of Official Requirements on Signing Judgments).

No. CCLX.

Final Judgment under Order XIV.

(O. 41, r. 1 ; Y. S. C. P., and A. P., App. F., No. 5.)

[*Heading as in writ.*]

The 9th day of June, 1898.

The defendant having appeared to the writ of summons herein, and the plaintiff having by the order of Master   , dated the 9th day of June, 1898, obtained leave to sign judgment under the Rules of the Supreme Court, Order XIV., Rule 1, for the amount indorsed on the writ, with interest, if any [*or*, possession of the land in the indorsement on the writ described as No. 11, Davies Street, Marylebone, in the County of London], and 6*l*. 10*s*. costs [*or*, costs to be taxed].

It is this day adjudged that the plaintiff recover against the defendant 46*l*. 13*s*. [*or*, possession of the land in the indorsement on the writ described as No. 11, Davies Street, Marylebone, in the County of London], and 6*l*. 10*s*. costs [*or*, costs to be taxed].

[The above costs have been taxed and allowed at 7*l*. 16*s*. 6*d*., as appears by a Taxing Officer's certificate dated the 23rd day of June, 1898].

No. CCLXI.

Final Judgment under Order XIV. against Married Woman.

(O. 41, r. 1; Y.S.C.P., App. F., No. 1c; and A. P., App. F., No. 5a.)

[*Heading as in writ.*]

The 3rd day of August, 1896.

The defendant, Sarah Ann Morrison, having appeared to the writ of summons herein, and the plaintiff having by order of Master   , dated the 2nd day of August, 1896, obtained leave to sign judgment under the Rules of the Supreme Court, Order XIV., Rule 1, for the amount indorsed on the writ, with interest, if any, and costs to be taxed, and such order directing that execution be limited to the separate property of the said Sarah Ann Morrison, not subject to any restriction against anticipation (unless by reason of section 19 of the Married Women's Property Act, 1882, such property shall be liable to execution notwithstanding such restriction):

It is this day adjudged that the plaintiff recover 121*l*. 4*s*. 3*d*. and costs to be taxed against the said defendant, such sum and costs to be payable out of her separate property and not otherwise. And it is ordered that execution hereon be limited to the separate property of the said defendant Sarah Ann Morrison not subject to any restriction against anticipation (unless by reason of section 19 of the Married Women's Property Act, 1882, the property shall be liable to execution notwithstanding such restriction).

The above costs have been taxed and allowed at 9*l*. 2*s*. 6*d*., as appears by a Taxing Officer's certificate, dated the 11th day of August, 1896.

No. CCLXII.

Final Judgment under Order XIV. on Conditional Order.

[*Heading as in writ.*]

The 6th day of December, 1897.

The defendant having appeared to the writ of summons herein, and the plaintiff having by order of Master, , dated the 20th day of November, 1897, obtained leave to sign judgment under the Rules of the Supreme Court, Order XIV., Rule 1, for the amount indorsed on the writ, with interest, if any, and costs to be taxed, unless the defendant paid into court the sum of 80*l.* on or before the 4th day of December, 1898 [*or*, within fourteen days from the date of the said order] and default having been made in payment into court as conditioned by the said order—

It is this day adjudged that the plaintiff recover against the defendant 82*l.* 11*s.* 2*d.* and costs to be taxed.

The above costs have been taxed and allowed at 8*l.* 4*s.*, as appears by a Taxing Officer's certificate, dated the 21st day of December, 1897.

No. CCLXIII.

Judgment after Trial with Jury.

(O. 41, r. 1 ; Y. S. C. P., and A. P., App. F., No. 7.)

[*Heading as in writ.*]

DATED and entered the 13th day of November, 1897.

The action having on the 12th and 13th November, 1897, been tried before the Honourable Mr. Justice with a common [*or*, special] jury of the County of Middlesex, and the jury having found (*a*) a verdict for the plaintiff for 100*l.* [*or*, for the defendant], and the said Mr. Justice having ordered (*b*) that judgment be entered for the plaintiff for 100*l.* and costs [*or*, for the defendant]—

Therefore it is adjudged that the plaintiff recover against the defendant 100*l.* and his costs to be taxed [*or*, that the plaintiff recover nothing against the defendant, and that the defendant recover against the plaintiff his costs of defence to be taxed].

The above costs have been taxed and allowed at 57*l*. 18*s*. 4*d*., as appears by a Taxing Officer's certificate, dated the 17th day of December, 1897.

W. H. BOWERS,
solicitor for the plaintiff [*or*, defendant].

(*a*) The findings of the jury as stated in the officer's certificate should be set out. See O. 36, r. 42, and Yearly Supreme Court Practice and the Annual Practice, App. B., No. 17.

(*b*) The direction of the judge, as set out in the certificate, should be followed.

No. CCLXIV.

Judgment after Trial without Jury.

(O. 41, r. 1 ; Y. S. C. P., and A. P., App. F., No. 11.)

[*Heading as in writ.*]

DATED and entered the 8th day of July, 1894.

This action having on the 8th day of July, 1894, been tried before the Honourable Mr. Justice   , without a jury, in the County of Middlesex, and the said Mr. Justice   on the 8th day of July, 1894, having ordered that judgment be entered for the plaintiff for 170*l*. [*or*, for the defendant]—

It is this day adjudged that the plaintiff recover from the defendant 170*l*. and costs to be taxed [*or*, that the defendant recover against the plaintiff his costs of defence to be taxed].

The above costs have been taxed and allowed at 83*l*. 4*s*. 8*d*. as appears by a Taxing Officer's certificate, dated the 31st day of July, 1894.

BLACKBURN and JAMESON,
solicitors for the plaintiff [*or*, defendant].

See also Yearly Supreme Court Practice and the Annual Practice, App. F., No. 6.

No. CCLXV.

Judgment in Court for Amount to be Ascertained.

(A. P., App. F., No. 7A.)

[Heading as in writ.]

DATED the 9th day of December, 1897.

The action having on the 9th day of December, 1897, been tried before the Honourable Mr. Justice   , and the said Mr. Justice   having ordered that judgment be entered for the plaintiff for such amount as shall be found due by the official referee for damages [*or as the case may be, following the terms of reference*]—

It is this day adjudged that the plaintiff recover against the defendant such amount as shall be found due by the official referee for damages [*or as the case may be*] and costs to be taxed.

The official referee having certified the amount due to the plaintiff hereunder at 84*l*., it is adjudged that the plaintiff recover against the defendant the said sum of 84*l*. and costs to be taxed (*a*).

The above costs have been taxed and allowed at 92*l*. 12s. 6d., as appears by a Taxing Officer's certificate, dated the 23rd day of March, 1898.

(*a*) This paragraph to be added to both the original and the office copy judgment after the official referee has certified the amount.

No. CCLXVI.

Judgment after Trial before Referee.

(O. 41, r. 1; Y. S. C. P., and A. P., App. F., No. 8.)

[Heading as in writ.]

30th November, 1896.

The action having on the 29th and 30th November, 1896, been tried before   Esq., an official referee; and the said   having ordered that judgment be entered for the defendant—

JUDGMENT OF DISMISSAL. 187

It is this day adjudged that the plaintiff recover nothing against the defendant, and that the defendant recover against the plaintiff his costs of defence, to be taxed.

The above costs have been taxed and allowed at 41*l.* 13*s.* 8*d.*, as appears by a Taxing Officer's certificate, dated the 17th day of December, 1896.

No. CCLXVII.

Judgment after Trial of Questions of Account by Referee.

(O. 41, r. 1 ; Y. S. C. P., and A. P., App. F., No. 9.)

The 23rd day of July, 1897.

The questions of account in this action having been referred to   Esq. [an official referee], and he having found that there is due from the defendant to the plaintiff the sum of 73*l.* 2*s.* 9*d.*, and directed that the defendant do pay the costs of the reference :

It is this day adjudged that the plaintiff recover against the defendant 73*l.* 2*s.* 9*d.* and costs to be taxed.

The above costs have been taxed and allowed at 39*l.* 7*s.* 6*d.*, as appears by a Taxing Officer's certificate dated the 11th day of August, 1897.

See the Arbitration Act, 1889, s. 14.

No. CCLXVIII.

Judgment of Dismissal on Non-appearance of Plaintiff.

(O. 36, r. 32 ; A. P., App. F., No. 11A.)

DATED and entered the 3rd day of February, 1898.

This action having on the 3rd day of February, 1898, been called on for hearing before the Honourable

Mr. Justice   , and the plaintiff having failed to appear, and the defendant having thereupon become entitled under Order XXXVI, Rule 32, to judgment dismissing the action, and the said Mr. Justice   having ordered that judgment be entered accordingly:

Therefore it is adjudged that this action do stand dismissed out of this court with costs.

And it is further adjudged that the defendant recover against the plaintiff his costs to be taxed.

The above costs have been taxed and allowed at 47*l*. 16*s*., as appears by a Taxing Officer's certificate, dated the 1st day of March, 1898.

No. CCLXIX.

Judgment on Motion after Trial of Issue.

(O. 40, r. 7; Y. S. C. P., and A. P., App. F., No. 18.)

[*Heading as in writ.*]

DATED and entered the 13th day of May, 1898.

The issues [*or*, questions] of fact arising in this action, by the order of Master   , dated the 13th day of January, 1898, ordered to be tried before   , having on the 23rd day of April, 1898, been tried before the said   , and the said   having found that the wheat, the subject matter of the action, was up to sample: Now on motion before the court for judgment on behalf of the plaintiff, the court having ordered that judgment be entered for the plaintiff for 117*l*. 3*s*. 6*d*. and costs:

It is this day adjudged that the plaintiff recover against the defendant the sum of 117*l*. 3*s*. 6*d*. and costs to be taxed.

The above costs have been taxed and allowed at 43*l*. 2*s*. 8*d*., as appears by a Taxing Officer's certificate, dated the 8th day of June, 1898.

No. CCLXX.
Judgment on Warrant of Attorney.
(Y. S. C. P., App. F., No. 20; and A. P., App. F., No. 19.)

[*Heading as in writ.*]

The 6th day of July, 1897.

The defendant having executed a Warrant of Attorney, bearing date the 4th day of March, 1897, whereby the above-named plaintiff was authorised to enter up judgment against the said defendant for 105*l*. and costs of suit:

It is this day adjudged that the plaintiff recover against the said defendant 105*l*., and 3*l*. 10*s*. costs.

Original Warrant of Attorney, }
filed the 10th day of March, 1897.}

No. CCLXXI.
Memorandum to be Indorsed on Judgment or Order where Act Ordered to be Done.
(O. 41, r. 5.)

If you, the within-named John Henry Stokes, neglect to obey this judgment [*or*, order] by the time therein limited, you will be liable to process of execution for the purpose of compelling you to obey the same judgment [*or*, order].

No. CCLXXII.
Order by Consent for Judgment.
(O. 41, r. 9.)

[*Heading as in No. CI.*]

Upon hearing the solicitors on both sides [and upon reading the affidavit of Joseph Abrahams, filed the 18th day of May, 1898, and the affidavit, etc.] and by consent, it is ordered that the plaintiff be at liberty to sign final judgment herein for the amount indorsed on the writ of summons with interest, if any, and costs to be taxed, and that the costs of this application be costs in the cause.

DATED the 23rd day of May, 1898.

No. CCLXXIII.

Consent of Defendant to Order.

(O. 41, r. 10.)

I, THE within-named defendant, hereby consent to an order being made in the terms within-mentioned, and I request Mr. Henry A. Jones, solicitor of the Supreme Court, to act on my behalf, and witness my signature hereto.

DATED the 22nd day of May, 1898.

ROBERT H. STONE.

SIGNED by the within-named defendant in my presence, whilst acting on his behalf as his solicitor; and I hereby attest his signature to the above-written consent pursuant to Order XLI., Rule 10, of the Rules of the Supreme Court.

HENRY A. JONES.

No. CCLXXIV.

Judgment by Consent.

(O. 41, r. 9.)

[*Heading as in writ.*]

The 26th day of May, 1898.

PURSUANT to the order of Master   , dated the 23rd day of May, 1898, whereby, upon hearing the solicitors on both sides [and upon reading the affidavit of, etc.] and by consent, it was ordered that the plaintiff be at liberty to sign final judgment herein for the amount indorsed on the writ of summons with interest, if any, and costs to be taxed—

It is this day adjudged that the plaintiff recover against the defendant 173*l*. 11*s*. 9*d*. and costs to be taxed.

The above costs have been taxed and allowed at 8*l*. 14*s*., as appears by a Taxing Officer's certificate, dated the 7th day of June, 1898.

CHAPTER XXI.

EXECUTION.

The following references to forms of and præcipes for writs of execution, other than those given in this and succeeding chapters, may be found useful:

	Y. S. C. P.	and A. P.
Writ of Elegit	App. H., No. 3.	
Præcipe for Elegit	,,	G., No. 2.
Writ of Venditioni Exponas	,,	H., No. 4.
Præcipe for ,, ,,	,,	G., No. 3.
Writ of Fieri Facias de Bonis Ecclesiasticis	,,	H., No. 5.
Præcipe for ,, ,, ,,	,,	G., No. 4.
Writ of Fieri Facias de Bonis Ecclesiasticis during Vacancy of Bishop's See	,,	H., No. 6.
Writ of Sequestrari Facias de Bonis Ecclesiasticis	,,	H., No. 7.
Præcipe for Sequestrari Facias de Bonis Ecclesiasticis	,,	G., No. 5.
Writ of Sequestration	,,	H., No. 13.
Præcipe for ,,	,,	G., No. 6.
Writ of Distringas against Ex-sheriff	,,	H., No. 14.
Præcipe of Distringas against Ex-sheriff	,,	G., No. 11.
Writ of Restitution	A. P. ,,	H., No. 8A.

See also Table of Official Requirements on Issuing Executions, Annual Practice, Part III.

No. CCLXXV.

Summons for Leave to Issue Execution.

(O. 42, rr. 9, 23 ; O. 48A, rr. 8, 10.)

[*Formal parts as in No. C.*]

the plaintiff for an order that he be at liberty to issue execution against the defendant on the judgment herein, dated the 12th day of March, 1892, and that the costs of this application be paid by the defendant to the plaintiff.

For the cases where leave to issue execution is necessary, see the orders and rules cited above. In general the application should be by summons, but in some cases leave may be granted on an *ex parte* application. An affidavit will usually be necessary, showing the right of the applicant to apply, and the special circumstances of the case. See the notes to the above rules in the Yearly Supreme Court Practice and the Annual Practice.

If the person entitled or liable to execution is not the original plaintiff or defendant, the form of summons will be varied by inserting the name of such person.

No. CCLXXVI.

Præcipe for Writ of Fieri Facias.

(O. 42, r. 12 ; Y. S. C. P., and A. P., App. G., No. 1.)

[*Heading as in writ.*]

SEAL [in pursuance of the order dated the 27th day of November, 1897] (*a*), a writ of *fieri facias* directed to the sheriff of Middlesex, to levy against James Petersen the sum of 119*l*. and interest thereon at the rate of 4*l*. per centum per annum from the 13th day of November, 1897 [and 37*l*. 14*s*. 8*d*. costs].

Judgment dated the 13th day of November, 1897.

[Order (*b*) dated the 27th day of November, 1897.]

[Taxing Officer's certificate dated the 4th day of December, 1897.]

BIRD and LESLIE,
solicitors for the plaintiff.

(*a*) This is to be inserted where execution is issued by leave.

(*b*) If the execution is issued after leave obtained, the date of the order giving leave must be inserted, as well as the date of the judgment.

No. CCLXXVII.

Writ of Fieri Facias.

(O. 42, r. 14 ; Y. S. C. P., and A. P., App. II., No. 1.)

[*Heading as in writ.*]

VICTORIA, by the grace of God of the United Kingdom of Great Britain and Ireland, Queen, Defender of the Faith, to the sheriff of City and County of the City of Exeter (*a*) greeting : ᵃ

We command you that of the goods and chattels of Hubert Green in your bailiwick, you cause to be made the sum of 150*l*. (*b*), and also interest thereon at the rate of 4*l*. per centum per annum from the 8th day of February, 1898 (*c*), which said sum of money and interest were lately before us in our High Court of Justice in a certain action [*or*, certain actions] † wherein Walter Merry Johnstone is plaintiff, and Hubert Greene, defendant, by a judgment of our said court, bearing date the 8th day of February, 1898, adjudged to be paid by the said Hubert Greene to Walter Merry Johnstone, together with certain costs in the said judgment mentioned, and which costs have been taxed and allowed by one of the taxing officers of our said court at the sum of 53*l*. 12*s*. 6*d*., as appears by the certificate of the said Taxing Officer, dated the 28th day of February, 1898. And that of the goods and chattels of the said Hubert Greene in your bailiwick you further cause to be made the said sum of 53*l*. 12*s*. 6*d*. [costs] together with interest thereon at the rate of 4*l*. per centum per annum from the 8th day of February, 1898 (*d*), and that you have that money and interest before us in our said court immediately after the execution hereof to be paid to the said Walter Merry Johnstone in pursuance of the said judgment. And in what manner you shall have executed this our writ, make appear to us in our said court immediately after the execution thereof. And have there then this writ.

Witness HARDINGE STANLEY, EARL OF HALSBURY, Lord High Chancellor of Great Britain, the third day of

March, in the year of Our Lord one thousand eight hundred and ninety-eight.

[*The following to be indorsed on the writ.*]

Levy 204*l*. 2*s*. 9*d*. (*e*) and 1*l*. 10*s*. for costs of execution, etc., and also interest on 203*l*. 12*s*. 6*d*. (*f*) at 4*l*. per centum per annum from the 3rd day of March, 1898, until payment ; besides sheriff's poundage, officers' fees, costs of levying, and all other legal incidental expenses.

This writ was issued by James and Jobson, of 16, New Street, in the City of Exeter [agents for, etc.], solicitors for the plaintiff.

The defendant is a merchant, and resides at Hurst Bank, Norwich Road, in your bailiwick.

(*a*) For forms of direction to various sheriffs, see the Annual Practice, Part III., Table of Official Requirements on Issuing Execution.

(*b*) The amount of the judgment debt.

(*c*) The date of the judgment or order, or day on which the money is directed to be paid, or from which interest is directed by the order to run, as the case may be.

(*d*) The date of the judgment or order ; not, as formerly, date of certificate of taxation.

(*e*) The aggregate amount of (1) judgment debt, (2) costs, and (3) interest on judgment debt and costs from date of judgment to date of issue of writ of *fieri facias*.

(*f*) The amount of judgment debt and costs.

No. CCLXXVIII.

Writ of Fieri Facias against Married Women.

(Y. S. C. P., and A. P., App. II., No. 1A.)

[*As in No. CCLXXVII. to* *.]

WE COMMAND you that of the goods and chattels of Amelia Elizabeth Birkett (being her separate property not subject to any restriction against anticipation as hereinafter mentioned) in your bailiwick, you cause to be made the sum of 81*l*. 10*s*. and 12*l*. 9*s*. 8*d*. costs, and also interest thereon at the rate of 4*l*. per centum per annum from the 16th day of December, 1897, which said sums of money and interest were lately before us in our High Court of Justice in a certain action there depending wherein Herbert Avery Baxter is plaintiff and Amelia Elizabeth Birkett defendant by a judgment of our said court bearing date the 16th day of December, 1897, adjudged to be paid by the said Amelia Elizabeth Birkett to Herbert Avery Baxter, out of her separate property not subject to any restriction against anticipation (unless by reason of section 19 of the Married Women's Property Act, 1882, the property should be liable to execution notwithstanding such restriction) and that you have that money, etc. [*as in No. CCLXXVII.*].

No. CCLXXIX.

Writ of Fieri Facias for Costs.

(O. 42, r. 18 ; Y. S. C. P., and A. P., App. II., No. 2.)

[*As in No. CCLXXVII. to* *.]

WE COMMAND you that of the goods and chattels of Henry Williams in your bailiwick you cause to be made the sum of 41*l*. 19*s*. 6*d*. for certain costs, which by an order of our High Court of Justice dated the 3rd day of May, 1898, were ordered to be paid by the said Henry Williams to Jacob Benson, and which have been taxed and allowed at the said sum, and interest on the said sum at the rate of 4*l*. per centum per annum from the 3rd day of May, 1898, and that you have the said sum and interest before us in our said court immediately after the execution hereof, to be rendered to the said Jacob Benson. AND in what manner, etc. [*as in No. CCLXXVII.*].

No. CCLXXX.

Præcipe for Writ of Possession.

(O. 47, r. 1 ; Y. S. C. P., and A. P., App. G., No. 7.)

[*Heading as in writ.*]

SEAL a writ of possession, directed to the Sheriff of Middlesex, to deliver possession to Percy Thorneycroft of the premises in the judgment herein mentioned.

Judgment dated the 13th day of December, 1897.

WALTER BRISCOE,
solicitor for the plaintiff.

No. CCLXXXI.

Writ of Possession.

(O. 47, rr. 1, 2 ; Y. S. C. P., and A. P., App. H., No. 8.)

[*As in No. CCLXXVII. to* *.]

WHEREAS lately in our High Court of Justice, by a judgment of the Queen's Bench Division of the same court, Paul Simpson recovered [*or*, Charles Philip Cutler was ordered to deliver Paul Simpson] possession of all that land, messuage and premises known as No. 171, Southwark Park Road, in the County of London, with the appurtenances, in your bailiwick : THEREFORE WE COMMAND you that you omit not by reason of any liberty of your county, but that you enter the same, and without delay you cause the said Paul Simpson to have possession of the said land and premises with the appurtenances. AND in what manner, etc. [*as in No. CCLXXVII.*].

For the contents of affidavit to be filed on suing out a writ of possession, see O. 47, r. 2, and notes thereto.

No. CCLXXXII.
Præcipe for Writ of Possession and Fieri Facias.
(O. 47, r. 3; A. P., App. G., No. 7A.)

[*Heading as in writ.*]

SEAL a writ of possession and *fi. fa.* combined, directed to the Sheriff of Kent, to deliver possession to the plaintiff of the land and premises in the judgment [*or*, order] herein mentioned [described as No. 61, Forest Road, Beckenham, in the County of Kent] (*a*).

AND ALSO to levy against William Burton, of No. 17, High Street, Beckenham, in the County of Kent, the sum of [35*l*. debt and] 27*l*. 1*s*. 4*d*. costs, and interest at the rate of 4*l*. per centum per annum on the said amount [s] from the 13th day of July, 1896.

Judgment [*or*, order] dated the 13th day of July, 1896.

Taxing Master's certificate dated the 27th day of July, 1896.

DATED the 29th day of July, 1896.

GEORGE ABUD MANLEY, of 131, Lombard Street, in the City of London, solicitor for the plaintiff.

(*a*) This to be added where possession of part only of the premises is to be given.

No. CCLXXXIII.
Writ of Possession and Fieri Facias.
(O. 47, r. 3; Y. S. C. P., App. H., No. 8A, and A. P., App. H., No. 7A.)

[*As in No. CCLXXVII. to* *.]

WHEREAS lately in our High Court of Justice, by judgment [*or*, order] of the Queen's Bench Division of the same court, it was adjudged [*or*, ordered] that the plaintiff recover possession of all that land and premises known as No. 61, Forest Road, Beckenham, in the

County of Kent, with the appurtenances, in your bailiwick: THEREFORE WE COMMAND you that you omit not by reason of any liberty of your county, but that you enter the same, and without delay you cause the said Robert Haslam to have possession of the said land and premises with the appurtenances. AND WE FURTHER COMMAND you that of the goods and chattels of the said William Burton, in your bailiwick, you cause to be made the sum of 35*l*., and also interest thereon at the rate of 4*l*. per centum per annum, from the 13th day of July, 1896, which said sum of money and interest were in the said action by the judgment therein adjudged [*or*, order dated the 13th day of July, 1896, ordered] to be paid by the said William Burton to the said Robert Haslam, together with certain costs in the said judgment [*or*, order] mentioned, and which costs have been taxed and allowed by one of the taxing officers of our said court at the sum of 27*l*. 1*s*. 4*d*., as appears by the certificate of the said taxing officer, dated the 27th day of July, 1896. AND that of the goods and chattels of the said William Burton in your bailiwick you further cause to be made the said sum of 27*l*. 1*s*. 4*d*., together with interest thereon, from the 13th day of July, 1896, and that you have that money and interest before us in our said court immediately after the execution hereof to be paid to the said Robert Haslam in pursuance of the said judgment [*or*, order]. AND in what manner you have executed this our writ make to appear to us in our High Court of Justice immediately after the execution thereof. AND have there then this writ.

Witness HARDINGE STANLEY, EARL OF HALSBURY, Lord High Chancellor of Great Britain, the twenty-ninth day of July, in the year of our Lord one thousand eight hundred and ninety-six.

This writ was issued by GEORGE ABUD MANLEY, of 131, Lombard Street, in the City of London [agent for, etc.], solicitor for the plaintiff, who resides at Oakdene, Chislehurst, in the County of Kent.

The defendant is a grocer, and resides at No. 17, High Street, Beckenham, in your bailiwick.

Cause possession to be delivered to the plaintiff of the within-mentioned premises [described as, etc.] (a).
And levy 62l. 3s. 5d. (b) and interest on 62l. 1s. 4d. at 4l. per centum per annum, from the 29th day of July, 1896, and 1l. 10s. for costs of execution besides poundage fees and expenses of execution.

(a) See note to No. CCLXXXII.
(b) See No. CCLXXVII., note (e).

No. CCLXXXIV.

Writ of Fieri Facias by Executors of Plaintiff.

(O. 42, r. 23.)

[*As in No. CCLXXVII. to †.*]

wherein Walter Merry Johnson, deceased, was plaintiff and Hubert Greene defendant by a judgment of our said court, bearing date the 8th day of February, 1898, adjudged to be paid by the said Hubert Greene to the said Walter Merry Johnson, together with certain costs in the said judgment mentioned, and the said Walter Merry Johnson having died since the date of the said judgment, whereupon by order of Master   , dated the 23rd day of February, 1898, on an application to him, it was ordered that Thomas Atkinson and Henry Graves Bidwell, as executors of the last will and testament of the said Walter Merry Johnson, should be at liberty to issue execution on the said judgment for the amount thereof, together with the costs of the said application, and the costs in the said judgment mentioned together with the costs of the said application having been taxed and allowed by one of the taxing officers, etc.

[*Conclude as in No. CCLXXVII., substituting the names of the executors for the name of the plaintiff.*]

See also Table of Official Requirements on Issuing Executions Annual Practice, Part III.

No. CCLXXXV.

Notice of Renewal of Writ of Fieri Facias.

(O. 42, r. 20 ; Y. S. C. P., and A. P., App. B., No. 21,)

[*Heading as in writ.*]

TAKE NOTICE that the writ of *fieri facias* issued in this action, directed to the Sheriff of Sussex, and bearing date the 18th day of March, 1897, has been renewed for one year from the 3rd day of March, 1898.

DATED the 3rd day of March, 1898.

     FRANKLIN WEBSTER, of 16, Cross Street, Brighton [agent for, etc.], solicitor for the defendant.

To the Sheriff of Sussex.

No. CCLXXXVI.

Application for Stay of Execution.

(O. 42, r1. 17 (b), 27.)

[*Formal parts as in No. C.*]

  the plaintiff for an order that execution herein on the judgment dated the 5th day of February, 1897, be stayed.

Where this application is made to a Master in chambers, it should be supported by an affidavit showing the grounds on which it is made.

No. CCLXXXVII.

Præcipe for Writ of Delivery.

(O. 42, r. 6 ; O. 48, r. 1 ; Y. S. C. P., and A. P., App. G., No. 8.)

[*Heading as in writ.*]

SEAL a writ of delivery directed to the Sheriff of Middlesex to make delivery to James Hodgson of the following chattels, that is to say, grand piano, dining-table, and set of twelve chairs.
JUDGMENT dated the 2nd day of December, 1897.
NEWMAN and WOOD,
solicitors for the plaintiff.

No. CCLXXXVIII.

Writ of Delivery.

(O. 42, r. 6 ; O. 48 ; Y. S. C. P., and A. P., App. H., No. 10.)

[*As in No. CCLXXVII. to* *.]

WE command you, that without delay you cause the following chattels, that is to say, grand piano, dining-table, and set of twelve chairs to be returned to James Hodgson, which the said James Hodgson, lately in our High Court of Justice recovered against Elizabeth Jane Purcell [*or,* Elizabeth Jane Purcell was ordered to deliver to the said James Hodgson] in an action in the Queen's Bench Division of our said court. And we further command you, that if the said chattels cannot be found in your bailiwick, you distrain the said Elizabeth Jane Purcell by all her land and chattels in your bailiwick, so that neither the said Elizabeth Jane Purcell nor anyone for her do lay hands on the same until the said Elizabeth Jane Purcell render to the said James Hodgson the said chattels [*or,* (*a*) And we further command you that if the said chattels cannot be found in your bailiwick, of the goods and chattels of the said

Elizabeth Jane Purcell in your bailiwick you cause to be made 105*l*.] (*b*).

[And we further command you that of the goods and chattels of the said Elizabeth Jane Purcell in your bailiwick, you cause to be made the sum of 30*l*. (*c*). And also interest thereon at the rate of 4*l*. per centum per annum, from the 3rd day of March, 1897, which said sum of money and interest were in the said action by the judgment therein dated the 3rd day of March, 1897, adjudged to be paid by the said Elizabeth Jane Purcell to James Hodgson, together with certain costs, etc.—*as in No. CCLXXVII. to the words* " in pursuance of the said judgment" (*d*).]

And in what manner etc. [*conclude as in No. CCLXXVII.*]

The application for leave to issue a writ of delivery is made *ex parte* to a Master, and is supported by an affidavit of the facts.

(*a*) This paragraph to be substituted for the preceding where the sheriff is commanded to levy on defendant's goods the assessed value of the chattels, instead of distraining until the chattels are returned.

(*b*) The assessed value of the chattels.

(*c*) The amount of damages.

(*d*) This paragraph to be added where it is wished to include damages, costs, and interest.

CHAPTER XXII.

ATTACHMENT OF PERSONS AND DEBTS.

No. CCLXXXIX.

Notice of Motion for Leave to Issue Writ of Attachment (*a*).

(O. 44 ; O. 52, r. 4.)

[*Heading as in writ.*]

TAKE NOTICE that this Honourable Court will be moved on Wednesday, the 9th day of November next, at 10.30 o'clock in the forenoon, or so soon thereafter as counsel can be heard by [Mr.   of] counsel for the plaintiff on his behalf for an order that he be at liberty to issue a writ of attachment against you, the above-named defendant [or alternatively, that you, the above-named defendant, be committed to prison] on the ground of your contempt in having broken an undertaking not to carry on your business of a butcher at No. 61, New Cross Road, in the County of London, contained in an order made herein on the 13th day of July, 1898. And that you do pay to the plaintiff the costs of this application, and of the issuing and execution of the said writ of attachment.

DATED the 5th day of November, 1898 (*b*).

Yours, etc.,
HENRY A. PEARCE,
solicitor the above-named
plaintiff.

To the above-named defendant, Richard Hudson,
and to Messrs. LANG and DALE,
his solicitors.

(*a*) There must be an affidavit in support of the application.

(*b*) There must be two clear days between the service of the notice of motion and the day named for hearing (O. 52, r. 5).

No. CCXC.

Summons for Leave to Issue Writ of Attachment.

(O. 44.)

[*Formal parts as in No. C.*]

            the plaintiff, that he be at liberty to issue a writ of attachment against the defendant on the ground that the defendant has failed to answer the interrogatories herein administered to him by the plaintiff, which the defendant was ordered to answer, and that the costs of this application and of the issuing and execution of the said writ of attachment be paid by the defendant to the plaintiff.

The application, when made by summons, must be to the Judge in Chambers (O. 54, r. 12 (a)).

No. CCXCI.

Order Giving Leave to Issue Writ of Attachment.

(O. 44.)

[*Formal parts as in No. CI.*]

It is ordered that the plaintiff be at liberty to issue a writ of attachment against the defendant for his contempt in not paying to the plaintiff's solicitor before the 13th day of December last, the sum of 6*l.* 6*s.*, pursuant to the order of Master   , made herein on the 6th day of December, 1898. And that the costs of this application and of the issuing and execution of the said writ of attachment be paid by the defendant to the plaintiff.

The order must be drawn up (O. 52, r. 14). It should state the nature of the contempt of which the person to be attached is guilty.

No. CCXCII.

Præcipe for Writ of Attachment.
(O. 44 ; Y. S. C. P., and A. P., App. G., No. 10.)

[*Heading as in writ.*]

SEAL in pursuance of order dated the 2nd day of February, 1897, an attachment directed to the Sheriff of Middlesex, against John Burnett, for not paying to Robert John Burn the sum of 6*l*. 6*s*. in the said order mentioned.

ORDER dated the 2nd day of February, 1897.

HERBERT ANDERSON,
solicitor for the plaintiff.

No. CCXCIII.

Writ of Attachment.
(O. 44 ; Y. S. C. P., and A. P., App. H., No. 12.)

[*As in No. CCLXXVII. to* *.]

WE COMMAND you to attach John Burnett so as to have him before us in the Queen's Bench Division of our High Court of Justice, wheresoever the said Court shall then be, there to answer to us, as well touching a contempt which he, it is alleged, hath committed against us, as also such other matters as shall be then and there laid to his charge, and further to perform and abide such order as our said court shall make in this behalf, and hereof fail not, and bring this writ with you.

WITNESS, etc. [*as in No. CCLXXVII.*].

[*The following to be added as a footnote to the writ.*]

NOTICE TO SHERIFF.—This writ, if issued for default in payment of money, is subject to the following limitation :

If under section 4 of the Debtors' Act, 1869, it does not authorise imprisonment for any longer period than One Year.

ATTACHMENT OF PERSONS AND DEBTS.

[*The following to be indorsed.*]

THIS writ was issued by Harvey and Wilkinson, of 16, Cross Street, in the City of London, [agents for, etc.] solicitors for the plaintiff, who resides at 12, Lindow Gardens, Streatham, in the County of Surrey, and was issued pursuant to order dated the 2nd day of February, 1897, for such default as is therein mentioned [not] being a default in payment of money [under section 4 of the Debtors' Act, 1869].

No. CCXCIV.

Summons for Examination of Judgment Debtor.

(O. 42, r. 32.)

1897. C. No. 2351.

IN THE HIGH COURT OF JUSTICE,
Queen's Bench Division.

BETWEEN James Richard Cadman - judgment creditor,
and
Bertram Mason - - judgment debtor.

LET all parties concerned attend the Master in Chambers, Central Office, Royal Courts of Justice, Strand, London, on Thursday, the 13th day of January, 1898, at 11 o'clock in the forenoon, on the hearing of an application on the part of the judgment creditor for an order that the above-named judgment debtor may attend at such time and place as may be appointed, and be orally examined as to whether any and what debts are owing to him, and whether he has any and what other property or means of satisfying the judgment obtained against him in this action, and that he may be ordered to produce on such examination any books or documents in his possession or power relating to the same. And that the costs of this application and of the said examination may be paid by the judgment debtor.

DATED, etc. [*as in No. C., substituting judgment creditor and debtor, for plaintiff and defendant.*]

No. CCXCV.

Order for Examination of Judgment Debtor.

(O. 42, r. 32 ; Y. S. C. P., and A. P., App. K., No. 38.)

[*Heading as in No. CCXCIV., with the addition of the words,*
"Master , Master in Chambers."]

UPON hearing the solicitors on both sides, and upon reading the affidavit of Henry Petch, filed the 10th day of January, 1898 [and the affidavit of, etc.],

IT IS ORDERED that the above-named judgment debtor attend and be orally examined as to whether any and what debts are owing to him, and whether the debtor has any other and what property or means of satisfying the judgment, before one of the Masters of the Supreme Court of Judicature at such time and place as he may appoint, and that the said judgment debtor produce any books or documents in his possession or power relating to the same before the said Master at the time of the examination.

DATED the 13th day of January, 1898.

See also No. CCXCVI.

No. CCXCVI.

Order for Examination touching Means.

(O. 42, r. 32 ; O. 45, r. 1 ; Y. S. C. P., and A. P. App. K., No. 46.)

[*Heading as in No. CCXCV.*]

UPON hearing the solicitor for the judgment creditor and the judgment debtor,

IT IS ORDERED that the above-named judgment debtor attend before one of the Masters of the Supreme Court of Judicature at such time and place as such Master may appoint, and be orally examined as to whether any and what debts are owing to him, and whether he has any and what other property or means of satisfying the judgment signed herein; and that the said judgment debtor produce any books or other documents in his possession or power relating to the same before the said Master at the time of the examination.

DATED the 13th day of January, 1898.

Ses also No. CCXCV.

No. CCXCVII.

Affidavit in Support of Application for Garnishee Order.

(O. 45, r. 1 ; Y. S. C. P., and A. P., App. B., No. 25.)

1897. H. No. 897.

IN THE HIGH COURT OF JUSTICE,
   Queen's Bench Division.

BETWEEN Alfred Harris (a)   -   - judgment creditor,

and

William Morris Young   - judgment debtor.

I, ALFRED HARRIS, of 64, Queen Street, Kensington, in the County of London, gentleman [or, I, etc., solicitor for], the above-named judgment creditor, make oath and say as follows:

1. By a judgment of the court given in this action, and dated the 19th day of November, 1897, it was adjudged that I [or, the above-named judgment creditor] should recover against the above-named judgment debtor, William Morris Young [the sum of 64l. 10s. and] costs to be taxed, and the said costs were by a Master's certificate, dated the 3rd day of December, 1897, allowed at 33l. 14s. 4d.

2. The said judgment still remains unsatisfied to the extent of 46l., and interest amounting to 3s. 5d.

3. [I am informed and verily believe that] Robert Hurley, of 12, Moor Lane, in the City of London, bookbinder, is indebted to the judgment debtor, William

Morris Young, in the sum of 50l. or thereabouts [or, in a sum, the particulars whereof I have been unable to ascertain].

4. The said Robert Hurley is within the jurisdiction of this court (b).

SWORN, etc.

Filed on behalf of the judgment creditor.

(a) Where the plaintiff is the debtor (e.g., for costs) the affidavit will be entitled "Between (the *defendant*) judgment creditor, [or, creditor by order] and (the *plaintiff*) judgment debtor [or, debtor by order].

(b) In the case of partners "carry on business within the jurisdiction of this court."

No. CCXCVIII.

Garnishee Order Nisi.

(O. 45, r. 1 ; Y. S. C. P., and A. P., App. K., No. 39.)

1897. H. No. 897.

IN THE HIGH COURT OF JUSTICE,
 Queen's Bench Division.
Master , in Chambers.

BETWEEN Alfred Harris - - - judgment creditor,
      and
  William Morris Young - judgment debtor.
  Robert Hurley - - - garnishee.

UPON hearing the solicitor for the judgment creditor, and upon reading the affidavit of Alfred Harris, filed the 5th day of December, 1897,

IT IS ORDERED that all debts due, owing, or accruing due from the above-named garnishee to the above-named judgment debtor be attached to answer a judgment recovered against the said judgment debtor by the above-named judgment creditor in the High Court of Justice

on the 19th day of November, 1897, for the sum of
98*l*. 4*s*. 4*d*., on which judgment the [said] sum of 46*l*.
remains due and unpaid.

AND IT IS FURTHER ORDERED that the said garnishee
attend the Master in Chambers, Central Office, Royal
Courts of Justice, Strand, London, on Friday, the 16th
day of December, 1897, at 11 o'clock in the forenoon, on
an application by the said judgment creditor, that the
said garnishee pay the debt due from him to the said
judgment debtor, or so much thereof as may be sufficient
to satisfy the judgment.

DATED the 9th day of December, 1897.

No. CCXCIX.

Garnishee Order Absolute.

(O. 45 ; Y. S. C. P., and A. P., App. K., No. 40.)

[*Heading as in No. CCXCVIII.*]

UPON hearing the solicitors for the judgment creditor
and the garnishee, and upon reading the affidavit of
George Jenkins, filed the 14th day of December,
and the order *nisi* made herein, dated the 9th day
of December, 1897, whereby it was ordered that
all debts owing, or accruing due from the above-
named garnishee to the above-named judgment
debtor should be attached to answer a judgment
recovered against the said judgment debtor by the
above-named judgment creditor in the High Court of
Justice on the 19th day of November, 1897, for the
sum of 98*l*. 4*s*. 4*d*., on which judgment the [said]
sum of 46*l*. remained due and unpaid,

IT IS ORDERED that the said garnishee do forthwith pay
the said judgment creditor 50*l*., the debt due from him
to the said judgment debtor (or so much thereof as may
be sufficient to satisfy the judgment debt), and that in
default thereof execution may issue for the same [and

that the costs of this order be taxed and added to the judgment obtained by the said judgment creditor against the said judgment debtor.]

DATED the 16th day of December, 1897.

No. CCC.

Order for Issue between Judgment Creditor and Garnishee.

(O. 45, r. 4 ; Y. S. C. P., and A. P., App. K., No. 40A.)

[*Heading as in No. CCXCVIII.*]

UPON hearing the solicitors for the judgment creditor and the garnishee, and upon reading the affidavit of Robert Hurley, filed the 13th day of December, 1897, and the order *nisi* herein, dated the 9th day of December, 1897,

IT IS ORDERED that the judgment creditor and the garnishee proceed to the trial of an issue wherein the said judgment creditor shall be plaintiff and the said garnishee shall be defendant, and that the question to be tried shall be whether the garnishee was indebted to the judgment debtor in any and what amount at the time the said order *nisi* was served. AND IT IS FURTHER ORDERED that the issue be prepared and delivered by the plaintiff therein within ten days from this date, and be returned by the defendant therein within seven days, and be tried at Middlesex, and that the question of costs and all further questions be reserved until the trial of the said issue.

DATED the 16th day of December, 1897.

No. CCCI.
Issue between Judgment Creditor and Garnishee.
(O. 45, r. 4.)

IN THE HIGH COURT OF JUSTICE,
Queen's Bench Division.

BETWEEN Alfred Harris - - - plaintiff,
and
Robert Hurley - - - defendant.

ISSUE for trial pursuant to order of Master , dated the 16th day of December, 1897.

1. By a judgment, dated the 19th day of November, 1897, in an action in the Queen's Bench Division of the High Court of Justice, wherein the above-named plaintiff was plaintiff and one William Morris Young was defendant, it was adjudged that the above-named plaintiff should recover against the said William Morris Young the sum of 64l. 10s. and costs, which said costs were taxed and allowed at 33l. 14s. 4d.

2. On the 9th day of December, 1897, the said judgment remained unsatisfied to the extent of 46l. and interest amounting to 3s. 5d.

3. By order of Master , dated the 9th day of December, 1897, it was ordered that all debts due, owing or accruing due from the above-named defendant to the said William Morris Young should be attached to answer the said judgment, and that the above-named defendant should attend on an application by the above-named plaintiff that the above-named defendant should pay the debt due from him to the said William Morris Young, or so much thereof as should be sufficient to satisfy the said judgment.

4. On the hearing of the said application, by order of Master , dated the 16th day of December, 1897, it was ordered that the above-named plaintiff and the above-named defendant should proceed to the trial of an issue, and that the question to be tried should be whether the above-named defendant was indebted to the said William Morris Young in any and what amount at

the date when the said order, dated the 9th day of December, 1897, was served upon him.

5. The said order, dated the 9th day of December, 1897, was served upon the above-named defendant on the said 9th day of December, 1897.

6. The above-named plaintiff affirms and the above-named defendant denies that a sum of money was due from the said defendant to the said William Morris Young on the 9th day of December, 1897.

Therefore let the said question be tried.

Delivered the 11th day of January, 1898, by WILLIAM CROKER, of 3, New Inn, in the County of London, solicitor for the above-named plaintiff.

See also No. CCXI.

CHAPTER XXIII.

CHARGING ORDERS.

No. CCCII.

Affidavit on Application for Charging Order (a).

(O. 46, r. 1.)

[*Heading as in No. CCLIII.*]

I, HENRY ALFRED JONES, of Whittlesea Villa, Balham, in the County of Surrey, merchant, the above-named plaintiff, make oath and say as follows:

1. The defendant is justly and truly indebted to me in the sum of 142*l*. 13*s*. 6*d*., under a judgment recovered by me herein on the 7th day of May, 1896, whereby I recovered against him the said sum of 100*l*. and 42*l*. 13*s*. 6*d*. costs.

2. [I am informed and verily believe that] there are now standing in the defendant's name (b) in his own right 500 fully paid 1*l*. shares in a certain public company, called the General Industrial Trust Company, Limited, and [that] the defendant is entitled to the same for his own use and benefit.

SWORN, etc.

Filed on behalf of the plaintiff.

(a) See note to No. CCCIII.

(b) If the shares are held in trust for the defendant —"in the names of Alfred Richardson and William George Murchison, in trust for the defendant . . . is beneficially entitled to the dividends thereon for his own use and benefit."

No. CCCIII.

Charging Order Nisi (a).

(O. 46, r. 1 ; Y. S. C. P., and A. P., App. K., No. 27.)

[*Heading as in No. CI.*]

UPON hearing the solicitor for the plaintiff, and upon reading the affidavit of the plaintiff, filed the 14th day of June, 1896, whereby it appears that the plaintiff recovered a judgment against the defendant on the 7th day of May, 1896, for the sum of 100*l*. and 42*l*. 13*s*. 6*d*. costs, that the said defendant is still indebted to the plaintiff in the said sums so recovered, and that there are standing in the defendant's name in his own right 500 fully-paid 1*l*. shares in the General Industrial Trust Company, Limited :

IT IS ORDERED that unless sufficient cause be shown to the contrary before the Judge in chambers, Central Office, Royal Courts of Justice, Strand, London, on Tuesday, the 22nd day of June, 1896, at eleven o'clock in the forenoon, the defendant's interest in the said shares so standing as aforesaid shall, and that it in the meantime do, stand charged with the payment of the above-mentioned amounts due on the said judgment.

DATED the 15th day of June, 1896.

(*a*) This is obtained by *ex parte* application to a Master in chambers, on affidavit (see No. CCCII.). The charging order absolute is made by the Judge in chambers (O. 54, r. 12 (1)). For forms relating to charging partnership property, see Nos. CCCXLIV. and CCCXLV.

No. CCCIV.

Charging Order Absolute.

[*Heading as in No. CI.*]

UPON hearing the solicitors on both sides, and upon reading the affidavit of the plaintiff filed the 14th day of June, 1896 [and the affidavit of etc.], and an order *nisi* made herein on the 15th day of June, 1896, reciting the [said] affidavit of the plaintiff, whereby it appeared that the plaintiff recovered a judgment against the defendant on the 7th day of May, 1896, for the sum of 100*l*. and 42*l*. 13*s*. 6*d*. costs, that the said defendant is still indebted to the plaintiff in the said sums so recovered, and that there are standing in the defendant's name in his own right, five hundred fully paid 1*l*. shares in the General Industrial Trust Company, Limited:

IT IS ORDERED that the defendant's interest in the said shares so standing as aforesaid, stand charged with the payment of the above-mentioned amounts due on the said judgment.

DATED the 22nd day of June, 1896.

See note to CCCIII.

No. CCCV.

Affidavit as to Stock.

(O. 46, rr. 4, 5; Y. S. C. P., and A. P., App. B., No. 27.)

IN THE MATTER OF the will of John Simpson, bearing date the 16th day of May, 1890,
and
In the matter of the Act of Parliament, 5 Vict. c. 5.

I (*a*), HENRY MORSE JACKSON, of 12, Earl's Court Terrace, in the County of London, stockbroker, make oath and say that according to the best of my knowledge, information and belief, I am beneficially interested in the stock comprised in the will above-mentioned, which stock, according to the best of my knowledge and

NOTICE AS TO STOCK. 217

belief, now consists of the stock specified in the notice hereto annexed (b).

SWORN, etc.

This affidavit is filed on behalf of Henry Morse Jackson, whose address for service is at the office of Messrs. WILLIAMSON and BRADLEY, of 16, Parliament Street, Westminster, in the County of London.

(a) The affidavit may be made by the solicitor of the party claiming to be interested (O. 46, r. 4), in which case the above form must be varied accordingly.

(b) For form of notice, see No. CCCVI.

No. CCCVI.

Notice as to Stock.

(O. 46, r. 4 ; Y. S. C. P., and A. P., App. B., No. 22.)

To the Governor and Company of the Bank of England.

TAKE NOTICE that the stock comprised in and now subject to the trusts of the will referred to in the affidavit (a) to which this notice is annexed, consists of the following, that is to say :

The sum of 5,000l. 3l. per cent. consolidated annuities.

This notice is intended to stop the transfer of the stock only, and not the receipt of the dividends [or, the receipt of the dividends on the stock, as well as the transfer of the stock].

DATED the 17th day of May, 1898.

       HENRY MORSE JACKSON.

Witness (b) to the signature } HENRY A. Moss,
of Henry Morse Jackson, } of 16, Newgate Street, in the City of London, solicitor.

(a) See No. CCCV.

(b) The Bank of England require the witness to be a practising solicitor.

218   CHARGING ORDERS.

No. CCCVII.

Summons to Discharge Notice as to Stock.

(O. 46, r. 9.)

[*Heading as in No. CCCV., with the following addition.*]

and

In the matter of a notice filed on the 17th day of May, 1898, pursuant to Order XLVI., Rule 4, of the Rules of the Supreme Court.

LET all parties concerned attend the Master in chambers, Central Office, Royal Courts of Justice, Strand, London, on Wednesday, the 25th day of May, 1898, at 12 o'clock noon, on the hearing of an application on the part of Frederick Norham, for an order that the operation of the above-mentioned notice do cease.

DATED, etc. [*as usual*].

No. CCCVIII.

Request for Withdrawal of Notice as to Stock.

(O. 46, r. 9.)

[*Heading as in No. CCCVII.*]

To the Governor and Company of the Bank of England.

TAKE NOTICE that the above-mentioned notice is, and I hereby request that the same be, withdrawn.

DATED the 28th day of June, 1898.

WITNESS (a), etc. [*as in No. CCCVI.*].

HENRY MORSE JACKSON.

(*a*) The Bank of England require the witness to be a practising solicitor.

CHAPTER XXIV.

INTERPLEADER PROCEEDINGS.

No. CCCIX.

Affidavit by Applicant for Interpleader Order (a).

(O. 57, rr. 1, 2; Y. S. C. P., and A. P., App. B., No. 26.)

[*Heading as in writ.*] (b).

I, RICHARD MARNER, of 21, King's Road, Chelsea, in the County of London, grocer, the defendant in the above action, make oath and say as follows :

1. The writ of summons herein was issued on the 8th day of March, 1898, and was served on me on the 9th day of March, 1898.

2. The action is brought to recover certain goods and chattels. The said goods and chattels are in my possession, but I claim no interest therein.

3. The right to the said subject-matter of this action has been, and is claimed in the letter now produced and shown to me marked " A," by one Mary Burgess, who threatens to sue me for the recovery of the said goods and chattels.

4. I do not in any manner collude with the said Mary Burgess, or with the above-named plaintiff, but I am ready to [bring into court or to pay or] dispose of or

transfer the said goods and chattels in such manner as the court may order or direct.

Sworn, etc.

Filed on behalf of the defendant.

(*a*) Where the applicant is sheriff, an affidavit is not necessary, and unless he has been ordered to make it, he will not be allowed the costs of it.

(*b*) Where no action has already been commenced, the affidavit should be headed thus:

In the matter of the Rules of the Supreme Court, 1883,
and
In the matter of an application by A. B. for relief against a claim by C. D. and E. F. to certain goods and chattels in the possession of the said A. B.

The form of the affidavit will be varied accordingly, attention being directed to the requirements of O. 57, r. 2.

No. CCCX.

Interpleader Summons by Defendant.

(O. 57, r. 5.)

1898. S. No. 573.

IN THE HIGH COURT OF JUSTICE (*a*),
Queen's Bench Division.

BETWEEN George Stevens- - - plaintiff,
and
Richard Marner - - defendant,
and
Mary Burgess - - - claimant.

LET all parties concerned attend before the Master in Chambers, Central Office, Royal Courts of Justice, Strand, London, on Wednesday, the 13th day of March, 1898, at 11 o'clock in the forenoon, on the hearing of an application on the part of* the defendant, that the plaintiff and Mary Burgess, the above-named claimant, do appear and state the nature and particulars of their claims to the subject-matter of this action, and either maintain or relinquish such claims. And that the costs of the defendant of this application be taxed and paid out of the subject-matter of this action.

DATED, etc. [*as usual*].

(*a*) For the form of heading where no action has been commenced, see note (*b*) to form No. CCCIX.

No. CCCXI.
Interpleader Summons by Sheriff.
(O. 57, r. 5.)

[*As in No. CCCX. to**.]

the sheriff of Middlesex, that the above-named plaintiff and the above-named claimant do appear and state the nature and particulars of their claims to the goods and chattels seized by the above-named sheriff under the writ of *fieri facias* issued herein, and either maintain or relinquish the same, and abide by such order as may be made herein, and that in the meantime all further proceedings be stayed.

DATED, etc. [*as usual*].

No. CCCXII.
Interpleader Order (No. 1), Barring Claimant.
(O. 57; Y. S. C. P., and A. P., App. K., No. 50.)

1897. P. No. 1761.

IN THE HIGH COURT OF JUSTICE,
   Queen's Bench Division.
      Master   in Chambers.
      BETWEEN Walter Phillips - - plaintiff,
            and
            Henry George Jackson, - defendant.
   AND BETWEEN Morton Pound - - claimant,
            and
            Walter Phillips - - respondent.

UPON hearing the solicitors for the plaintiff, the claimant, and the sheriff of Middlesex, and upon reading the affidavit of, etc. [*as usual*],

IT IS ORDERED that the claimant be barred, and that no action be brought against the above-named sheriff of Middlesex, and that the costs of this application be paid by the claimant.

DATED the 3rd day of August, 1897.

No. CCCXIII.

Interpleader Order (No. 1a), that Sheriff Withdraw.

(O. 57; Y. S. C. P., and A. P., App. K., No. 50A.)

1897. P. No. 1761.

IN THE HIGH COURT OF JUSTICE,
Queen's Bench Division.
Master   , Master in Chambers.

BETWEEN Walter Phillips   -   - plaintiff,
and
Henry George Jackson   - defendant,
Morton Pound   -   - claimant.

UPON hearing the solicitors for the plaintiff, the claimant, and the sheriff of Middlesex, and reading the affidavit of, etc. [as usual],*

IT IS ORDERED that the sheriff withdraw from the possession of the goods seized by him under the writ of *fieri facias* herein and claimed by the claimant, that no action be brought.

AND THAT the plaintiff pay to the claimant the costs of the interpleader to be taxed, and possession money to the sheriff.

DATED, etc. [as usual].

No. CCCXIV.

Interpleader Order (No. 2), Substituting Claimant as Defendant.

(O. 57, r. 7; Y. S. C. P., and A. P., App. K., No. 51.)

[*Heading as in No. CCCXIII.*]

UPON hearing the solicitors for the plaintiff, the defendant, and the claimant, and upon reading the affidavit, etc. [as usual],

IT IS ORDERED that the above-named claimant be substituted as defendant in this action in lieu of the present defendant, and that the costs of this application be costs in the action.

DATED, etc. [as usual].

No. CCCXV.
Interpleader Order (No. 3), for Sale and Trial of Issue.
(O. 57, rr. 7, 12 ; Y. S. C. P., and A. P., App. K., No. 52.)

1897. P. No. 1761.

IN THE HIGH COURT OF JUSTICE,
Queen's Bench Division.
Master   , Master in Chambers.

BETWEEN Walter Phillips   -   -   plaintiff,
                        and
            Henry George Jackson   -   defendant.
AND BETWEEN Morton Pound   -   -   claimant,
            and the said
            Walter Phillips, execution
            creditor, and the sheriff
            of Middlesex   -   -   respondents.

UPON hearing the solicitors for the plaintiff, the claimant and the sheriff of Middlesex, and upon reading the affidavit of, etc. [*as usual*],*

IT IS ORDERED that the said sheriff proceed to sell the goods seized by him under the writ of *fieri facias* issued herein and claimed by the claimant, and pay the net proceeds of the sale, after deducting the expenses thereof, into court in this cause, to abide further order herein.

†AND IT IS FUTHER ORDERED that the parties proceed to the trial of an issue in the High Court of Justice, in which the said claimant shall be the plaintiff, and the said execution creditor shall be the defendant, and that the question to be tried shall be whether at the time of the seizure by the sheriff the said goods were the property of the claimant as against the execution creditor.

AND IT IS FURTHER ORDERED that this issue be prepared and delivered by the plaintiff therein within seven days from this date, and be returned by the defendant within four days, and be tried at Middlesex.

AND IT IS FUTHER ORDERED that the question of costs and all further questions be reserved until the trial of the said issue, and that no action shall be brought against the said sheriff for the seizure of the said goods.

DATED the 3rd day of August, 1897.

No. CCCXVI.

Interpleader Order (No. 4), for Payment into Court by Claimant and Trial of Issue. A.

(O. 57, r. 7; Y. S. C. P., and A. P., App. K., No. 53.)

[*As in No. CCCXV. to *.*]

It is ordered that upon payment of the sum of 50*l.* into Court by the said claimant within seven days from this date, or upon his giving within the same time security to the satisfaction of the Master for the payment of the same amount by the said claimant according to the directions of any order to be made herein, and upon payment to the above-named sheriff of the possession money from this date, the said sheriff do withdraw from the possession of the goods seized by him under the writ of *fieri facias* herein and claimed by the claimant.

And it is further ordered that unless such payment be made or security given within the time aforesaid, the said sheriff proceed to sell the said goods, and pay the proceeds of the sale, after deducting the expenses thereof and the possession money from this date, into Court in the cause to abide further order herein.

[*Continue and conclude as in No. CCCXV. from †.*]

No. CCCXVII.

Interpleader Order (No. 5), for Payment into Court by Claimant and Trial of Issue. B.

(O. 57, r. 7; Y. S. C. P., and A. P., App. K., No. 54.)

[*As in No. CCCXV. to *.*]

It is ordered that upon payment of the sum of 75*l.* into Court by the said claimant, or upon his giving security to the satisfaction of the Master for the payment of the same amount by the claimant according to the directions of any order to be made herein, the above-named sheriff withdraw from the possession of the goods seized by him under the writ of *fieri facias* issued herein.

AND IT IS FURTHER ORDERED that in the meantime, and until such payment made or security given, the sheriff continue in possession of the goods, and the claimant pay possession money for the time he so continues, unless the claimant desire the goods to be sold by the sheriff, in which case the sheriff is to sell them and pay the proceeds of the sale, after deducting the expenses thereof, and the possession money from this date, into court in the cause, to abide further order herein.

[*Continue and conclude as in No. CCCXV. from †.*]

No. CCCXVIII.

Interpleader Order (No. 6), on Summary Decision by Consent.

(O. 57, r. 8; Y. S. C. P., and A P., App. K., No. 55.)

[*Heading as in No. CCCXV.*]

THE CLAIMANT and the execution creditor having requested and consented that the merits of the claim made by the claimant be disposed of and determined in a summary manner, now upon hearing the solicitors for the claimant and the execution creditor and upon reading the affidavit of etc. [*as usual*],

IT IS ORDERED that the above-named sheriff withdraw from possession of the goods seized by him under the writ of *fieri facias* herein upon payment to him by the execution creditor of possession money to the date hereof, and that the claimant be at liberty to enter judgment for the recovery of the said goods [*or as the case may be*].

And that the costs of the claimant and of the sheriff of this application be paid by the execution creditor.

DATED the 2nd day of August, 1897.

No. CCCXIX.

Interpleader Order (No. 7), for Sale and Payment of Execution Creditor and Claimant.

(O. 57, r. 12 ; Y. S. C. P., and A. P., App. K., No. 56.)

[*As in No. CCCXV. to* *.]

IT IS ORDERED that the above-named sheriff proceed to sell enough of the goods seized under the writ of *fieri facias* issued in this action to satisfy the expenses of the said sale, the rent (if any) due, the claim of the claimant, and this execution.

AND IT IS FURTHER ORDERED that out of the proceeds of the said sale (after deducting the expenses thereof, and rent, if any) the said sheriff pay to the claimant the amount of his said claim, and to the execution creditor the amount of his execution, and the residue, if any, to the defendant.

AND IT IS FURTHER ORDERED that no action be brought against the said sheriff, and that the costs of this application be paid by the execution creditor.

DATED the 2nd day of August, 1897.

No. CCCXX.

Interpleader Order (No. 8), Remitting to County Court.

(O. 57 ; Y. S. C. P., and A. P., App. K., No. 56A.),

[*As in No. CCCXIII. to* *.]

IT IS ORDERED that upon payment of the sum of 60*l.*, and possession money from the date of this order to the said sheriff by the said claimant within seven days from this date the sheriff do withdraw from the possession of the goods seized by him under the writ of *fieri facias* herein, and claimed by the claimant.

AND IT IS FURTHER ORDERED that unless such payment be made within the time aforesaid, the said sheriff proceed to sell the said goods, and retain the proceeds of the said sale, after deducting the expenses thereof and the possession money from this date.

AND IT IS FURTHER ORDERED that the said sum of 60*l*., or the proceeds of the said sale (as the case may be), do abide the order of the judge of the county court to whom the interpleader proceedings herein are hereinafter ordered to be transferred.

AND IT IS FURTHER ORDERED that the interpleader proceedings herein be transferred to the County Court of Middlesex, holden at Brentford.

AND IT IS FURTHER ORDERED that the costs of this application be costs in the interpleader proceedings, and that no action be brought against the said sheriff for the seizure of the said goods.

DATED the 2nd day of August, 1897.

No. CCCXXI.
Notice to Sheriff of Claim by Claimant.
(O. 57, r. 16.)

1898. B. No. 861.

[IN THE HIGH COURT OF JUSTICE,
   Queen's Bench Division.

BETWEEN Alfred Beeston - - plaintiff,
               and
    Maurice Henry Parker - defendant.]

TAKE NOTICE that, by virtue of a Bill of Sale, dated the 16th day of September, 1897, and made between [the above-named] Maurice Henry Parker of the one part, and Philip Tanner of the other part, the said Philip Tanner claims the goods taken in execution by you [in this action] at No. 16, Broad Street, Kilburn, in the County of London.

DATED the 12th day of August, 1898.
               Moss and CROWTHER, 16, Old Jewry,
                 E.C., solicitors for the said Philip
                 Tanner.
To the Sheriff of Middlesex,
   and his officers.

No. CCCXXII.

Notice by Sheriff to Execution Creditor of Claim.

(O 57, rr. 1, 16; Y. S. C. P., and A. P., App. B., No. 28.)

[*Heading as in writ.*]

TAKE NOTICE that Philip Tanner has claimed the goods taken in execution by the sheriff of Middlesex, under the warrant of execution issued in this action, by virtue of a Bill of Sale, dated the 16th day of September, 1897. You are hereby required to admit or dispute the title of the said Philip Tanner to the said goods and give notice thereof in writing to the said sheriff, within four days from the receipt of this notice, failing which, the said sheriff may issue an interpleader summons. If you admit the title of the said Philip Tanner to the said goods and give notice thereof in manner aforesaid to the said sheriff, you will only be liable for any fees and expenses incurred prior to the receipt of the notice admitting the claim.

DATED the 13th day of August, 1897.
(Signed)
Sheriff of Middlesex.
To the plaintiff.

No. CCCXXIII.

Notice by Execution Creditor to Sheriff Admitting or Disputing Claim.

(O. 57, r. 16 ; Y. S. C. P., and A. P., App. B., No. 29.)

[*Heading as in writ.*]

TAKE NOTICE that I admit [*or*, dispute] the title of Philip Tanner to [certain of] the goods [namely, etc.] seized by you under the execution issued under the judgment in this action.

ROBERT P. WILLIAMS, of 18, Chancery Lane, W.C., solicitor for the plaintiff.
To the Sheriff of Middlesex,
and his officers.

CHAPTER XXV.

ORDERS AS TO PROPERTY. INJUNCTIONS. RECEIVERS.

No. CCCXXIV.
Application for Order for Preservation or Interim Custody of Property, etc.
(O. 50, rr. 1, 7.)

This must now be made, except in cases to which O. 30 does not apply, on application for further directions (see No. CXLVI). It will be in the following or some similar form:

THAT AN ORDER be made for the preservation or interim custody of the subject-matter of this action [*or*, that the jewellery, the subject-matter of this action, be lodged in court; *or*, that the amount in dispute in this action be brought into court; *or as the case may be*].

No. CCCXXV.
Application for Order for Sale of Perishable Goods.
(O. 50, rr. 2, 6.)

[*Formal parts as in No. C.*]

THAT the goods, the subject-matter of this action, being of a perishable nature, be sold in open market by the defendant, and that the proceeds of such sale be brought into court to abide the result of the action, and that the costs of this application be costs in the action.

In the case of perishable goods the application will generally be made at an early stage of the action, *i.e.*, before the summons for directions, in which case it will be made by ordinary summons. Otherwise it should be included in the summons for directions.

No. CCCXXVI.

Application for Inspection of Property.

(O. 57, rr. 3, 5, 6.)

This will be made, except in cases to which O. 30 does not apply, on the summons for directions (see No. CXLII.), or on application for further directions. It may be in some such form as the following :

Inspection of real or personal property. That the plaintiff be at liberty by himself or by his agents [or, by the jury before whom this action will be tried] to inspect the goods and chattels [or, property], the subject-matter of this action.

For a form of order for view by jury, see Yearly Supreme Court Practice, App. K., No. 26B, and the Annual Practice, App. K., No. 68.

No. CCCXXVII.

Order for Interim Injunction.

(O. 50, r. 6 ; Y. S. C. P., App. K., No. 26F, and A. P., App. K., No. 66.)

[*Heading as in writ.*]

UPON HEARING the solicitor for the plaintiff (*a*) and upon reading the affidavit (*b*) of George Pile, filed the 3rd day of April, 1896, and the plaintiff by his said solicitor undertaking to abide by any order the court or a judge may make as to damages in case the court or a judge should hereafter be of opinion that the defendant shall have sustained any by reason of this order which the plaintiff ought to pay :

IT IS ORDERED that the defendant, his agents and servants and every of them be restrained, and an injunction is hereby granted restraining them and every of them from entering upon the land described on the writ of summons herein until after the trial of this action or until further order, [*or*, until the 18th day of April, 1896, and that the plaintiff be at liberty to issue and serve a summons to extend this injunction,] and that the costs of this application be reserved.

DATED the 4th day of April, 1898.

(*a*) Applications for interim injunctions under the Judicature Act, 1873, s. 25, (8), may be made *ex parte*.
The application must be made to the Judge in Chambers, O. 54, r. 12 (h).
(*b*) The affidavit in support should show (1) the nature of the claim ; (2) the right alleged to be infringed ; (3) the infringement ; (4) the actual or anticipated damage.

No. CCCXXVIII.

Interum Order for Appointment of Receiver.

(O. 50, r. 6 ; Y. S. C. P., App. K., No. 26H, and A. P., App. K., No. 62.)

[*Heading as in writ.*]

UPON the application of the solicitor for the plaintiff, and the plaintiff by his said solicitor undertaking to be answerable for all sums to be received by the receiver hereinafter named,

IT IS ORDERED that James Bowden, of 51, Lombard Street, in the City of London, chartered accountant, be appointed without security to receive the rents and profits of the property the subject-matter of this action, but without prejudice to the rights of any prior incumbrancer or his possession (if any), and the tenants of the said estate are (without prejudice as aforesaid) to attorn and pay their rents in arrear and growing rents to the said James Bowden, so long as he shall continue to be such receiver, and that all questions as to passing his accounts and payments thereunder and all further questions be reserved until further order.

Defendant to be at liberty to apply in the meantime.

DATED the 15th day of November, 1897.

No. CCCXXIX.

Application for Delivery Up of Property where Lien is Claimed.

(O. 50, r. 8.)

This will be made, except in cases to which O. 30 does not apply, on application for further directions, in some such form as follows :

That the plaintiff be at liberty to pay into court the amount of money in respect of which the lien [*or*, security] mentioned in paragraph 6 of the defence herein is claimed and such further sum (if any) for interest and costs as the court may direct, and that upon such payment into court being made, the furniture, the subject-matter of this action, be given up to the plaintiff.

No. CCCXXX.

Application for Order for Private Sale.

(O. 43, rr. 8, 9.)

[*Formal parts as in No. C.*]

the plaintiff, the execution creditor herein, for an order that the sheriff of Lincolnshire, be at liberty to sell the goods and chattels seized by him under the writ of *fieri facias* herein by private contract, on the ground that on a sale by public auction in the district wherein the said goods and chattels are, the said goods and chattels would realise much less than their proper value.

No. CCCXXXI.

Order for Private Sale.

(O 43, r. 8; Y. S. C. P., App. K., No. 26D, and A.P., App. K., No. 69.)

[*Formal parts as in No. CI.*]

It is ordered that the sheriff of Lincolnshire be at liberty to sell the goods and chattels seized by him under the writ of *fieri facias* in this action by private contract.

CHAPTER XXVI.

APPEALS.

(See also Nos. XCIX., CCLVI., CCLVII., CCCLVIII.)

No. CCCXXXII.

Notice of Appeal from Master to Judge in Chambers.
(O. 54, r. 21.)

[*Heading as in writ.*]

TAKE NOTICE that the above-named plaintiff, [*or*, defendant] intends to appeal against the decision of Master   , given on the 15th day of March, 1898, ordering [*or*, refusing to order] that this action be remitted to the county court of Oxfordshire, holden at Banbury, and that the costs of the application be costs in the cause.

AND FURTHER TAKE NOTICE that you are required to attend before the Judge in Chambers, at the Central Office, Royal Courts of Justice, Strand, London, on Saturday, the 19th day of March, 1898 (*a*), at 11 o'clock in the forenoon, on the hearing of an application by the said plaintiff [*or*, defendant] that the said order may be set aside or varied by ordering that the action be remitted to the Bow County Court of Middlesex, and that the costs of this appeal and of the application to the Master may be paid by the defendant [*or*, plaintiff] to the plaintiff [*or*, defendant].

[And further take notice that it is the intention of the plaintiff [or, defendant] to attend by counsel.]

DATED the 16th day of March, 1898.
    BRADSHAW and FORBES,
      of 196, Strand, W.C., solicitors
      for the plaintiff [or, defendant].

To the defendant [or, plaintiff] and to
  MR. HERBERT READY,
    his solicitor.

See also No. XCIX.

(a) The appeal must be not only entered but heard within four days.

No. CCCXXXIII.

Notice of Appeal from Judge in Chambers.

(O. 54, r. 23 ; O. 58, rr. 3, 15.)

1898. A. No. 297.

IN THE COURT OF APPEAL.

BETWEEN Richard Austin - - plaintiff,
    and
  Martin Parker Hope - defendant.

TAKE NOTICE that this Honourable Court will be moved on Tuesday the 30th day of March, 1898, at 10.30 o'clock in the forenoon or so soon thereafter as counsel can be heard by [Mr. , of] counsel for the above-named defendant on his behalf, that the order of the Honourable Mr. Justice , made herein on the 19th day of March, 1898, whereby it was ordered that the order of Master , dated the 15th day of March, 1898, ordering that this action be remitted to the County Court of Oxfordshire, holden at Banbury, be set aside and that the action be remitted to the Bow County Court of Middlesex, be set aside, and that the order of Master be restored, and that the costs of this application and of the application to the judge be paid by the plaintiff to the defendant.

 DATED the 26th day of March, 1898.
   Yours, etc.,
    GEORGE H. WILKINSON,
     of 12, Craven Street, Strand,
     W.C., defendant's solicitor.
To Messrs. BURTON and DOWNES,
 plaintiff's solicitors.

As to the appeals which are to be made to the Court of Appeal, see Judicature Act, 1894, s. 1 (4) and notes. Where the appeal is to a divisional court, substitute " In the High Court of Justice, Queen's Bench Division " for " In the Court of Appeal " in the heading above.

As regards the time for appeals from the Judge in Chambers, the rules are as follows :

(1.) In appeals to the divisional court, the motion must be made within eight days, or, if no court be sitting within eight days, on the first day on which a court be sitting (O. 54, r. 24). There must be two clear days between the service of a notice of motion and the day named for the hearing (O. 52, r. 5).

(2.) In appeals to the Court of Appeal, the appeal must be brought (*i.e.*, the notice of appeal served) within fourteen days (O. 58, r. 15). The notice of appeal from an interlocutory order is a four days' notice (O. 58, r. 3).

No. CCCXXXIV.

Notice of Appeal from Judge in Court.

(O. 58, rr. 1, 3, 15.)

[*Heading as in No. CCCXXXIII.*]

TAKE NOTICE that this Honourable Court will be moved on Thursday, the 14th day of February, 1897, at 10.30 o'clock in the forenoon or so soon thereafter as counsel can be heard by [Mr. , of] counsel for the above-named plaintiff on his behalf* that the judgment of the Queen's Bench Division of the High Court of Justice herein dated the 18th day of December, 1896, whereby it was adjudged [*or*, so much of the judgment of . . . 1896, as adjudged] that the defendant should recover against the plaintiff 45*l.* and costs to be taxed, may be reversed, and that it may be adjudged that the plaintiff recover against the defendant 150*l.*, and that the costs of this appeal and in the court below may be paid by the defendant to the plaintiff.

DATED, etc. [*conclude as in* No. *CCCXXXIII.*]

For notices of motion to set aside judgment directed, see Nos. CCLVI, CCLVII.

No. CCCXXXV.

Memorandum of Entry of Appeal.

(O. 58, r. 8 ; Y. S. C. P., and A. P., App. G., No. 23.)

[*Heading as in writ.*]

ENTER this appeal from the judgment of Mr. Justice   in this action, dated the 18th day of December, 1896.

DATED the 31st day of January, 1897.

ARTHUR COLES, of 19 New Street, Bloomsbury, W. C., plaintiff's solicitor.

No. CCCXXXVI.

Notice of Cross-Appeal by Respondent.

(O 58, rr. 6, 7.)

[*Heading as in* No. *CCCXXXIV.*]

TAKE NOTICE that the above-named defendant intends at the hearing of the appeal from the Queen's Bench Division of the High Court of Justice, whereof notice of motion, dated the 31st day of January, 1897, has been served upon the defendant, to contend that the decision of the court below should be varied by, etc. [*according to circumstances.*]

DATED, etc. [*conclude as in* No. *CCCXXXIV.*]

No. CCCXXXVII.
Notice of Motion for Security for Costs.
(O. 58, r. 15.)

[*As in No. CCCXXXIV to* *.]

for an order that the plaintiff give security for the costs of the appeal herein from the judgment of the Queen's Bench Division of the High Court of Justice, dated the 18th day of December, 1896, and that until such security be given the said appeal be stayed, and that the costs of this application may abide the event of the said appeal.

DATED, etc. [*conclude as in No. CCCXXXIV.*]

No. CCCXXXVIII.
Notice of Motion for New Trial.
(O. 39.)

[*As in No. CCCXXXIV to* *.]

for an order that the judgment obtained in this action be set aside and a new trial had between the parties on the ground [s] that [*here insert such one or more of the following or other grounds as may be applicable*] the verdict was against the weight of evidence [and perverse] [*or*, the learned judge misdirected the jury in directing them that, etc. ; *or*, the evidence of, etc. as to, etc., was improperly admitted (*or*, rejected) ; *or*, the question whether, etc., was not left to the jury ; *or*, the damages are excessive] and that in the meantime all further proceedings be stayed.

DATED, etc. [*conclude as in No. CCCXXXIV.*]

As to the time for service of the notice of motion, and the length thereof, see O. 39, r. 4.

No. CCCXXXIX.
Notice of Motion on Appeal from County Court.
(O. 59, rr. 10, 12.)

IN THE HIGH COURT OF JUSTICE,
Queen's Bench Division.
On appeal for the County Court of Yorkshire, holden at Wakefield.

TAKE NOTICE that this court will be moved on Wednesday the 16th day of February, 1896, or so soon thereafter as counsel can be heard by [Mr.   , of] counsel for the above-named plaintiff on his behalf that the order of His Honour Judge   , made herein at the trial [before himself and a jury] on the 18th day of January, 1898, whereby he directed that judgment should be entered for the defendant with costs, may be set aside, and that in lieu thereof judgment may be entered for the plaintiff for the sum of 35*l*. and costs or a new trial had between the parties.

The following are the grounds of the appeal:
(1) That the learned Judge was wrong in law in holding, etc.
(2) That the evidence of, etc. was improperly admitted [*or*, rejected, *or as the case may be.*]

DATED the 7th day of February, 1898.

BETTS and WILKINSON,
solicitors for the above-named plaintiff.
To the defendant, and to
Mr. JNO. HUTCHINSON,
his solicitor.

The notice of motion is an eight days notice (O. 59, r. 10), and it must be served and the appeal entered within twenty-one days from the date of the judgment, etc., complained of (O. 59, r. 12).

CHAPTER XXVII.

PARTNERSHIP PROCEEDINGS.

See also the following forms :

No. LIV. - Entry of Appearance by Partners Sued in Firm Name.
No. LV. - Entry of Appearance under Protest by Person Served as Partner.
No. LXIX. - Affidavit of Service of Writ on Partner on behalf of Firm.
No. LXX. - Affidavit of Service or Writ upon Person in Control of Partnership Business.
No. LXXI. - Notice of Service upon Person in Control of Partnership Business.
No. LXXII. - Notice of Service on Partnership where Capacity of Party Served is Uncertain.
No. CCLXXV. Summons for Leave to Issue Execution (O. 48A, rr. 8, 10).

No. CCCXL.

Summons for Disclosure of Names of Partners.

(O. 48A, r. 1.)

[*Formal parts as in No. C.*]

the plaintiff for an order that the defendants do furnish the plaintiff with a statement in writing, verified by affidavit, of the names and addresses of the persons who were at the time of the accruing of the cause of action co-partners in the defendant firm.

See also O. 48A, r. 2; and Forms No. CCCXLII., and CCCXLIII.

No. CCCXLI.

Order for Disclosure of Names of Partners.

(O. 48A, r. 1 ; Y. S. C. P., and A. P., App. K., No. 11.)

[*Formal parts as in No. CI.*]

IT IS ORDERED that the defendants furnish the plaintiff with a statement in writing, verified by affidavit, setting forth the names and addresses of the persons who were at the time of the accruing of the cause of action co-partners in the defendant firm, and that the costs of this application be costs in the action.

No. CCCXLII.

Demand for Names of Plaintiff Firm.

(O. 48A, r. 2.)

[*Heading as in writ.*]

PURSUANT to Order 48A, Rule 2, of the Rules of the Supreme Court, we hereby demand on behalf of the above-named defendant [James Headlam] a statement in writing of the names and places of residence of all the persons constituting the plaintiff firm.

DATED the 23rd day of August, 1897.

       FRITH and GREENE,
  solicitors for the above-named defendant.
To Mr. WILLIAM WILLIAMSON,
  solicitor for the plaintiffs.

No. CCCXLIII.

Declaration of Names of Plaintiff Firm.

(O. 48A, r. 2.)

[*Heading as in writ.*]

PURSUANT to demand in writing, dated the 23rd day of August, 1897, we hereby declare the names and places of residences of all the persons constituting the plaintiff firm to be as follows:

Names.	Places of Residence.
Herbert John Buckland	12, Grove Road, Streatham, S.W.
George Wilkinson	Highstead, Oxford Road, Hornsey, N.W.
Harold Baker	31, North Road, Enfield.

WILLIAM WILLIAMSON,
solicitor for the plaintiffs.

To Messrs. FRITH and GREENE,
defendant's solicitors.

No. CCCXLIV.

Summons for Order to Charge Partnership Property.

(O. 46, r. 1A.)

[*Formal parts as in No. C.*]

the plaintiff, the execution creditor herein, for an order charging the interest of the defendant [Joseph Robinson] in the partnership property and profits of the firm of Bryant and Co. with payment of the amount of the judgment debt and costs and interest thereon [and for an order that Henry Morton, of 37, Cheapside, in the City of London, chartered accountant, may be appointed receiver of the defendant's share in the said profits, and for an order that all necessary accounts and enquiries may be taken and made as the circumstances of the case may require].

See the Partnership Act, 1890, s. 23 (2). The application is made to the Judge in chambers.

ORDER CHARGING PARTNERSHIP PROPERTY.

No. CCCXLV.

Order Charging Partnership Property.

(O. 46, r. 1A.)

[*Heading as in writ.*]

UPON hearing the solicitors for the plaintiff and defendant, and upon reading the affidavit of the plaintiff, filed the 19th day of November, 1898, whereby it appears that the plaintiff recovered a judgment against the defendant on the 26th day of October, 1898, for the sum of 187*l*. 10*s*., and 32*l*. 4*s*. 8*d*. costs, and that the said defendant is still indebted to the plaintiff in the said sums so recovered, and that the said defendant is a partner in the firm of Bryant and Co.,

IT IS ORDERED THAT the interest of the defendant in the partnership property and profits of the said firm of Bryant and Co. do stand charged with payment of the amount of the said sums so recovered and interest thereon [and that Henry Morton be appointed receiver of the share of the defendant in the said profits (whether already declared or accruing) and of any other money which may be coming to him in respect of the partnership, and that all necessary accounts and enquiries be taken and made as the circumstances of the case may require,] and that the costs of this application be paid by the defendant to the plaintiff.

DATED the 21st day of November, 1898.

# CHAPTER XXVIII.

ARBITRATIONS AND REFERENCES.

See also the following Forms :
No. CCLXVI.   Judgment after Trial before Referee.
No. CCLXVII.   „   „   of Questions of Account by Referee.

No. CCCXLVI.

Submission to Arbitration.

MEMORANDUM OF AGREEMENT made the 16th day of April, 1897, BETWEEN James Morgan Hobbs, of 16, Bryant Road, Limehouse, in the County of London, coal factor, of the one part, and Robert Burton, of 99, Eastcheap, in the City of London, contractor, of the other part, whereby it is agreed as follows :

1. The said James Morgan Hobbs and the said Robert Burton agree to submit all matters in dispute between them in respect of a contract made between them dated the 9th day of December, 1895, to the arbitration of Alfred John Barker, of 112, City Road, in the County of London, merchant [and George Hensman, of   , etc.] [*or*, to   , Esq., Official Referee].

2. The said Alfred John Barker [and George Hensman] shall have all the powers conferred on a single arbitrator [*or*, arbitrators] by the Arbitration Act, 1889.

3. The said Alfred John Barker [and George Hensman] may obtain such professional or other assistance as he [*or*, they] shall think fit.

4. The costs of the said arbitration and award shall follow the event of the said award.

5. This submission shall continue in force notwithstanding the death of either the said Alfred John Barker or the said George Hensman.

JAS. M. HOBBS.
ROBERT BURTON.

Witness, H. A. ASTBURY,
16, Budge Row, E.C.,
solicitor.

See Arbitration Act, 1889, ss. 1—12.

No. CCCXLVII.

Summons to Stay Proceedings where there is a Submission.

[*Formal parts as in No. C.*]

the defendant for an order that all further proceedings herein be stayed pursuant to section 4 of the Arbitration Act, 1889, and that the costs of this action and of this application be paid by the plaintiff to the defendant.

The defendant must show by his affidavit in support of this application that he " was, at the time when the proceedings were commenced, and still remains, ready and willing to do all things necessary to the proper conduct of the arbitration."

No. CCCXLVIII.

Notice to Appoint Arbitrator.

In the matter of an arbitration between James Helmsley and Alfred Norman Buxton,
and
In the matter of the Arbitration Act, 1889.

TAKE NOTICE that I have appointed Henry Burgess, of 116, Queen Victoria Street, in the City of London, electrical engineer, to act on my behalf pursuant to the terms of the submission herein, dated the 17th day of August, 1896.

AND FURTHER TAKE NOTICE that you are hereby required, within seven days of the service of this notice upon you, to appoint an arbitrator to act on your behalf pursuant to the terms of the said submission herein, and that in default of your so doing I shall appoint the said Henry Burgess to act as sole arbitrator.

JAMES HELMSLEY.

To ALFRED NORMAN BUXTON, Esq.

See Arbitration Act, 1889, s. 6.

No. CCCXLIX.

Summons for Appointment of Arbitrator.

[*Heading as in No. CCCXLVIII.*]

[*Other formal parts as in No. C.*]

James Hedley, that   , esquire, barrister-at-law, or some other fit and proper person, be appointed arbitrator herein.

See Arbitration Act, 1889, s. 5.

No. CCCL.

Summons for Leave to Enforce Award.

(O. 42, r. 31A ; O. 54, r. 4F.)

[*Heading as in No. CCCXLVIII.*]

[*Other formal parts as in No. C.*]

Alfred Norman Buxton for leave to enforce the award, dated the 29th day of November, 1896, in the above arbitration in the same manner as a judgment or order to the same effect.

See Arbitration Act, 1889, s. 12.

No. CCCLI.

Notice of Motion to Set Aside Award.

(O. 52, r. 4 ; O. 64, r. 12.)

IN THE HIGH COURT OF JUSTICE,
Queen's Bench Division.
In the matter of an arbitration between James Karslake
and The West Riding Colliery Company, Limited,
and
In the matter of the Arbitration Act, 1889.

TAKE NOTICE that this Honourable Court will be moved on Wednesday, the 13th day of July, 1893, at 10.30 o'clock in the forenoon, or so soon thereafter as counsel can be heard, by [Mr.   , of] counsel for the above-named James Karslake on his behalf for an order that the award of John Humphreys, civil engineer, to whom the matters in dispute between the said James Karslake and the West Riding Colliery Company, Limited, were, by a submission dated the 17th day of October, 1892, referred, be set aside on the following grounds :

(1.) That the arbitrator refused to allow the witness, James Smith, who gave evidence on the part of the West Riding Colliery Company, Limited, to be cross-examined.

(2.) That the arbitrator had an interest in the subject-matter in dispute.

DATED the 9th day of July, 1893.

PANTIN AND HOOD, of 12, Bishopsgate
Street Within, E.C., solicitors for
the above-named James Karslake.

To Messrs. GEORGE and BIRCH,
solicitors for the above-named
West Riding Colliery Company, Limited.

See Arbitration Act, 1889, ss. 11—13, 16.

No. CCCLII.

Order of Reference under S. 13 of Arbitration Act, 1889.

(Y. S. C. P., and A. P., App. K., No. 32.)

[*Formal parts as in No. CI.*]

IT IS ORDERED that the following question arising in this action, namely, whether or not the dilapidations to the premises, the subject-matter of this action, arose during the occupation of the defendant of the said premises, be referred for inquiry and report to an official referee [*or*, to Henry Arthur Smith, esquire, as special referee], under section 13 of the Arbitration Act, 1889, and that the costs of this application be costs in the action.

No. CCCLIII.

Order of Reference under S. 14 of Arbitration Act, 1889.

(Y. S. C. P., App. K., No. 33, and A. P., App. K., No. 33A.)

[*Formal parts as in No. CI.*]

IT IS ORDERED that the whole of this cause be tried before an official referee, who shall have all the powers of certifying and amending of a judge of the High Court of Justice, and shall direct judgment to be entered and otherwise deal with the whole action pursuant to Order XXXVI.

See also the Annual Practice, App. K., No. 33.

For form of Order of Reference to Master, see the Yearly Supreme Court Practice and the Annual Practice, App. K., No. 34.

No. CCCLIV.

Special Case by Referee or Arbitrator.

[*Heading as in writ, or as in No. CCCXLVIII., according to whether the reference is under order of the court, or by consent out of court.*]

Special Case.

The following special case is [under order of Master ———, dated the 13th day of April, 1897], stated for the opinion of the court pursuant to section 19 of the Arbitration Act, 1889:

1. [*Here set out the material facts, according to circumstances.*]

2.

3.

Etc., etc.

The question[s] for the opinion of the court is [*or*, are] :

1. Whether [or not], etc.

[2. Whether [or not], etc.]

DATED the 19th day of July, 1897.

CHAPTER XXIX.

PROCEEDINGS IN DISTRICT REGISTRIES.

See also : No. III. Writ of Summons, General Form, District Registry.
  No. IV. Writ of Summons, Specially Indorsed, District Registry.
  Y. S. C. P., and A. P., App. A., No. 7. Writ of Summons, District Registry for Service out of the Jurisdiction, General Form.
  Y. S. C. P., and A. P., App. A., No. 8. Writ of Summons, District Registry for Service out of the Jurisdiction, Specially Indorsed.
  Y. S. C. P., and A. P., App. A., No. 10. Notice of Writ from District Registry in lieu of Service to be Given out of the Jurisdiction.
  No. CCXLVIII. *Subpœna ad Testificandum*, Assizes.

No. CCCLV.

Title in District Registry Proceedings.

1898. S. No. 239.

IN THE HIGH COURT OF JUSTICE,
  Queen's Bench Division.
    Leeds District Registry.

BETWEEN Mary Anne Soames - plaintiff,
    and
  The Collotype Company,
    Limited - - - defendants.

No. CCCLVI.

Notice of Entry of Appearance in District Registry.

[*Heading as in No. CCCLV.*]

TAKE NOTICE that I, as [agent for, etc.] solicitor for the above-named George Jackson, have this day entered an appearance at the office of the Registrar of the Ipswich District Registry for the defendant, George Jackson, to the writ of summons in this action.

[*Continue as in No. LII.*]

No. CCCLVII.

Summons in District Registry.

(O. 35, r. 7.)

[*Heading as in No. CCCLV.*]

LET all parties concerned attend the District Registrar on Thursday, the 7th day of March, 1897, at the office of the Norwich District Registry, No. 12, Castle Meadow, Norwich, at 11 o'clock in the forenoon, on the hearing of an application on the part of [*conclude as in No. C.*]

No. CCCLVIII.

Notice of Appeal from District Registrar to Judge.

(O. 35, r. 9.)

[*Heading as in No. CCCLV.*]

[*Continue as in No. CCCXXXII., substituting for "Master   ," "Mr. Registrar   [one of] the District Registrar[s] of Leeds."*]

No. CCCLIX.
Notice of Removal from District Registry to London.
(O. 35, rr. 13, 14.)

[*Heading as in No. CCCLV.*]

TAKE NOTICE, that the above-named defendant [Charles Hammond] desires this action to be removed to London.

DATED the 8th day of February, 1898.

HARRIS and BARNABY,
solicitors for the above-named defendant [Charles Hammond].

To the District Registrar of Maidstone, and to the above-named plaintiff.

No. CCCLX.
Certificate of Non-Delivery of Defence.
(O. 35, r. 15.)

[*Heading as in No. CCCLV.*]

I HEREBY CERTIFY that the defence of the above-named defendant [Charles Hammond] herein has not been delivered, and that the time for delivery of the same has not expired.

DATED the 8th day of February, 1898.

HARRIS and BARNABY,
solicitors for the above-named defendant [Charles Hammond].

No. CCCLXI.
Summons to Remove Action to District Registry.
(O. 35, r. 17.)

[*Formal parts as in No. C.*]

the defendant, for an order that this action be removed to the District Registry of Bristol.

Sometimes the application will be made on the summons for directions (see No. CXLII.), or on application for further directions (see No. CXLVI). The form above may readily be adapted to meet either case.

No. CCCLXII.

Summons to Remove Action from District Registry.

(O. 35, r. 16.)

[*Formal parts as in No. CCCLVII.*]

the defendant, for an order that this action be removed to London.

See note to No. CCCLXI.

No. CCCLXIII.

Notice of Defendant's Address for Service in London.

(O. 35, r. 18.)

1897. T. No. 1079 (*a*).

IN THE HIGH COURT OF JUSTICE,
Queen's Bench Division.
BETWEEN James Philip Perkins   -   plaintiff,
and
Archibald Benson   -   -   defendant.

TAKE NOTICE that the address for service in London of the above-named defendant is at our offices, situate at No. 39, Fetter Lane, in the County of London.

DIXON and BERRY,
Agents for Hubert Jennings,
of 12, New Street, Worcester,
defendant's solicitors.

To the plaintiff, and to
Messrs. HART and JOHNSTONE,
his solicitors.

(*a*) After removal of an action to London, a fresh distinctive mark is given to it.

CHAPTER XXX.

MISCELLANEOUS FORMS.

No. CCCLXIV.

Affidavit of Registration of Bill of Sale.

(See Y. S. C. P., and A. P., App. B., No. 24.)

1897. W. No. 241.

IN THE HIGH COURT OF JUSTICE,
    Queen's Bench Division.

I, JOHN WILLIAM THOMPSON, of No. 12, Abchurch Lane, in the City of London, a solicitor of the Supreme Court, make oath and say as follows:

1. The paper writing hereto annexed, and marked "A," is a true copy of a bill of sale, and of every schedule or inventory thereto annexed or therein referred to, and of every attestation of the execution thereof, as made and given and executed by Stephen Wilson.

2. The said bill of sale was made and given by the said Stephen Wilson, on the 8th day of February, 1897.

3. I was present and saw the said Stephen Wilson duly execute the said bill of sale, on the said 8th day of February, 1897.

4. The said Stephen Wilson resides at 168, Walworth Road, in the County of London, and is a grocer.

5. The name "Jno. W. Thompson," subscribed to the said bill of sale as that of the witness attesting the due execution thereof, is in the proper handwriting of me this deponent.

AFFIDAVIT ON ENTRY OF SATISFACTION. 255

[6. I am a solicitor of the Supreme Court, and reside at 121, Blackheath Road, Lee, in the County of Kent.

7. Before the execution of the said bill of sale by the said Stephen Wilson, I fully explained to him the nature and effect thereof] (*a*).

SWORN, etc.

(*a*) Paragraphs 6 and 7 are only necessary in cases within the Bills of Sale Act, 1878, that is to say, where the bill of sale is given otherwise than as security for the payment of money.

No. CCCLXV.

Affidavit on Entry of Satisfaction on Bill of Sale.

(O 61, r. 26.)

[*Heading and commencement as in No. CCCLXIV.*]

1. On the 14th day of April, 1898, I was present and saw James Hobday, of 21, Cross Street Islington, in the County of London, bookseller, sign the consent hereunto annexed marked "A," to an order that a memorandum of satisfaction should be written upon the registered copy of a bill of sale dated the 8th day of February, 1897, and made between Stephen Wilson, of 168, Walworth Road, in the County of London, grocer, and the said James Hobday, the debt for which such bill of sale was made or given, having been satisfied or discharged.

2. The name signed to the said consent is in the proper handwriting of the said James Hobday, who is the same person as James Hobday mentioned in the said bill of sale.

3. The name "J. R. Turner" set and subscribed as witness to the signature of the said James Hobday, is in the proper handwriting of me this deponent.

4. I am a solicitor of the Supreme Court, and reside at Court Lodge, Enfield, in the County of Middlesex.

See also Yearly Supreme Court Practice, App. B., No. 24E.

No. CCCLXVI.

Summons for Entry of Satisfaction on Bill of Sale.

(O. 61, r. 27 ; Y. S. C. P., and A. P., App. K., No. 58.)

IN THE HIGH COURT OF JUSTICE.

IN the Matter of a Bill of Sale by Stephen Wilson to James Hobday, dated the 8th day of February 1897, and registered on the 11th day of February, 1897.

LET all parties concerned attend the Registrar of Bills of Sale at the Central Office, Royal Courts of Justice, London, on the 19th day of May, 1898, at 2 o'clock in the afternoon on the hearing of an application on the part of Stephen Wilson, that satisfaction be entered on the above-named bill of sale.

DATED, etc. [as usual].

For order for entry of satisfaction, see Yearly Supreme Court Practice, App. K., No. 59, and the Annual Practice, App. K., No. 58A.

No. CCCLXVII.

Affidavit on Renewal of Registration of Bill of Sale

[*Heading as in No. CCCLXIV.*]

I, JAMES PHILLIPS, of 12, South Avenue, Hampstead, in the County of London, a solicitor of the Supreme Court, do swear that a bill of sale bearing date the 8th day of February, 1897, and made between Stephen Wilson, of 168, Walworth Road, in the County of London, grocer, and James Hobday, of 21, Cross Street, Islington, in the County of London, bookseller, and [a copy of] which said bill of sale was registered on the 11th day of February, 1897, is still a subsisting security.

SWORN, etc.

See also Yearly Supreme Court Practice, App. B., No. 24A.

For form of order to register or re-register bill of sale, see Yearly Supreme Court Practice, App. K., No. 60, and the Annual Practice, App. K., No. 59.

No. CCCLXVIII.

Summons for Security for Costs.

(O. 65, r. 6; Y.' S. C. P., App. K., No. 9D.)

[*Formal parts as in No. C.*]

the defendant for an order that the plaintiff give security for the defendant's costs herein to the satisfaction of the Master, and that in the meantime all further proceedings be stayed.

For form of order, see Yearly Supreme Court Practice, App. K., No. 9E, and the Annual Practice, App K., No. 70.

No. CCCLXIX.

Summons to Review Taxation of Costs.

(O. 65, r. 27 (41).)

[*Formal parts as in No. C.*]

the defendant for an order that the taxation of costs herein by Master   be reviewed, and that the objections numbered 1, 3, 4, and 5, respectively, made by the defendant to the allowance [*or*, disallowance] of the several items specified in the said objections be allowed, and the said items disallowed [*or*, allowed], and that the costs of this application be paid by the plaintiff to the defendant.

This application is made to the Judge in Chambers (O. 54, r. 12 (k)).

No. CCCLXX.

Order for Arrest under Debtors Act.

(O. 69, r. 1; Y. S. C. P., and A. P., App. K., No. 31.)

[*Formal parts as in No. CI.*]

IT IS ORDERED that the defendant [Charles Frederick Hamilton] be arrested and imprisoned for the term of six weeks from the date of his arrest, including the day of such date, unless and until he shall sooner deposit in

C.F.   8

court the sum of 100*l*., or give to the plaintiff a bond executed by him and two sufficient sureties in the penalty of 100*l*., or some other security satisfactory to the plaintiff, that the defendant will not go out of England without the leave of the court.

AND IT IS FURTHER ORDERED, that the sheriff of Middlesex do within one calendar month from the date hereof, including the day of such date and not afterwards, take the defendant for the purpose aforesaid if he shall be found in the said sheriff's bailiwick.

This application must be made to the Judge in Chambers (O. 54, r. 12 (a)). The affidavit in support of the application, which is made *ex parte*, must be in accordance with s. 6 of the Debtors Act, 1869, as to which, see the notes to O. 69, r. 1, in the Yearly Supreme Court Practice and the Annual Practice.

No. CCCLXXI.

Summons to Set Aside Proceedings on the Ground of Irregularity.

(O. 70, rr. 1—3.)

[*Formal parts as in No. C.*]

the defendant for an order that the writ of summons herein may be set aside for irregularity, on the ground that separate causes of action by the plaintiffs have been improperly joined.

Applications to set aside irregularities, occurring after the summons for directions under O. 30, will be made on application for further directions (see No. CXLVI.).

TABLE OF STAMPS.

See also the tables of Court Fees and Stamps in the Yearly Supreme Court Practice, and in the Annual Practice, Vol. II., Part II.

Imp. = Impressed.   Adh. = Adhesive.

Summonses, Writs, Notices, Commissions and Warrants.

		s.	d.	
On sealing writ of summons		10	0	Imp.
Ditto	concurrent, renewed, or amended writ of summons	2	6	Imp.
Ditto	third party notice (O. 16, r. 48)	2	6	Imp. or Adh.
Ditto	writ of mandamus	20	0	Imp.
Ditto	writ of subpœna for not exceeding three witnesses	5	0	Imp.
Ditto	writ of execution and all other writs	5	0	Imp.
Ditto	any originating summons	10	0	Imp.
On amending any originating summons		5	0	Adh.
On sealing or issuing summons for directions under O. 30		10	0	Imp. or Adh.
On sealing or issuing any other summons		3	0	Imp. or Adh.
On sealing or issuing taxing master's warrant		3	0	Imp. or Adh.
On sealing or issuing commission		20	0	Imp.

Appearances.

	s.	d.	
On entering an appearance, for each person	2	0	Imp.
On amending same	2	0	Imp.

Filing.

	s.	d.	
On filing special case or petition of right	20	0	Imp.
Ditto affidavit, deposition, or set of depositions, including exhibits	2	6	Imp. or Adh.
Ditto statement of claim in default of appearance	2	6	Imp. or Adh.
Ditto referee's certificate	2	6	Imp. or Adh.
Ditto submission to arbitration, or award	2	6	Imp. or Adh.
Ditto writ of execution with return	2	6	Imp. or Adh.
On depositing documents for safe custody, if not more than five	5	0	Adh.
On depositing documents for safe custody, if more than five	10	0	Adh.
On receipt for such documents, when delivered out	2	6	Adh.
On filing affidavit and notice as to stock (O. 46, r. 4)	10	0	Imp.
On filing bill of sale and affidavit, not exceeding 100*l*.	5	0	Imp.
On filing bill of sale and affidavit, exceeding 100*l*., and not exceeding 200*l*.	10	0	Imp.

On filing bill of sale and affidavit,   s.   d.
above 200l.   -   -   -   -   20   0   Imp,

On filing any other document under
the Bills of Sale Acts   -   10   0   Imp.

Ditto   affidavit of re-registration
of Bill of Sale   -   -   10   0   Imp.

Ditto   fiat of satisfaction   -   -   5   0   Imp.

Certificates.

On certificate of appearance, or of
pleading, affidavit, or proceeding,
entered, filed, or taken   -   -   2   6   Imp. or Adh.

On certificate of appearance, or of
pleading, affidavit, or proceeding,
entered, filed, or taken for use in
foreign country -   -   .   -   5   0   Imp. or Adh.

On certificate of proceedings under
O. 61, r. 24   -   -   -   -   5   0   Imp. or Adh.

On certificate of Taxing Master or
District Registrar of result of
proceeding or taxation of costs
before him   -   -   -   -   10   0   Imp.

Searches and Inspections.

Appearance or Affidavit   -   -   1   0   Imp.

Index, pleading, judgment, decree,
order, or other record, for each
hour or part of an hour occupied -   2   6   Imp.

Not exceeding on one day   -   -   10   0   Imp.

Examination of Witnesses.

On memorandum of appointment
before examiner of court   -   -   5   0   Adh.

262   TABLE OF STAMPS.

	s.	d.	
On every witness examined at examiner's office, per hour - -	10	0	Adh.
On examination of witnesses away from office, per day - - -	60	0	Adh.

Hearing.

On entering and setting down action (in London or at assizes), appeal, or special case - -	40	0	Imp. or Adh. at Associate's offices; otherwise Imp.
On entering and certifying directions of judge at trial (O. 36, rr. 41, 42) - - - - -	20	0	Imp. or Adh.

Judgments, Decrees, and Orders.

On drawing up and entering judgments, etc., if made in court (including Court of Appeal) after hearing - - - - -	20	0	Imp.
On drawing up and entering judgments, etc., if without hearing in court - - - - -	10	0	Imp.
On drawing up and entering judgments, etc., under O. 15; O. 32, r. 6; O. 33, r. 2 - - -	10	0	Imp.
On drawing up and entering any other order - - - -	5	0	Imp.
On signing note or memorandum of order not drawn up (O. 52, r. 14) - - - - -	3	0	Imp. or Adh.

References and Inquiries.

	s.	d.	
On reference or inquiry before Master or District Registrar, per hour - - - - - -	10	0	Imp. or Adh.
On reference before Official Referee, per hour - - - - -	10	0	Imp. or Adh.
On reference before Official Referee, elsewhere than in London or Middlesex, further, per night	31	6	Imp. or Adh.
On reference before Official Referee, elsewhere than in London or Middlesex, for his clerk - -	15	0	Imp. or Adh.

Taxation of Costs.

	s.	d.	
On taxing bill of costs where amount allowed does not exceed 4*l*. - - - - - -	2	0	Imp. or Adh.
On taxing bill of costs over 4*l*., for every 2*l*. or part thereof allowed-	1	0	Imp. or Adh.
On certificate of result - - -	10	0	Imp.

Pay Office Proceedings.

	s.	d.	
On certificate of amount, etc., of money, funds, or securities, including request - - - -	1	0	Imp.
On transcript of account for each opening, including request - -	2	0	Imp.
On request for paying, lodging, transferring, or depositing money, etc., in court without an order; for paying out without order or certificate - - - - -	1	0	Imp.

	s.	d.	
On request for information in writing as to money, etc., in court-	1	0	Imp. or Adh.
On request for information in writing as to money, etc., not dealt with for 15 years	2	6	Imp. or Adh.
On affidavit under 10 & 11 Vict. c. 96	1	0	Imp.
On preparing power of attorney	3	0	Imp.

Miscellaneous.

	s.	d.	
On a commitment-	5	0	Imp.
On an application to produce judge's notes-	5	0	Imp.

INDEX.

ABATEMENT,
certificate of, 88.

ABROAD,
order for appointment of special examiner to take evidence, 169.

ACCEPTANCE
of money paid into court, notice of, 133.
judgment for costs after, 134.

ACCOUNT,
judgment after trial of questions of, by referee, 187.

ACCOUNT STATED,
special indorsement for, 14, 17.

ADD DEFENDANT,
order to, 75.
summons to, 74.

ADDED PLAINTIFF OR NEXT FRIEND,
consent of, 77.

ADDRESS
for service in London, notice of defendant's, 253.

[1]

INDEX.

ADMINISTRATOR,
claim by or against, 6.

ADMISSION,
affidavit of signature of, 139.
of facts pursuant to notice, 138.
voluntary notice of, 135.

ADMIT
documents, notice to, 136.
facts, notice to, 137.

ADMITTING CLAIM,
notice by execution creditor to sheriff, 228.

AFFIDAVIT,
agreement to take evidence by, 157.
for leave to appear by party not named as defendant, 50.
   entry of appearance as guardian, 79.
in answer to interrogatories, with objections, 125.
on application for appointment of guardian, 78.
         order to carry on proceedings, 86.
         charging order, 214.
of default of defence, 121.
on application to deliver further defence, 115.
by one deponent, 176.
by two or more deponents, 177.
as to documents, 126.
on application to inspect documents, 130.
   entry of satisfaction of bill of sale, 255.
   application to sue *in formâ pauperis*, 80.
         for garnishee order, 208.
by applicant for interpleader order, 219.
under Order XIV., plaintiff's, 65
         defendant's, 66.
application for leave to prove particular facts by, 157.

INDEX.

AFFIDAVIT.—*continued.*
   on registration of bill of sale, 254.
   renewal of registration of bill of sale, 256.
   application for renewal of writ, 42.
   of service of notice of motion, 121.
               of writ, 58.
               to produce, 140.
            subpœna, 174.
            summons and affidavit under Order XIV., 66.
            writ, personal, 53.
                  substituted, 54.
                  on company, 54.
                     partner on behalf of firm, 55.
                     person in control of partnership, 56.
   of signature of admissions, 139.
   as to stock, 216.
   for order for substituted service, 40.
   on application to issue third party notice, 81.
   of verification of copies of business books, 131.
   for leave to issue writ for service out of the jurisdiction, 36.

AGREEMENT
   as to result of special case, 144.
   to take evidence by affidavit, 157.

AMEND PLEADING,
   order to, 110.
   summons to, 110.

AMENDMENT
   summons to disallow, 111.

ANSWERS
   to interrogatories, 125.
      application for further, 126.

[3]

INDEX.

APPEAL,

cross, notice of, 237.
from county court, notice of motion on, 239.
    district registrar to judge, notice of, 251.
    judge in chambers, notice of, 235.
        court, notice of, 236.
    master to judge, notice of, 234.
        under Order XIV., 72.
memorandum of entry of, 237.

APPEARANCE,

entry of, 45.
    by defendant incompletely described on writ, 46.
        guardian, affidavit for, 79.
        landlord named in writ, 49.
        partners sued in firm name, 47.
        party not named as defendant, by leave, 51.
            affidavit for, 50.
            order for, 51.
        party served with order to continue action, 52.
        person served as partner under protest, 47.
        third party, 47.
        third person to counterclaim, 48.
    limiting defence, 49.
judgment in default of, 58, 59.
    against married woman, 63.
    final, after assessment of damages, 61.
    interlocutory, 59.
    recovery of land, 62.
notice of, 46.
    by party not named as defendant, 52.
    in district registry, 251.

APPLICATION. *See* VARIOUS TITLES.

APPOINT

arbitrator, notice to, 245.

APPOINTMENT

of arbitrator, summons for, 246.
    guardian, affidavit on application for, 78.
        notice of application for, 77.
    receiver, interim order for, 231.
    special examiners to take evidence abroad, order for, 169.

ARBITRATION,

submission to, 244.
    summons to stay proceedings where there is, 245.

ARBITRATION ACT

reference under, 248.

ARBITRATOR,

notice to appoint, 245.
special case by, 249.
summons for appointment of, 246.

ARREST,

order for, under Debtors Act, 257.

ASSAULT,

general indorsement for, 8.

ASSESSMENT

of damages. *See* DAMAGES.

ATTACHMENT,

writ of, 205.
    notice of motion for leave to issue, 203.
    order for leave to issue, 204.
    præcipe for, 205.
    summons for leave to issue, 204.

ATTORNEY,
judgment on warrant of, 189.

AUTHORITY
of plaintiff for payment out of court, 133.
to solicitor to use name of next friend, 77.

AWARD,
notice of motion to set aside, 247.
summons for leave to enforce, 246.

B.

BANKERS' BOOKS. *See* BOOKS.

BANKRUPT,
description of, on writ, 5.

BILL OF COSTS,
order under Order XIV. in action on, 70.
special indorsement for, 33.

BILL OF EXCHANGE,
foreign, special indorsement for, 25, 26.
inland,   „   „   21 –24.

BILL OF SALE,
affidavit on registration of, 254.
        renewal of registration of, 256.
        entry of satisfaction of, 255.
summons for,   „   „   256.

BOOKS,
bankers', application for inspection of, 170.
business, affidavit of verification of copies of, 131

INDEX.

BUILDING CONTRACT,
  special indorsement for, 14.

BUSINESS BOOKS. *See* BOOKS.

C.

CARRRIAGE
  of goods by railway, special indorsement for, 15.
    sea, special indorsement for, 16.

CARRY ON PROCEEDINGS. *See* PROCEEDINGS.

CASE,
  special. *See* SPECIAL CASE.

CERTIFICATE OF
  abatement, 88.
  change of interest, 89.
  non-delivery of defence, 252.

CHANGE OF
  interest, certificate of, 89.
  venue, application for, 152.

CHARGING ORDER,
  absolute, 216.
  affidavit on application for, 214.
  nisi, 215.
  on partnership property, 243.
    summons for, 242.

CHEQUE,
  special indorsement for, 26, 27.

INDEX.

CLAIM,

    judgment for part of, 120.
    notice of, by claimant to sheriff, 227.
                   sheriff to execution creditor, 228.
    statement of. *See* STATEMENT OF CLAIM.

COMMERCIAL LIST,

    order for directions, 102.
    summons for directions, 101.

COMMISSION,

    application for, 159.
    general indorsement for, 7.
    order for letter of request for, 166.
        long, 161,
        short, 160.
    request for, 167.
                 undertaking by solicitors as to costs of, 168.
    special indorsement for, 15, 32.
    writ of, 164.

COMPANY,

    affidavit of service of writ on, 54.
    allotment money and calls upon shares, special indorsement
        for, 15.
    description of, on writ, 5.

CONDITIONAL

    order under Order XIV., final judgment on, 184.

CONFESSION

    of defence, 116.
        judgment for costs after, 116.

CONSENT

    for withdrawal of action after entry for trial, 150.
    judgment by, 190.

CONSENT.—*continued.*
of defendant to order, 190.
added plaintiff or next friend, 77.
guardian, 80.
order by, for judgment, 189.
special case by, 142.
to countermand notice of trial, 154.

CONSOLIDATE,
order refusing to, 93.
to, 92.
summons to, 91, 92.

CONSOLIDATED
actions, heading or title of, 93.

CONTRACT,
breach of, general indorsement for, 8.

COPIES
of business books, affidavit of verification of, 131.

CORPORATION,
application to deliver interrogatories to, 124.
description of, on writ, 5.

COSTS,
bill of, order under Order XIV. in action on, 70.
special indorsement for, 33.
judgment for, after acceptance of money paid into court, 134.
confession of defence, 116.
defendant's, on discontinuance after notice, 149.
by order, 150.
of request for commission, undertaking by solicitors as to, 168.
security for, notice of motion for, 238.
summons for, 257.

COSTS.—*continued.*
    taxation of, summons to review, 257.
    writ of *fi. fa.* for, 195.

COUNCIL,
    county or parish, description of, on writ, 5.

COUNTERCLAIM, 105.
    entry of appearance by third person to, 48.
    notice of, to person not a party, 114.
    summons to disallow, 111.

COUNTERMAND,
    notice of trial, application for leave to, 155.
    consent to, 154.

COUNTERMANDING,
    notice of trial, notice, 155.

COUNTY COUNCIL,
    description of on writ, 5.

COUNTY COURT,
    appeal from, notice of motion on, 239.
    interpleader order remitting action to, 226.
    order under Order XIV. remitting action to, 71.

COURT,
    payment into. *See* PAYMENT INTO COURT.

CREDITOR,
    execution. *See* EXECUTION CREDITOR.
    judgment. *See* JUDGMENT CREDITOR.

CROSS-APPEAL,
    notice of, 237.

INDEX.

CUSTODY,
interim, of property, application for order for, 229.

D.

DAMAGES,
general indorsement for, 7.
final judgment in default of appearance after assessment of, 61.
judgment in court for amount to be ascertained, 186.
notice of evidence in mitigation of, 175.
writ of inquiry for assessment of, 60.

DEBTOR,
judgment, order for examination of, 207.
    summons „ „ 206.
              touching means, 207.

DEBTORS ACT,
order for arrest under, 257.

DECLARATION
of names of firm, 242.

DEFAULT,
judgment by, against third party, 84.
 summons to set aside, 122.
of appearance, judgment in, 58, 59.
 against married woman, 63.
 final, after assessment of damages, 61.
 interlocutory, 59.
 recovery of land, 62.
of defence, affidavit of, 121.
 judgment in, 118, 119.
  notice of motion for, 120.
  recovery of land, 119.
of notice of trial, application by defendant to dismiss in, 154.

INDEX.

DEFENCE, 105.
   application for leave to withdraw, 149.
      payment into court after, 132.
   certificate of non-delivery of, 252.
   confession of, 116.
      judgment for costs after, 116.
   default of, affidavit of, 121.
      judgment in, 118, 119.
         notion of motion for, 120.
         recovery of land, 119.
   entry of appearance limiting, 49.
   notice limiting, 50.
   notice of special, 97.
   summons to deliver further, 115.
      affidavit in support of, 115.

DEFENDANT,
   order to add, 75.
   summons to add, 74.
   party not named as, affidavit by, for leave to appear, 50.
      entry of appearance by, 51.
      notice of appearance by, 52.
      order for appearance by, 51.

DELIVERY,
   writ of, 201.
      præcipe for, 201.

DELIVERY UP,
   of property where lien claimed, application for, 232.

DEMAND,
   for names of firm, 241.

DEPONENT
   affidavit by one, 176.
      two or more, 177.

INDEX.

DEPOSIT,
> return of, special indorsement for, 20.

DESCRIPTION
> of parties on writ, 4.

DETENTION,
> general indorsement for, 8.

DIRECTIONS,
> notice of application for further, 103.
> order for, 100.
>> as to third party, 86.
>> commercial list, 102.
>> further, 104.
>> under Order XIV. with, 71.
> summons for, 99.
>> as to third party, 85.
>> commercial list, 101.

DISALLOW,
> amendment, summons to, 111.
> counterclaim, summons to, 111.

DISCHARGE,
> notice as to stock, summons to, 218.

DISCLOSURE,
> of names of partners, order for, 241.
>> summons for, 240.

DISCONTINUANCE,
> judgment for defendant's costs on, after notice, 149.
> notice of, 147.

INDEX.

DISCONTINUE,

application by plaintiff for leave to, 148.
order giving plaintiff leave to, 148.

DISCOVERY,

of documents, application for, 126.

DISMISS,

application by defendant to, in default of notice of trial, 154.
for want of prosecution, order to, 117.
    summons to, 117.
notice of motion to, 113.

DISMISSAL,

judgment of, for want of prosecution, 118.
    on non-appearance of plaintiff, 187.
    pursuant to order, 114.
wrongful, general indorsement for, 8.

DISPUTING CLAIM,

notice by execution creditor to sheriff, 228.

DISTRICT REGISTRAR,

notice of appeal to judge from, 251.

DISTRICT REGISTRY,

notice of entry of appearance in, 251.
    removal from, 252.
summons in, 251.
    to remove action from, 253.
        to, 252.
title in proceedings in, 250.
writ of summons, general form, 3.
    specially indorsed, 4.
    for service out of the jurisdiction, 36.
        notice in lieu of, 39.

DISTRINGAS,
   writ of, 191.
   præcipe for, 191.

DISUNITE,
   causes of action, summons to, 90.

DOCUMENTS,
   admit, notice to, 136.
   affidavit as to, 126.
   discovery of, application for, 126.
   inspect, notice to, 129.
   not mentioned in pleadings, application to inspect, 130.
      affidavit in support of, 130.
   produce, notice to, 139.
         for inspection, notice to, 128.

E.

EJECTMENT,
   general indorsement for, 8.
   special indorsement for, 29.

ELEGIT,
   writ of, 191.
   præcipe for, 191.

ENFORCE
   award, summons for leave to, 246.

ENTRY
   for trial. *See* TRIAL.
   of appeal, memorandum of, 237.
      appearance. *See* APPEARANCE.
      satisfaction. *See* SATISFACTION.
      special case, memorandum of, 144.

EVIDENCE

abroad, order for appointment of special examiner to take, 169.
agreement to take, by affidavit, 157.
in mitigation of damages, notice of, 175.
taken in another cause, notice of intention to read, 158.

EXAMINATION OF

judgment debtor, summons for, 206.
    order for, 207.
    touching means, 207.
witness before examiner, application for, 158.
    order for, 159.

EXAMINER,

application for examination of witness before, 158.
order for examination of witness before, 159.
special, order for appointment of, to take evidence abroad, 169.

EXCLUDE

cause of action, summons to, 90.

EXECUTION

creditor, notice by sheriff of claim to, 228.
    to sheriff, admitting or disputing claim, 228.
leave to issue, summons for, 191.
stay of, application for, 200.

EXECUTOR,

claim by or against, 6.
writ of *fi. fa.* by, 199.

F.

FACT,

issue of, 145.
  application for trial of, 146.

INDEX.

FACTS,

admission of, pursuant to notice, 138.
voluntary notice of, 135.
application for leave to prove, by affidavit, 157.
notice to admit, 137.

FIERI FACIAS,

de bonis ecclesiasticis, writ of, 191.
præcipe for, 191.
præcipe for writ of, 192.
writ of, 193.
    against married woman, 194.
    and possession, 197.
    by executors, 199.
    for costs, 195.
    notice of renewal of, 200.

FINAL JUDGMENT

in default of appearance after assessment of damages, 61.
under Order XIV., 182.
    against married woman, 183.
    on conditional order, 184.
    summons for, 64.

FIRM,

declaration of names of, 242.
demand for names of, 241.
description of, on writ, 5.
entry of appearance by, 47.
See also PARTNERS; PARTNERSHIP.

FOREIGN

bill of exchange, special indorsement for, 25, 26.
judgment, special indorsement for, 19.

FORMA PAUPERIS,

affidavit on application for leave to sue in, 80.

INDEX.

FRAUDULENT MISREPRESENTATION,
general indorsement for, 8.

FREIGHT,
special indorsement for, 16.

FRIENDLY SOCIETY,
description of, on writ, 6.

FURTHER
answer to interrogatories, application for, 126.
defence, summons to deliver, 115.
      affidavit in support of, 115.

FURTHER DIRECTIONS,
notice of application for, 103.
order for, 104.

G.

GARNISHEE,
issue between judgment creditor and, 212.
order for, 211.
order, absolute, 210.
  affidavit on application for, 208.
nisi, 209.

GENERAL INDORSEMENT, 6.
assault, etc., 8.
goods sold and carriage, 7.
contract, 8.
damages and other claims, 7.
detention, 8.
dismissal, wrongful, 8.
ejectment, 8.
fraudulent misrepresentation, 8.

INDEX.

GENERAL INDORSEMENT—*continued.*
    libel and injunction, 8.
    money claims, 6.
        obtained by fraud or lent, 7.
    negligence, 8, 9.
    repairs, 9.
    salary and commission, 7.
    trespass and injunction, 9.
    work done and money paid, 7.

GOODS,
    sold and carriage, general indorsement for, 7.
    delivered, special indorsement for, 17.
    perishable, application for order for sale of, 229.

GOVERNMENT
    department, description of, on writ, 6.

GUARANTEE,
    special indorsement for, 18.

GUARDIAN,
    appointment of, affidavit on application for, 78.
    notice of application for, 77.
    entry of appearance as, affidavit for, 79.
    of infant, consent of, 80.

H.

HABEAS CORPUS,
    ad testificandum, writ of, 173.

HIRE
    of furniture, special indorsement for, 18.

HUSBAND AND WIFE,
    description of, on writ, 5.

INDEX.

I.

INDORSED,
 memorandum to be, on judgment, etc., where act ordered to be done, 189.
 specially, writ of summons, 3.
  district registry, 4.

INDORSEMENT,
 general. *See* GENERAL INDORSEMENT.
 for trial without pleadings, 95, 96.
 of representative character of parties, 6.
 special. *See* SPECIAL INDORSEMENT.

INFANT,
 description of, on writ, 5.
 guardian of, consent of, 80.
  affidavit for entry of appearance as, 79.
   on application for appointment of, 78.
  notice of application for appointment of, 77.

INJUNCTION,
 general indorsement for, 8, 9.
 interim, order for, 230.

INLAND,
 bill of exchange, special indorsement for, 21—24.

INQUIRY,
 writ of, for assessment of damages, 60.
  præcipe for, 60.

INSPECT
 documents, notice to, 129.
  not mentioned in pleadings, application to, 130.
  affidavit on, 130.

[20]

INDEX.

INSPECTION,
  notice to produce documents for, 128.
  of bankers' books, application for, 170.
  property, application for, 230.

INTENTION
  to read evidence in another cause, notice of, 158.

INTEREST,
  certificate of change of, 89.
  when claimable on special indorsement, 12.

INTERIM,
  custody of property, application for order for, 229.
  injunction, order for, 230.
  order for appointment of receiver, 231.

INTERLOCUTORY JUDGMENT
  in court, 186.
  default of appearance, 59.

INTERPLEADER
  order, affidavit by applicant for, 219.
  orders, various, 221—226.
  summons by defendant, 220.
      sheriff, 221.

INTERROGATORIES, 123.
  affidavit in answer to, with objections, 125.
  application for further answer to, 126.
    to deliver, 123.
        to a corporation, 124.
  where more than one plaintiff or defendant, 124.

IRREGULARITY,
  summons to set aside for, 258.

ISSUE,

between judgment creditor and garnishee, 212.
    order for, 211.
    judgment on motion after trial of, 188.
    notice of motion for judgment after trial of, 181.
    of fact, 145.
        application for trial of, 146.

J.

JUDGE,

in chambers, notice of appeal from, 235.
                to, from district registrar, 251.
                master, 234.
                Order XIV., 72.
in court, notice of appeal from, 236.

JUDGMENT

after trial by referee, 186.
                of questions of account, 187.
    with jury, 184.
    without jury, 185.
against third party after trial, 84.
                decision without trial, summons for, 85.
                by default, 84.
application for leave to set down motion for, 181.
by consent, 190.
by default, summons to set aside, 122.
directed, notice of motion to set aside, 179, 180.
for costs after acceptance of money paid into court, 134.
        confession of defence, 116.
    on discontinuance after notice, 149.
            by order, 150.
for part of claim unanswered by defence, 120.
in court for amount to be ascertained, 186.

[22]

INDEX.

JUDGMENT—*continued.*
in default of appearance, 58, 59.
after assessment of damages, 61.
against married women, 63.
interlocutory, 59.
recovery of land, 62.
in default of defence, 118, 119.
notice of motion for, 120.
recovery of land, 119.
memorandum to be indorsed on, where act ordered to be done, 189.
notice of motion for, 179.
after trial of issue, 181.
of dismissal for want of prosecution, 118.
on non-appearance of plaintiff, 187.
pursuant to order, 114.
on motion, 122.
after trial of issue, 188.
on special case, 145.
warrant of attorney, 189.
order by consent for, 189.
special indorsement for, 19.
under Order XIV., 182.
against married woman, 183.
on conditional order, 184.
summons for, 64.

JUDGMENT CREDITOR AND GARNISHEE,
issue between, 212.
order for, 211.

JUDGMENT DEBTOR,
examination of, order for, 207.
summons for, 206.
touching means, 207.

JURISDICTION,
service out of the. *See* SERVICE.

[23]

INDEX.

JURY,
  notice of special, 153.
  trial with, judgment after, 184.
      notice of, by defendant, 153.
  trial without, judgment after, 185.

LANDLORD,
  named in writ, entry of appearance by, 49.

LAW,
  points of, application to set down, 141.

LETTER
  of request for commission, order for, 166.

LIBEL
  and injunction, general indorsement for, 8.

LIEN,
  where claimed, application for delivery up of property, 232.

LIMITED
  liability company, description of, on writ, 5.

LIMITING
  defence, entry of appearance, 49.
      notice, 50.

LONG ORDER
  for commission, 161.

LORD CAMPBELL'S ACT,
  claim under, 6.

LUNATIC,
  appointment of guardian for, affidavit on application for, 78.
      notice of application for, 77.
  description of, on writ, 5.

[24]

INDEX.

M.

MARRIED WOMAN,
description of, on writ, 5.
judgment in default of appearance against, 63.
under Order XIV. against, 183.
order under Order XIV. against, 69.
writ of *fi. fa.* against, 194.

MASTER,
notice of appeal to judge from order of, 234.
Order XIV., 72.

MEANS,
order for examination touching, 207.

MEMORANDUM. *See* PRÆCIPE.
of entry of appeal, 237.
special case, 144.
to be indorsed on judgment where act ordered to be done, 189.

MISREPRESENTATION,
general indorsement for, 8.

MITIGATION
of damages, notice of evidence in, 175.

MONEY
claim, general indorsement for, 6.
lent, special indorsement for, 20.
obtained by fraud or lent, general indorsement for, 7.
paid, general indorsement for, 7.
special indorsement for, 20.
received by agent, special indorsement for, 21.

C.F. U [25]

INDEX.

MOTION
>for judgment, application for leave to set down, 181.
>judgment on, 122.
>>after trial of issue, 188.
>notice of, affidavit of service of, 121.
>>for judgment, 179.
>>>after trial of issues, 181.
>>>in default of defence, 120.
>>for leave to issue writ of attachment, 203.
>>>new trial, 238.
>>>security for costs, 238.
>>on appeal from county court, 239.
>>to set aside award, 247.
>>>judgment directed, 179, 180.
>>to strike out or dismiss, 113.

MUNICIPAL CORPORATION,
>description of, on writ, 5.

N.

NAMES
>of partners in firm, declaration of, 242.
>>demand for, 241.
>>order for disclosure of, 241.
>>summons for disclosure of, 240.

NEGLIGENCE,
>general indorsement for, 8, 9.

NEGOTIABLE INSTRUMENTS,
>special indorsement for, 21—28.

NEW TRIAL,
>notice of motion for, 238.

NEXT FRIEND,
>authority to solicitor to use name of, 77.
>consent of, 77.

INDEX.

NON-APPEARANCE

of plaintiff, judgment of dismissal on, 187.

NON-DELIVERY

of defence, certificate of, 252.

NOTICE,

    admission of facts pursuant to, 138.
    as to stock, 217.
        request for withdrawal of, 218.
        summons to discharge, 218.
    by claimant to sheriff, of claim, 227.
        execution creditor to sheriff, admitting or disputing claim, 228.
        sheriff to execution creditor, of claim, 228.
    judgment for defendant's costs on discontinuance after, 149.
    limiting defence, 50.
    of acceptance of money paid into court, 133,
        address for service in London, 253.
        admission of facts, voluntary, 135.
        appeal from district registrar to judge, 251.
        appeal from judge in chambers, 235.
            court, 236.
            master to judge, 234.
                Order XIV., 72
    appearance, 46.
        by party not named as defendant, 52.
        in district registry, 251.
    application for appointment of guardian, 77.
        further directions, 103.
    counterclaim to person not a party, 114.
    cross-appeal by respondent, 237.
    discontinuance, 147.
    evidence in mitigation of damages, 175.
    intention to read evidence taken in another cause, 158.
    motion. *See* MOTION.
    payment into court, 132.

INDEX.

NOTICE—*continued.*
   of place of trial, 151.
      removal from district registry, 252.
      renewal of writ of *fi. fa.*, 200.
      service of writ on partnership, where capacity of party served uncertain, 57.
      service of writ on person in control of partnership business, 57.
      special defence, 97.
          jury, 153.
      trial, 152.
         application for leave to countermand, 155.
            to dismiss in default of, 154.
         consent to countermand, 154.
         notice countermanding, 155.
         with jury by defendant, 153.
         without pleadings, 96.
      writ, affidavit of service of, 58.
         in lieu of service out of the jurisdiction, 39.
           district registry, 39.
   third party. *See* THIRD PARTY.
   to admit documents, 136.
         facts, 137.
   to appoint arbitrator, 245.
   inspect documents, 129.
   produce documents, 139.
      affidavit of service of, 140.
      for inspection, 128.

O.

OBJECTIONS
   to answer interrogatories, 125.

OFFICER,
   public, claim by or against, 6.
      description of, on writ, 6.

INDEX.

OFFICIAL REFEREE. *See* REFEREE.

ORDER. *See* VARIOUS TITLES.
    particulars delivered pursuant to, 109.

ORDER XIV.,
    affidavit of defendant on summons under, 66.
        plaintiff on summons under, 65.
        service of summons and affidavit under, 66.
    final judgment under, 182.
        against married woman, 183.
        on conditional order, 184.
    order under, various, 67—72.
    summons under, 64.

P.

PARISH COUNCIL,
    description of, on writ, 5.

PART
    of claim, judgment for, 120.

PARTICULARS
    delivered pursuant to order, 109.
    exceeding three folios, 12, 106.
    in special indorsement, 11.
    of counterclaim, order for, 109.
    order for, 108.
    summons for, 108.

PARTIES,
    description of, on writ, 4.
    representative character of, indorsement of, 6.

INDEX.

PARTNERS,
    affidavit of service of writ on, 55.
    entry of appearance by, sued in firm name, 47.
                         person served as, under protest, 47.
    names of, declaration of, 242.
        demand for, 241.
        order for disclosure of, 241.
        summons for disclosure of, 240.

PARTNERSHIP,
    description of, on writ, 5.
    property, order charging, 243.
        summons to charge, 242.
    service of writ on person in control of, affidavit of, 56.
        notice of, 57.

PAYMENT INTO COURT,
    application for, after defence delivered, 132.
    judgment for costs after acceptance of, 134.
    notice of, 132.
        acceptance of, 133.

PAYMENT OUT OF COURT,
    authority of plaintiff for, 133.

PEER,
    description of, on writ, 5.

PERISHABLE GOODS,
    application for order for sale of, 229.

PERSONAL
    service of writ, affidavit of, 53.

PLACE OF TRIAL,
    notice of, 151.
    application for change of, 152.

INDEX.

PLAINTIFF,
 consent of added, or next friend, 77

PLEADINGS, 105.
 order to amend, 110.
 summons to amend, 110.
    plead after reply, 115.
    strike out, 112.
    where no reasonable cause of action, 112.
 trial without. *See* TRIAL.

POINTS OF LAW,
 application to set down, 141.

POSSESSION,
 writ of, 196.
   and *fi. fa.*, 197.
   præcipe for, 196.

POSTPONEMENT OF TRIAL,
 application for, 156.

PRÆCIPE
 for writ of attachment, 205.
    delivery, 201.
    distringas, 191.
    elegit, 191.
    fi. fa., 192.
    de bonis ecclesiasticis, 191.
    inquiry, 60.
    possession, 196.
    sequestrari facias de bonis ecclesiasticis, 191
    sequestration, 191.
    venditioni exponas, 191.
 of entry of appeal, 237.
 renewal of writ, 44.
 subpœna, 170.

INDEX.

PRESERVATION
of property, application for interim order for, 229.

PRIVATE SALE,
application for, 232.
order for, 233.

PROCEEDINGS,
order to carry on, 87.
    affidavit on application for, 86.
    summons to discharge, 87.
summons to compel representative of deceased party to carry on, 88.

PRODUCE,
notice to, affidavit of service of, 140.
    documents, 139.
        for inspection, 128.

PROMISSORY NOTE,
special indorsement for, 28.

PROPERTY,
delivery up of, where lien claimed, application for, 232.
inspection of, application for, 230.
partnership, order charging, 243.
    summons to charge, 242.
preservation or interim custody of, application for order for, 229.

PROSECUTION,
want of, judgment on dismissal for, 118.
    order to dismiss for, 117.
    summons to dismiss for, 117.

PROTEST,
entry of appearance under, by person served as partner, 47.

INDEX.

PROVE,
application for leave to, facts by affidavit, 157.

PUBLIC OFFICER,
claim by or against, 6.
description of on writ, 6.

R.

RECEIVER,
interim order for appointment of, 231.

RECOVERY OF LAND,
general indorsement for, 8.
judgment in default of appearance, 62.
defence, 119.
special indorsement for, 29.

REFEREE,
judgment after trial by, 186.
of questions of account by, 187.
special case by, 249.

REFERENCE,
order of, under Arbitration Act, 248.

REGISTRATION
of bill of sale, affidavit on, 254.
renewal of, 256.

REGISTRY
district. *See* DISTRICT REGISTRY.

REJOINDER,
summons for, 115.

INDEX.

REMOVAL,

from district registry, notice of, 252.

REMOVE,

from district registry, summons to, 253.
to district registry, summons to, 252.

RENEWAL,

of registration of bill of sale, affidavit on, 256.
writ, affidavit for, 42.
of *fi. fa.*, notice of, 200.
præcipe for, 44.

RENT,

special indorsement for, 30, 31.

REPAIRS,

general indorsement for, 9.

REPLY, 105.

summons to plead after, 115.

REPRESENTATIVE

capacity of parties, indorsement of, 6.
of deceased party, summons to compel, to proceed, 88.

REQUEST,

for commission, 167.
order for letter of, 166.
undertaking by solicitors as to costs of, 168.
for withdrawal of notice as to stock, 218.

RESPONDENT,

notice of cross-appeal by, 237.

RESTITUTION,
writ of, 191.

RESULT,
of special case, agreement as to, 144.

REVIEW
taxation of costs, summons to, 257.

S.

SALARY
and commission, general indorsement for, 7.
special indorsement for, 32.

SALE,
bill of. *See* BILL OF SALE.
of perishable goods, application for order for, 229.
private, application for order for, 232.
order for, 233.

SATISFACTION
of bill of sale, affidavit on entry of, 255.
summons for entry of, 256.

SCHOOL BILL,
special indorsement for, 33.

SECURITY
for costs, notice of motion for, 238.
summons for, 257.

SEQUESTRARI FACIAS
de bonis ecclesiasticis, writ of, 191.
præcipe for, 191.

INDEX.

SEQUESTRATION,
    writ of, 191.
        præcipe for, 191.

SERVICE,
    notice of address for, in London, 253.
    of notice of motion, affidavit of, 121.
        writ, affidavit of, 58.
        to produce, affidavit of, 140.
    of subpœna, affidavit of, 174.
    of summons and affidavit under Order XIV., affidavit of, 66.
    of writ on company, affidavit of, 54.
        partner on behalf of the firm, affidavit of, 55.
        partnership, where capacity of party served uncertain, notice of, 57.
        person in control of partnership, affidavit of, 56.
            notice of, 57.
    of writ, personal, affidavit of, 53.
        substituted, affidavit for order for, 40,
            of, 54.
        order for, 42.
    out of the jurisdiction, writ for, 35.
        affidavit on application to issue, 36.
        district registry, 36.
        notice in lieu of, 39.
            district registry, 39.
        order for leave to issue, 38.
        specially indorsed, 36.

SET ASIDE
    award, notice of motion to, 247.
    judgment by default, summons to, 122.
        directed, notion of motion to, 179, 180.
    for irregularity, summons to, 258.

SET DOWN
    motion for judgment, application to, 181.
    points of law, application to, 141.
    special case, application to, 143.

INDEX.

SHERIFF,
interpleader summons by, 221.
notice by, to execution creditor, of claim, 228.
       to, by execution creditor, admitting or disputing claim, 228.
       to, of claim, by claimant, 227.

SHORT
cause list, order under Order XIV. for entry of action in, 71.
order for commission, 160.

SIGNATURE
of admissions, affidavit of, 139.

SOLICITOR,
authority to, to use name of next friend, 77.
bill of costs, order under Order XIV. in action on, 70.
       special indorsement for, 33.

SPECIAL
case, agreement as to result of, 144.
    application for, 143.
       leave to set down, 143.
    by consent, 142.
    referee or arbitrator, 249.
    judgment on, 145.
defence, notice of, 97.
examiners to take evidence abroad, order for appointment of, 169.
indorsement, account stated, 14.
       bill of exchange. See below, "negotiable instruments."
       building contract, 14.
       carriage of goods by rail, 15.
       cheque. See below, "negotiable instruments."
       commission of traveller, 32.
           on sale of houses, 15.
       company, allotment money and calls upon shares, 15.

INDEX.

SPECIAL—*continued*.
   indorsement, freight, 16.
        goods sold and delivered and account stated, 17.
        guarantee, 18.
        hire of furniture, 18.
        interest, where claimable in, 12.
        judgment, 19.
        money lent and interest, 20.
            paid, 20.
            received by agent, 21.
        negotiable instruments, bill of exchange, inland, 21—24.
        negotiable instruments, bill of exchange, foreign, 25, 26.
                  cheque, 26, 27.
                  promissory note, 28.
        particulars in, 11.
        promissory note. See above, "negotiable instruments."
        recovery of land, 29.
        rent, 30, 31.
        salary and commission of traveller, 32.
        school bill, 33.
        solicitor's bill of costs, 33.
        warehouse charges, 34.
   jury, notice of, 153.

SPECIALLY
   indorsed writ of summons, 3.
        district registry, 4.
        for service out of the jurisdiction, 36.

STAMPS, 259—263.

STATEMENT OF CLAIM, 105.
   order for, 97.
   summons for, 96.

INDEX.

STAY

of execution, application for, 200.
proceedings, pending trial of test action, order to, 94.
  summons to, where there is a submission, 245.

STOCK,

affidavit as to, 216.
notice as to, 217.
  request for withdrawal of, 218.
  summons to discharge, 218.

STRIKE OUT

or dismiss, notice of motion to, 113.
party, order to, 76.
  summons to, 76.
pleading, summons to, 112.
  where no reasonable cause of action, 112.

SUBMISSION

to arbitration, 244.
summons to stay proceedings where there is, 245.

SUBPŒNA

ad testificandum, assizes, 172.
    general form, 171.
    high court, 171.
affidavit of service of, 174.
duces tecum, 172.
præcipe of, 170.

SUBSTITUTED

service, affidavit for order for, 40.
  affidavit of, 54.
  order for, 42.

SUMMONS. *See* VARIOUS TITLES.

writ of. *See* WRIT OF SUMMONS.

[39]

T

TAXATION
of costs, summons to review, 257.

TEST ACTION,
order staying proceedings, pending trial of, 94.

TESTIFICANDUM,
subpœna ad. *See* SUBPŒNA.
writ of *habeas corpus ad*. *See* HABEAS CORPUS.

THIRD PARTY
directions, order for, 86.
summons for, 85.
entry of appearance by, 47.
judgment against. after trial, 84.
by default against, 84.
notice, 82.
affidavit on application to issue, 81.
order giving leave to issue, 83.
summons by, to discharge order, 84.
for judgment against, after decision without trial, 85.

THIRD PERSON,
entry of appearance by, to counterclaim, 48.

TIME,
summons for, 106.

TITLE
in district registry proceedings, 250.
of consolidated actions, 93.

TRANSFER,
order to, 91.
summons to, 91.

INDEX.

TRESPASS
and injunction, general indorsement for, 9.

TRIAL,
before referee, judgment after, 187.
of questions of account, judgment after, 187.
entry for, 155.
consent for withdrawal of action after, 150.
new, notice of motion for, 238.
notice of, 152.
application by defendant to dismiss in default of, 154.
for leave to countermand, 155.
consent to countermand, 154.
notice countermanding, 155.
place of, 151.
with jury by defendant, 153.
of issue, judgment on motion after, 188.
notice of motion for judgment after, 181.
of fact, application for, 146.
postponement of, application for, 156.
with jury, judgment after, 184.
without jury, judgment after, 185.
pleadings, indorsement for, 95, 96.
notice of, 96.

TRUSTEE
of bankrupt, description of, on writ, 5.
will, claim by or against, 6.

U.

UNSOUND MIND,
person of, affidavit on application for appointment of guardian of, 78.
description of, on writ, 5.
notice of application for appointment of guardian of, 77.

UNDERTAKING
by solicitors as to costs of request for commission, 168.

C.F.   X   [41]

V.

VENDITIONI EXPONAS,
 writ of, 191.
  præcipe for, 191.

VENUE,
 application for change of, 152.

VERIFICATION
 of copies of business books, affidavit of, 131.

VOLUNTARY
 notice of admission of facts, 135.

W.

WARRANT
 of attorney, judgment on, 189.

WIFE,
 description of, on writ, 5.

WITHDRAWAL,
 consent for, after entry for trial, 150.
 of defence, application for, 149.
  notice as to stock, request for, 218.

WITNESS,
 application for examination of, before examiner, 158.
 order for examination of, before trial, 159.

WOMAN,
 description of, on writ, 5.

WORK
 done and money paid, general indorsement for, 7.

INDEX.

WRIT
  of attachment, 205.
          notice of motion for, 203.
          order for, 204.
          præcipe for, 205.
          summons for, 204.
  commission, 164.
  delivery, 201.
      præcipe for, 201.
  distringas against ex-sheriff, 191.
  elegit, 191.
  fi. fa., 193.
    against married woman, 194.
    and possession, 197.
    by executors, 199.
    for costs, 195.
    notice of renewal of, 200.
    præcipe for, 192.
  fi. fa. de bonis ecclesiasticis, 191.
  habeas corpus ad testificandum, 173.
  inquiry for assessment of damages, 60.
  possession, 196.
    and *fi. fa.*, 197.
    præcipe for, 196.
  restitution, 191.
  sequestrari facias de bonis ecclesiasticis, 191.
  sequestration, 191.
  summons for service out of the jurisdiction, 35.
    affidavit on application for, 36.
    district registry, 36.
    notice in lieu of, 39.
      district registry, 39.
    order for leave to issue, 38.
    specially indorsed, 36.
  summons, general form, 1.
          district registry, 3.
    renewal of, affidavit for, 42.
    renewed, præcipe for, 44.
    service of notice of, affidavit of, 58.

INDEX.

WRIT—*continued.*
    of summons, service of, notice of, on partnership, where
        capacity of party served uncertain, 57.
        service of, notice of, on person in control of
          partnership, 57.
        service of, on company, affidavit of, 54.
                partner on behalf of firm, 55.
                person in control of partnership,
                    56.
            personal, affidavit of, 53.
            substituted, affidavit of, 54.
        specially indorsed, 3.
            district registry, 4.
    of *venditioni exponas*, 191.

WRONGFUL DISMISSAL,
    general indorsement for, 8.

www.ingramcontent.com/pod-product-compliance
Lightning Source LLC
Chambersburg PA
CBHW021203230426
43667CB00006B/526